"Patricia Ireland is willing to pay the personal price for fighting inequality." —*San Francisco Chronicle*

"Smart, outspoken and passionate . . . an inspiring book." —*Cleveland Plain Dealer*

"Ireland writes compellingly." —*Fortune*

"Ireland chronicles some of the most dynamic legal and personal battles for women's rights." —*Minneapolis Star Tribune*

"A blueprint of how to live a life of social and political activism. Ireland is an expert architect." —*Bookpage*

"Ireland is intensely smart, deeply passionate, deliciously outspoken. . . . Women ought to want to read this book." —*Kirkus Reviews*

"An extremely sensible account of how Ireland came to be where she is." —*Philadelphia Inquirer*

PATRICIA IRELAND leads the quarter-million members of NOW and travels extensively as a speaker. She divides what time is left between Washington, D.C., and southern Florida.

"Intensely action-oriented, Ireland relates her growing awareness of discrimination against women in the airline industry, legal profession, and political sphere."
—*Utne Reader*

"Ireland writes with obvious passion and pain."
—*Los Angeles Times Book Review*

"This eminently readable autobiography, with its account of Ireland's life in the trenches, will inspire and enlighten activists of all stripes." —*Publishers Weekly*

"The perfect gift for a young woman . . . who does not yet realize what Patricia Ireland . . . won for her, and at what price." —*New York Times Book Review*

"One woman's journey through the politics of protest and power. . . . Ireland aptly describes dramatic triumphs and frustrating defeats in her fight for what women want." —*Columbus Dispatch*

"Ireland traces an interesting story . . . the book of an optimist." —*Minneapolis City Pages*

"Ireland urges women to answer the question "What do I want?" and to empower themselves to go out and get it."
—*Saint Paul Pioneer Press*

"Part memoir, part history, part call to action, *What Women Want* covers considerable ground."
—*Miami Herald*

"Sheds light on the reasoning behind some of NOW's most internally debated stances, namely political endorsements, gay and lesbian rights advocacy and pro-choice activism."
—*Baltimore Sun*

"Ireland comes across as smart, outspoken, and a passionate spokeswoman for women's rights."
—*Austin American-Statesman*

"For those interested in Ireland's progression from teenage bride and flight attendant to lawyer and women's rights activist, this is a straightforward account that includes a well-articulated version of feminist stands."
—*Sunday Oregonian*

"Interesting . . . Ireland writes in an easy, conversational style that loops forward and back in her life. It's an effective commentary on what one woman's life has been like in the second half of the 20th century, and what effect society and her individual role within it has played in the lives of the rest of us, male and female alike."
—*Wichita Eagle*

PATRICIA IRELAND

WHAT WOMEN WANT

A PLUME BOOK

PLUME
Published by the Penguin Group
Penguin Books USA Inc., 375 Hudson Street, New York, New York 10014, U.S.A.
Penguin Books Ltd, 27 Wrights Lane, London W8 5TZ, England
Penguin Books Australia Ltd, Ringwood, Victoria, Australia
Penguin Books Canada Ltd, 10 Alcorn Avenue, Toronto, Ontario,
Canada M4V 3B2
Penguin Books (N.Z.) Ltd, 182-190 Wairau Road, Auckland 10, New Zealand

Penguin Books Ltd, Registered Offices:
Harmondsworth, Middlesex, England

Published by Plume, an imprint of Dutton Signet,
a division of Penguin Books USA Inc.
Previously published in a Dutton edition.

First Plume Printing, June, 1997
10 9 8 7 6 5 4 3 2 1

 REGISTERED TRADEMARK—MARCA REGISTRADA

The Library of Congress has catalogued the Dutton edition as follows:

Ireland, Patricia.
    What women want / Patricia Ireland.
       p.   cm.
    ISBN 0-525-93857-5 (hc.)
    0-452-27249-1 (pbk.)
       1. Ireland, Patricia.   2. Feminists—United States—Biography.
3. Feminism—United States.   4. Women's rights—United States.
5. Women—United States—Social conditions.   I. Title.
HQ1413.I74A3   1996
305.42'092—dc20   96-5490
                                                          CIP

Printed in the United States of America
Original hardcover design by Stanley S. Drate/Folio Graphics Co., Inc.

ACKNOWLEDGMENTS

I owe thanks to so many people who helped move this book from concept to reality. I am grateful to all of these friends and colleagues.

To longtime family friends Shawn Miller, a journalist whose writing I admire, and Roger Leroy Miller, a successful business, law, and economics textbook writer. Without Roger's participation at the inception, this project would likely not have happened. Shawn's contribution to the writing and conceptualization of the book could only have come from someone who's known me since I was in law school. After two years the demands of Shawn's career compelled him to move on to other projects. The imagination, insight, and humor of his writing added immeasurably to the finished product.

To Meredith Bernstein, an agent Roger knew in New York City. Meredith's enthusiasm, energy, and experience got this project off the ground and have helped keep it on track.

To Carole DeSanti, the editor of this book and the ever resourceful and calm center of this project. I turned repeatedly to Carole for help in shaping the book and making its vision and voice my own. Carole not only devoted her own time and skill, she also knew when we needed other resources and where to find them. Every time we hit a snag, Carole's response was, "Don't worry; I have a backup plan." And she always made good on her promise.

To Jenifer Levin, one of the writers on the book. After reading *The Sea of Light*, I was excited by the prospect of her involvement on this project. Jenifer brought to the work her perspective as a woman, a feminist, and a successful author. Her passion, creativity, and talent brought the book closer to its final form.

To Amy Mintzer, who started out as an editor and generously expanded her job description to "do what must be done." Amy edited, drafted, collaborated, coordinated, and ended up being the magnet who pulled everything together to produce the final draft.

To Pat Silverthorn, who researched, wrote, and lived part of this story. Pat's critiques of various versions of the manuscript helped set the direction of the book. Her writing and her willingness for parts of her life to be included were especially helpful in crafting the introduction and reconstructing the atmosphere of life in Miami in the early eighties.

To Janet Canterbury for her courage, inspiration, and hard work. In addition to letting me share so much of her life in the book, Janet provided concrete help in reading draft after draft with an eye to the politics as well as the integrity of the story. And as cochair of NOW's national advisory committee, she shouldered substantial additional projects while I struggled with the writing.

To Chris Delboni, an increasingly successful writer in her home country, Brazil. Chris volunteered her time as a reliable and rigorous researcher and as a reader of the early drafts; she informed and improved the book significantly.

To Elizabeth McGee, who served as the staff researcher on the book. Her experience as a field organizer and chapter activist for NOW meant Elizabeth always understood the nuances of what we were looking for, why it was important, and where to find answers that were at first elusive. And to Trish Kelly and

Margie Singleton, who came into the NOW offices during the final weeks to do fact checking and to coordinate with Alex Swenson at Dutton, to whom I am also indebted.

To the officers and staff in NOW's national action center, without whom I could never have turned so much of my time and energy to this book. The other officers, Kim Gandy, Rosemary Dempsey, and Karen Johnson, carried many additional responsibilities that normally would have been mine. Their work gave me confidence that this project would not detract from, but rather enhance, our progress toward NOW's goals. Staff members Loretta Kane, Diane Minor, and Wanda Alston were also called upon to stretch themselves as we juggled this project with all the others on our agenda.

Others felt the ripple effect of the additional work, too: Robin Abb, Mea Arnold, Beth Beck, Lisa Bennet-Haigney, Linda Berg, Janet Black, Pat and Twiss Butler (who also shared valuable research files and history), Alice Cohan, Beth Corbin, Francine Dunmore, Cindy Hanford, Barbara Hays-Hamilton, Dixie Johnson, Valerie Jordan, Angela McArdell, Vernon McCaster, Mary Melchior, Jimmy Pipp, Veronika Rickard, Boden Sandstrom, Melinda Shelton, Deborah Sidbury, Toni Stroud, Marquita Sykes, Amy Tracy, Kyle Velte, Kim Ward, Mira Weinstein, Kirsten Xanthippe, Heidi Zimmerman. Ginny Montes and Faith Evans, who both left us much too soon, had a special impact on my politics and perspective and thus on this book.

To Ellie Smeal, who drew me into NOW and into politics at the national level. Ellie continues to provide valuable leadership, vision, and plain hard work to our common cause and I am privileged to count her as an ally. And to Toni Carabillo and Judith Meuli, and June B. Csida, who wrote and published *The Feminist Chronicles*. Until I wrote my own book, I had not fully appreciated how important a contribution their book is as a resource to trace the history of feminism in this country.

To James Humble, who has given me nearly three decades of support. He has sacrificed a great deal of his own privacy as I have become a public figure. I am grateful for his understanding that I cannot talk about my own life without talking some about his. I have tried to be respectful that his story is not mine to share, and at his request I have not included more.

To my parents and sisters, for whom I feel such great love and respect. To all of my family and friends, named and unnamed, thank you.

WHAT
WOMEN
WANT

INTRODUCTION

Whenever I prepare to lead a class or give a speech, I always learn as much as, if not more than, my audience does.

That's been my experience writing this book as well. I began it for the same reasons as the rest of the work I do: to speak to women and men who support women's rights, to share my experiences, to strategize ways to get around the pitfalls and over the obstacles we all face . . . and, I always hope, to spur some of my audience to action.

When I began writing, I saw this book as another form of media—like an extended magazine article or TV interview focusing on women's lives, on the ways we've changed society, on all that remains to be done. This would be a new vehicle, I thought, for discussing politics—another organizing project aimed at fighting for the things women want.

But like anything I've done that was really worth doing, this project has proved more difficult—and more satisfying—than I could have imagined.

Before I could write about what women want, friends and colleagues said, didn't I have to look at my own life and answer what *I* wanted? I resisted, but slowly I realized they were right.

I did have to answer a lot of questions myself. What had led me down this path of feminist politics in the first place? How did I grow from that person wearing the bland "may I help you" smile and flight attendant's pillbox hat into the determined woman being led away from a White House protest in handcuffs? After all, I haven't exactly traveled an ordinary road to political life.

Quite honestly, I wasn't at all sure I could answer the question "What do women want?" by looking at my own life. For one thing, I don't like talking about myself. I'm not the type who goes in for the public confessional, laying bare the personal experiences that have shaped me. Especially since, as a public figure, I have very little private life left. Then, too, introspection isn't my strong point. I'm generally a here-and-now type of person.

Gazing at two photographs—one of me in a stewardess uniform, the other of me in front of the White House with hands cuffed behind my back—I shook my head in some bewilderment. And I thought to myself: I don't know how all those changes happened! I don't know what the steps were. They just seemed the logical progression at the time.

Anyway, explaining the past has always seemed less important than figuring out how we want to steer the future. I wanted this book to give women something they could use in their everyday lives. I wasn't sure that examining the steps I'd taken toward getting what I wanted could provide insight into other women's wants and needs. After all, our needs and desires and passions are as diverse as our lives. And while I've committed my life to defending the whole spectrum of options for women, I feared that many would find themselves unable to identify with the choices I'd made for myself. I've chosen to live an untraditional life, to forgo having children, to pursue a life in politics, to take a lot of risks and chances—in my personal and professional life—that many people can't imagine taking.

Then, too, my life didn't necessarily seem worth emulating. As a young woman I was decidedly apolitical. I didn't begin my political career in college, or as an anti-war activist in the sixties. I didn't consciously become a feminist at all, for that matter, until I'd already spent some years in the workforce. My political consciousness came late, developing through trial and error and plenty of wrong turns and detours.

With all these reservations in mind, I nevertheless began to trace some of the steps I'd taken in my life—the big ones, anyway. In examining these stories—and now, in telling them to you—I've come to understand much more than I thought I would. Over time I realized that I couldn't hide behind a lot of political theory. I couldn't write a book that was all about politics but not about me. I would have to tell my story after all—how I first began to understand what I really wanted, how I finally went about getting it, how I came to be who I am. And in the end I decided that I wanted to tell something of my personal journey—because I think as women we are more alike than we might appear at first.

My political consciousness came late, I discovered, because it came from my life experiences—as part of a family, as a worker, and as a witness to events in my community. For many years I worked in traditional women's jobs—as a waitress, a chambermaid, and a flight attendant. I know firsthand that women's work is undervalued and underpaid. I've also worked as a corporate attorney, and I know how challenging it can be to break into a traditionally male field and how satisfying it can be to succeed.

Looking back has been bittersweet. But in examining my past with the question "What did this woman want?" in mind, I began to see a consistent (if not conscious) path leading toward feminism—not just as a philosophy but as a way of life. My last thirty years have been irrevocably shaped by the women's rights movement in our country. And although others may not have immersed themselves in the movement as fully as I have, we have all been profoundly affected by the changes the movement has brought.

The year I graduated from high school, people were still arguing that women didn't need or deserve equal pay for equal work, and no law required it. The arguments seem almost funny now: men had families to support, while women were said to work for "pin money," little extras near and dear to our hearts, but not necessary for our families' survival.

The year I got married, reproductive freedom was still not recognized as a constitutional right. Birth control was illegal, even for married couples, in some states, and illegal abortion was the leading cause of maternal death in this country.

The year I started law school, child care was still seen as a commie plot. In vetoing a child-care bill, Richard Nixon, in a message written by Pat Buchanan, called it "the Sovietization of American children."

When I was well into my legal career, head and master laws, which made husbands absolute rulers over their wives and families, were still in force in many states.

To those too young to remember, it may sound like I'm describing the Middle Ages. But these conditions were enshrined in law in this country until very recently—in some cases, less than twenty years ago.

So I want to review and celebrate with you the gains we've made in just my lifetime alone . . . and to remind ourselves about all that remains to be done.

W e should be proud of our progress, but we need to be vigilant to maintain and expand it. Because it is so easy to take our progress for granted, I need to sound an alarm about how quickly and how terribly our victories can be rolled back—and how very real is the threat that they will be.

Finally, I want to share some of the things I've learned about what women want. I can make generalizations, of course, and tell you what the polls say. I can describe some of my own experiences, and the experiences of other women who have told me about their lives and needs. But most of all, I want to encourage you to answer that question for yourself.

For me—and, I suspect, for many women—the question of what I wanted was never asked. We were socialized always to put others and their needs first. We were rarely encouraged to ask ourselves what *we* really wanted. Nor were we usually in positions to go after it, anyway. Or so it seemed. But I want us to look again.

The first step is to ask the question:

What do I want?

I worked hard for many years to avoid asking myself this. But I couldn't ever totally suppress my feelings of dissatisfaction and the sense that I wasn't being true to myself. I believe now that some vibrant, stubborn part of me also knew that deciding what I wanted and learning how to get it would require making enormous, maybe frightening, changes in my life.

I want to tell my story because I want to encourage others to ask the question anyway. I want to demonstrate that in spite of the risks and difficulties, the inevitable disruption and conflict, and the very real trade-offs and losses, the gains are so well worth the cost. I want to show that the confidence and optimism that come from gaining political and personal power—not over others but over yourself—the sense of community and self-worth that result, the feeling of living lovingly, honestly, and well, are enormous payoffs. When you decide what you want, when you add your own voice to those of other women, when we begin collectively to answer the question of what women want, we become stronger; we become that much more determined to get it.

Believe me, I know how difficult facing this question can be. In fact, the first step for me in deciding what I wanted was to allow myself to feel at all. For years I was afraid of my long-suppressed anger, afraid of all the other unresolved emotions I had about the death of my older sister in childhood and about my family. I was also afraid to lift the lid off my feelings of resentment at the ways I was treated as a woman.

In some sense, I was right to be afraid. Once I opened my eyes, I could not really, wholly, close them again.

If you had asked me before I became a flight attendant, I would have told you that I had never faced discrimination in my life. Once I shed the protective blinders I had been wearing, I began to see the sexual harassment and discrimination I faced on the job for the injustice it was, and a flood of painful memories came rushing back, viewed through the lens of my new consciousness.

I felt again the disappointment of being told that I couldn't be a crossing guard (or "patrol boy") in junior high and wondering why I didn't measure up to the job.

I felt the humiliation I had repressed when my college calculus professor responded to the first question I asked in class by slapping his forehead dramatically and sighing, "I don't know how they expect me to teach calculus to girls!" I never asked another question in that class, wound up with a D, and changed my major from math to liberal arts.

I recalled reporting to my biology instructor a change in my last name. When I explained that I was newly divorced, he made very explicit sexual advances. At the time I had felt guilty, wondering what I had done to make him think I wanted to have sex with him.

But reliving the shame and embarrassment of those incidents made me furious! And it wasn't only experiences from the past that I began to see in a new light. It was my current life as well. If I hadn't yet figured out what I wanted, I sure knew what I didn't want: the demeaning catcalls as we stewardesses walked through the hangar to emergency training, the airlines' advertising that depicted my coworkers and me as flirtatious diversions for business travelers, all of whom were presumed to be men. And I felt equally disgusted by the ad campaigns that depicted housewives as having no interests beyond removing ugly wax buildup from the kitchen floor and no worth beyond their relative abilities to remove ring-around-the-collar. Everywhere I looked, something made me angry.

Once my eyes were open, it was easy to see what I didn't

want. But only an actual need propelled me to action—and ultimately to an answer to the question of what I wanted.

I entered activism in the workplace propelled by a need for health coverage. I didn't seek out the fight so much as I hit a barrier, one that had a concrete impact on me and my family, and I had to fight to get what I needed. From that need I discovered feminism, the law, and politics.

Taking control of my life and recognizing the political context for my experiences didn't start as the lofty goals of a New Year's resolution. Instead, they were the result of realizing that if I was going to live a satisfying and worthwhile life, I was going to have to fight for it, and I knew I'd have to develop both the abilities and the stomach to fight hard.

While the years of work on this book, years of digging for answers to the question of what I wanted, what women want, haven't been easy, the process of telling these stories does lead me back to my original purpose for writing it—to organize for action, to better all of our lives, individually and together.

So I want to show, in the pages that follow, how I gained the power to control my own life and to make positive changes for myself and for other women. Because I believe without a doubt that you can do the same thing—in your own life, in your own way. And if you do, all of us will benefit immeasurably.

ONE

When I was five and living in Indianapolis, Indiana, I got into a fight with a neighborhood girl named Cynthia Kay Locke. I was passionately defending the status quo.

"Mommy *is* a doctor!" she shrieked, indignantly. "She *is!*"

"Liar!"

"Am not!"

I could be perfectly reasonable up to a point, but Cynthia Kay had gone too far. And I hated being lied to. It was simply a fact of life: Daddies could be doctors, mommies had to be nurses—everyone knew that. Snakes don't have legs.

In the clarity of my righteous rage, I noticed that Cynthia Kay was standing near a huge puddle left over from that morning's summer storm. I gave her a good shove, and she sprawled into the muddy waters.

Cynthia Kay started crying; I ran for home. I didn't want to be there when her mother—who, I later learned, was indeed an M.D.—came out to see what all the fuss was about. As I loped along, I felt absolutely no remorse. Liars got what they deserved.

I am still a fierce fighter for truth and justice, but I no longer believe in shoving—and some of my ideas about women have changed.

I was born at the end of World War II, when Rosie the Riveter—and thousands of women like her—were being pushed out of high-paying industrial jobs by GIs returning from military service. Throughout the 1930s and 1940s, women in this country had entered the workforce in unprecedented numbers and attained increased economic and social power. But by the end of the Second World War, both government and popular media—anxious to make room for demobilized soldiers in the peacetime workforce—trumpeted home and hearth as the proper place for women. This was very much in keeping with everything that I saw around me as I grew up: My father worked outside our home; my mother worked in it; and most of my friends' parents did the same.

The overwhelming prevalence of this lifestyle among the middle class in the 1950s—the emphasis on sameness, on not rocking the boat, on fitting in—had an insistent quality about it. At the same time, middle-class people felt optimistic: The economy was growing, and many could look forward to living a better life materially than their own parents had. Still, although women's participation in the paid workforce continued to increase, it remained primarily a workforce of men. Women weren't reflected in it much. A girl in the 1950s couldn't help but be aware of that. That's just the way it was.

For me, though, there were a few tantalizing hints that women could be powerful, nontraditional, even adventurous. I remember a faded photo of my Grandma Nell as a young woman, taking to the air in an open-cockpit biplane. She wore a leather helmet, a dashing white scarf. And she was holding my father—then a little boy no older than five—on her lap. I gazed at that picture in awe. It seemed almost impossible that the woman I knew—the old grandmother who doted on me—had ever desired adventure.

Throughout Nell's life, though, her daring streak had been bounded by a conservative upbringing. When Nell was still a child, her mother perished in a fire. Her father could not take care of her, and Nell was raised by a well-to-do Midwestern family. A self-conscious orphan, she took emotional refuge in social form and social skills. How a proper young lady sat, gazed, shook hands, and behaved in public were all terribly important to her, and, in her old age, she passed those social skills and expectations on to me. By the time I was old enough to understand that women were never supposed to be doctors, only nurses—and never pilots, only stewardesses—Nell was a slight, prim, pampered, cranky, gray-haired woman who reminded me more than once, "Whistling girls and crowing hens always come to some bad end." Her influence was both empowering and constricting. I adored her.

There was a special photo of her husband, too—this one a family treasure, because it shows Grandpa Ray at the Yalta Conference with Roosevelt, Churchill, and Stalin. As a young man he'd become an executive for Capital Air, one of the pioneer airlines of the 1930s. During World War II, he headed the army's new Air Transport Division, overseeing the movement of troops and supplies worldwide. At the end of the war, he coordinated flights to and from the Yalta Conference. After the war, the family moved to Chicago, where Ray became a vice president of United Airlines.

Thinking back on each separate photograph of these beloved grandparents, it's almost shocking to me that, even as a child, I never marked the contrast between what each of them had been in youth, and what they had become. While Ray's vistas broadened, Nell's shrank; while his power increased in the world outside the home, she became increasingly frail and tradition-bound inside it.

My father, an only child, grew up in Washington, D.C. Because he was sickly as a boy, during the summer he was often sent to stay with his grandfather in Michigan in the hope that getting him out of the muggy D.C. climate would improve his health. The time he spent with his grandfather—who was not only an atheist, but a proselytizing one to boot—shaped my father tremendously. He was healed physically, but his grandfather's influence left my father with few religious beliefs to fall back on when, as an adult, he could have used such support.

Unlike my father's parents, who both grew up with some economic privilege, my mother's parents called themselves shanty Irish. Their families had come to the United States during the nineteenth-century potato famine. My mother's grandfather had fought for the Union in the Civil War—not for ideals, but for money—earning what was then called a conscription fee by taking the place of a wealthy young man who'd been drafted, a practice common among impoverished young immigrants at that time. The poor—then as now—had fewer choices, dwelt closer to violence than others, and bore the brunt of war disproportionately.

My grandmother Beth Shay was an earthy, practical woman who exercised publicly throughout her first two pregnancies—almost unheard-of in 1918 and 1920—shocking the neighbors. A swollen belly was incontrovertible evidence of a woman's sexual maturity and activity; at a time when "confinement" was still a euphemism for pregnancy and "belly" was a dirty word, decent women simply did not parade it around for others to witness. But my grandmother, personally convinced that exercise and fresh air were important during pregnancy, made her own comfortable maternity clothes and ventured out anyway.

This act was every bit as radical then as burning a bra would be in the 1960s. Of course, her behavior may not have been viewed at the time as an attempt to strike a political blow for women's rights; but it cannot be shrugged off as individual eccentricity. I often wonder how many acts of rebellion, small statements of a desire for individual freedom, have been performed defiantly by women throughout history and have been dismissed by neighbors as mere displays of quirkiness. I'm willing to bet that these proud acts of free spirits, who refused to be completely suppressed, have been performed by many, many women throughout history. Many of these acts of defiance are lost to us, as those women and their yearnings have been lost. But these tiny acts helped women gain some measure of control over our lives. Such acts, collectively, have been an important part of changing history.

Grandma Shay also learned how to drive a car.

The Chicago police spoke to her husband, Harry, about it. It was dangerous, they said, not because she lacked any driving skills herself, but because male drivers on the road, unaccustomed to seeing a woman behind the wheel, were likely to crash. Mind you, there was no law against women driving. But the police insisted that she stop. My grandfather, who had himself taught her to drive, never did tell her to stop, and she kept right on driving.

But Grandma Shay had other things to keep her down. For one, she was staunchly Catholic and struggled to obey the Church's teachings even when they seemed against the best interests of herself and her family. After raising two children to adolescence (and using birth control for nearly a decade), she succumbed to her parish priest's guilt trip about committing the "sin" of having sex for anything but reproductive purposes. She and Grandpa Shay subsequently had two more children who they could neither practically nor emotionally afford. (My mother always claimed that it ruined her parents' marriage, and when she married she left the Church rather than obey its prohibition of birth control.)

M y mother was born in 1920—the year women won the right to vote. The women's rights movement, active and vibrant in the United States since the 1840s, reached a peak with this success. Not until the 1960s and '70s would the movement again make such dramatic change.

Though her family was far better off than many of their neighbors during the Great Depression, my mother grew up in an atmosphere of financial struggle. Her childhood home was not by any means unhappy, but it was strict, and her upbringing was punctuated with occasional episodes of violence: She remembers being sent to the woodpile to pick out the stick her mother would use to punish her. Grandma Shay became a strict disciplinarian after the birth of her third and fourth children. ("Quiet down, or heads will roll!" she would yell at my sisters and me, even in later years. When she said that, it was easy to imagine my head bouncing down the street.) Already an alcoholic, Grandpa Shay slid into a deep depression. Like other girls before and since, my mother assumed caretaking responsibilities in early adolescence, devoting substantial time to raising her two younger siblings. She grew up fearful of authority and anxious to comply with it. In her youth she was a devout Catholic, faithfully performing the Stations of the Cross. Her belief in the promised afterlife, in a fixed system of rewards and punishments, was great. But she expected some reward in this life, too.

My mother and father, who knew each other from high school, secretly married when she was only sixteen. When the two sets of parents discovered the secret, they were livid. His parents thought her family wasn't good enough and wanted to have the marriage annulled. Her parents felt they were too young, but that ultimately the two young people had to make up their own minds. Both sets of parents agreed that the newlyweds should live apart for a year, so my father stayed in college in Michigan and, over the summer, was sent to work on a ranch, where he learned to love horses. My mother stayed home and finished high school. My parents were reunited at the end of their forced separation. My father became a metallurgical engineer. My mother went to work in a tailor's shop. (She was sexually harassed on the job—although at the time there was no name for it and, of course, no recourse.) After the birth of their first child, my sister Kathy, my mother never worked outside our home again. She loved motherhood, and to this day says that the happiest time of her life was when Kathy and I were small. The role of 1950s wife and mother seemed to suit her to a tee. Still, she has said that if she'd been born in an era when women expected to have a career, she probably would have been a carpenter.

Even so, I believe that the message my mother inadvertently gave me throughout childhood and adolescence was not to comply with authority, but to challenge it. I've often wondered if giving me that mixed message was her unconscious way of trying to protect me from a repressive set of rules and regulations that she knew had limited her own life. One of my greatest joys was to climb as high as I could in our old backyard elm tree. This didn't faze my mother. She built me a tree house and encouraged me to keep on climbing . . . against the advice of Dr. Arnold, our family physician, who was very disapproving. From my high perch, I once overheard him warning her about all the bones he'd set in his time for children who fell out of trees. But she never once ordered me out of that tree unless it was time for dinner. And I never fell, either.

When I was four and a half, my family was changed forever.

My father had loved horseback riding ever since his summer on the ranch. Like many little girls, my sister and I also loved horses, and one day, when I was four and a half and Kathy was seven, my father took her riding for the first time. I remember standing in the backyard, watching them pull away down the driveway, waving good-bye with one hand and clutching in the other a prized piece of honeycomb I'd been given from my dad's hives as a consolation for being too young to go with them.

The details of that terrible day were conveyed to me by my parents: Kathy's horse bolted soon after they started out, and, screaming, she rode past my father's horse. At first he mistook her yells for laughter. But the next thing he knew she'd fallen. Her foot was caught in the stirrup, and the horse dragged her, at a full gallop, for half a mile before he could get to her. When he reached her she was still alive. My father carried Kathy's mangled body to the road for help. She died on the way to the hospital.

My memories of what followed are the memories of a grieving child; they're vague at best. And the truth is that I don't clearly know today how much of it is actual memory and how much can be attributed to things I've been told along the way by my parents and relatives. I do remember that I saw my father cry for the first time when my parents told me Kathy was dead; as a child, I never saw him cry again. After Kathy's death my parents decided that it would be best for me if they tried to keep day-to-day life as "normal" as possible. I did not attend the funeral. But this attempt to carry on as though nothing had happened was doomed from the start. Mourning finds expression in many ways, whether out in the open or below the surface.

In his grief, I think my father distanced himself emotionally from the pain by distancing himself from our family, although he and my mother stayed together another thirty-five years before he actually left. I think that he also developed a sort of permanent despair. How could there be a loving God, he'd argue over the years, when the world was so brutal? When tigers brought down and began to eat their wounded prey before the prey had even died—where was the beauty, where was the godliness, in that? Of course, the shadow of my sister's death hung over all of this; Kathy had died horribly, for no reason—where was the God in that? But those words remained unspoken.

My mother lost every remaining vestige of her Catholic faith. She tried going to college. She put me in Harmony Hall Nursery School and started taking classes at Butler University in Indianapolis. But her attempt at getting a degree was soon aborted when I came down with rheumatic fever—a serious childhood illness at the time—and strict bed rest was prescribed for six horrible weeks. The doctor was so worried about putting unnecessary strain on my heart that I wasn't even allowed a pillow. My mother dropped out of school to care for me, and she never went back. From that time on, I believe that she was determined to send me through college. She had a high school diploma, but my father was the one with an advanced degree from a prestigious institution—the University of Michigan. I think perhaps she linked his degree with the power he seemed to wield in the outside world. I wonder if, in the same way, she linked her own lack of a degree with a lack of power. I think many middle-class women of her age must have felt the same way. And, though they might have felt powerless when it came to the world outside the home, they were determined to equip their daughters for struggle in the world of knowledge, money, men.

And me? I was forbidden to ride horses. For years after Kathy's death, I had nighttime dreams of riding in which, every time, the horse would melt away beneath me. I know that I developed a strong desire to excel in order to somehow make up for my parents' unspeakable loss. Of course, this would be an impossible task, one that I'm sure I must have resented. In my teen years, both my desire to excel and my resentment at having to do so became evident. Throughout the rest of my life, regardless of circumstance, I would feel responsible for the welfare of everyone I knew, and I'd try to make people around me feel happy.

I probably would have tried to make people around me feel happy anyway; after all, I was a girl growing up in the fifties.

With Kathy's death, the family dynamics changed irrevocably. I had been the baby of the family; Kathy had been my protector in the gang of neighborhood kids, the big sister who linked me to all the others. Without her, I found myself terribly lonely. I once dreamt of her as an angel with golden wings. When I awoke from the dream, I asked my parents when they would bring me another sister.

My parents were in fact trying to bring me two new sisters

through adoption. Susan and Mary Lee, who were birth sisters, could have been adopted when Mary Lee was a newborn, but the foster-care bureaucracy created a nearly two-year delay. The caseworker said that policy would not allow Susan to be adopted until she had had surgery to correct her crossed eyes and that Mary Lee could not be adopted without her sister. Meanwhile, it apparently was consistent with their policy for the girls to languish in a foster home. My mother fought the system for a greater good; she was the first activist I ever studied. About a year and a half after my parents had initiated proceedings, my mother began calling the caseworker each Monday, politely but persistently pressing to bring Susan and Mary Lee into our family as quickly as possible. Using every connection she could think of, she finally found a judge who, working behind the scenes, forced the child welfare department to release the girls to my parents.

From the point of view of their own development, the delay was a tragedy for Susan and Mary Lee. As infants in foster care, both girls had suffered physically and emotionally. Susan, who had to endure a traumatic eye operation, seemed at first unable to learn colors and numbers. Mary Lee was physically weak; shortly after she came to live with us, she almost died of amoebic dysentery. I remember my father standing over her sickbed, wringing his hands, so afraid of losing another child.

As young children, my sisters and I were close. I enjoyed being the oldest, showing them around, protecting them. When a bully who sat across from Susan at the schoolroom table kicked her legs black-and-blue, I beat him up in the playground. But after I graduated to junior high, we never attended the same school again, didn't spend as much time together and would never be as close again.

Try as they might, my parents could not resurrect our family as it had been before the accident. My parents and I had never really recovered from the trauma of Kathy's death. Susan and Mary Lee probably needed more patience and carefree love than our particular family had to give.

Despite these problems, we had plenty of good times. My mother and father worked hard to be good parents. I remember Susan, Mary Lee, and me singing together all the time—on family camping trips, in the car—practicing harmony for hours. My father joined in; he and I both loved cowboy songs. (Roy Rogers was, in fact, my first crush.) "Ghost Riders in the Sky" was a favorite. We three girls put on dramas and ballets, played circus on our jungle gym, and invited all the neighborhood kids. We charged a penny for admission and two cents a cup for Kool-Aid.

Looking back, I see Kathy's death and much of what followed as a poignant reminder that we humans sometimes really *are* powerless. We cannot direct or control or enhance certain aspects of our lives. And too many of us—especially women—blame ourselves for what we cannot control. Illnesses, accidents, and acts of nature will always be beyond us. However, it's just as dangerous to refuse to take control of those areas of our lives in which we really can make positive changes. Neither role—superhero or perpetual victim—suits any of us well.

We cannot know the difference as children. But as adults we must.

I n the aftermath of Kathy's death my parents sought out new surroundings; it was just too painful to be reminded of her everywhere. We moved from Indianapolis to Valparaiso, Indiana, a rural town of about twenty thousand. Despite its proximity to the Gary/Chicago area, Valparaiso was almost entirely Republican and, with the exception of a few students at the university, entirely white. My grade school had two classrooms.

I watched my mother try to carry on normally. Mom had all the traditional skills. She could cook a mean casserole; she sewed clothes for my sisters and me—and our dolls—but she was no June Cleaver clone. She lugged fifty-pound bags of cement around and laid our side patio all by herself; she built us a sandbox and a jungle gym.

Right from the start I thought that Dad had the better deal. For one thing, he had an infinitely more interesting job and workplace. He loved his work as a metallurgical engineer, and when I was very young he'd take me to his plant in Indianapolis, where the possibilities for new discoveries seemed endless. I was allowed to play in a huge pile of white sand and to melt wire with a hot soldering gun. I loved the metallic smell of solder as it dripped in small puddles, hardening on the workbench before me.

My father also encouraged my fantasies of adventure, no matter how far-fetched they seemed. When I was five, I told him we ought to hike to Chicago to visit Grandma Nell and Grandpa Ray. Instead of sending me to go play with my dolls, he helped plan the expedition.

"It might take a few days," he warned. "We'd better bring my old army helmet. We can fill it with water to wash our faces every morning."

I agreed. Getting to use his hallowed army helmet was a bonus I hadn't counted on.

He went so far as to have my mother drive us to his plant, so we could train for the journey by hiking home together. Then he bragged to her for days about how far we'd made it before having to call a taxi.

Maybe he encouraged my rambunctious behavior. At any rate, I was a tomboy—and I liked it that way. At Valparaiso's two-room country school, I was thrilled to wear jeans instead of the skirts and dresses I'd been forced into in Indianapolis schools. It was obvious to me that you couldn't do fun things in a skirt. I liked playing dodgeball, tossing snowballs, being a roughneck. A lot of the other kids there came from impoverished households—tar paper shacks with no indoor plumbing and little or no electricity. One of my playmates at the time, Betty, came from such a home. She was a strong, athletic little kid: tough, short-haired, and in her denim jacket and worn-out jeans, markedly unintimidated—and unimpressed—by boys. She also wasn't afraid to act out bold adventures.

Together we played Ming the Emperor and Flash Gordon. We pretended to fly to distant planets in futuristic spaceships. One of my other favorite games was playing outlaw, riding the range on the Wild West frontier. I used to play with a boy named Corky sometimes. Once, we were being pursued by the sheriff. "I'm Jesse James!" Corky announced. I thought of all the Western heroes and outlaws I could; none of them were women. "Okay," I said, bewildered, "but who will I be?" Corky, trying to be helpful, kissed me. "Don't worry, Patty. You can be just who you are—my girlfriend," he said. I didn't know whether that was good or bad, but I felt like the boys had a real advantage—at least they got their own names.

My adventurous behavior had shown up in other kinds of play, too. During a family weekend at the country home of my father's boss, the boss's daughter and I (we were both about six years old) wandered off for private games. We stripped ourselves naked and were happily playing doctor by the time our parents found us.

During our drive back home, my mother addressed this topic (to her credit, very subtly) in a confidential tone.

"You know, Patty, not all boys fall in love with girls when they get older, and not all girls fall in love with boys. Some boys fall in love with other boys. Some girls fall in love with other girls. But this makes their lives very hard."

Her tone was entirely calm and matter-of-fact. I wonder now what lay beneath her studied equanimity. On the surface of things, there was absolutely no clue as to what had prompted the discussion. "Not many mommies and daddies tell their little girls about these things," she added.

I stared at the backs of their heads as we drove, swelling with pride that they considered me grown up enough for them to share such important bits of information. Obviously, they also trusted that I'd keep it secret.

That was the sum total of my knowledge about sex. I had no

idea there was so much more to learn. So when our cat became pregnant when I was seven, I watched in amazement as her belly grew and asked a lot of questions. My parents explained to me how the kittens had gotten inside. Several neighborhood kids joined my mother and me to watch the cat deliver.

"Is that how my mom had *me*?" asked Jimmy Wade.

"Yes, Jimmy." Mom beamed. "People have babies—just like that!"

"Uuueeoogggh!" His face contorted in sheer disgust. For a moment, I thought he'd vomit. "You mean *my* mom had to lick off all that stuff?"

In a way that was both unusual for and typical of the 1950s, my mother was superb at talking about girls falling in love with girls and how kittens are made, and at the same time she carefully avoided discussing the delicate subject of sex in personal terms. Society's views on sex hadn't changed all that dramatically since my grandparents' day. Growing up in the Indiana heartland hardly provided me with a foundation for clear and open thinking about sexual issues.

As I left my childhood behind, I began to feel a vague, not-quite-conscious discomfort. The world was a place that I suspected I didn't quite fit into. On the other hand, I desperately *wanted* to fit in, to be like the other girls at school, to be well liked. I just didn't know quite how to do it.

Early in adolescence, I discovered that not all authority figures were as easy to circumvent as old Dr. Arnold—especially for a girl. As badly as I wanted to direct traffic, I could never talk my way into wearing a Patrol Boy's coveted sash in junior high. Girls, it seemed, didn't quite measure up.

Seeing no apparent options, I learned to accept some of these limitations.

"You're too old to play football with the boys now!" Mom warned.

Thus began my transformation from tomboy to stereotypically feminine woman.

It wasn't easy. I was physically awkward, having suddenly

grown five inches (sprouting from 5'2" to 5'7") in junior high.
Having skipped sixth grade, I was a year younger than most
of my classmates, and physically slow to mature (I wore an
undershirt instead of a bra—a tremendous embarrassment in
gym class). But I had a sort of country kid's desire for popularity, a need for outside reinforcement of my own worth. So I
began to shed my tomboy garb, to wear skirts again, to follow
the traditional social path laid out for a schoolgirl in the late
1950s.

All the things that were expected seemed to suit me for a
while. I did well academically. The part of me that had always
wanted to be outstanding, to excel, was never suppressed. In
my heart I was fiercely competitive: I wanted to be the very
best at anything I cared about.

I was an aspiring social butterfly, too, and yearned to be a
cheerleader—that high school post which seemed to bring with
it such dizzying heights of popularity—but I could never get
my feet and arms to cooperate. So I turned to other areas: student council, clubs, parties. Still, I never lost that desire to become a cheerleader. Even now, the sensual pleasures of autumn
football games are among my most vivid memories of my high
school and college days in Indiana: dried leaves, wind, cider,
uniforms, and pom-poms. There's a certain irony in the fact
that as president of NOW, the National Organization for
Women, I finally lead giant rallies as a sort of cheerleader.

The late 1950s and early 1960s were my rebellious teenage
years. In Valparaiso that meant beer, cigarettes, and sex. Some
other girls may have been sexually active in high school, but
almost no one was blatant or open about it—except me, and
my parents worried. (Actually, the boys talked about it more
than they did it, and the girls talked about it less.) After struggling through my high school years my mother became a birth
control advocate and a founder of Northern Indiana Planned
Parenthood. But at the time, the extent of my mother's advice
to me was not to have sex until I was married.

I began to figure out that "free love" carried devastatingly different consequences for girls than for boys. Boys were not the ones who risked getting pregnant and who faced society's condemnation for being sexually active. As a teenager I knew that my openness was as rebellious as the activity, and there was a painful price to be paid. The guys I was with were admired by their peers, while I got socially trashed. For all these reasons, I struggled to sort through my own passionate, difficult conflicts about sex and sexual issues well into adulthood.

For me, nothing succeeded like excess. I got good grades, was popular, had a busy social life, and I loved good times, including partying with the boys. If part of the feminine game was to catch a guy, I would show just how well I could play.

I wasn't conscious of my motivations. In fact I had little or no self-awareness at all. (In any powerless state of being, like childhood and adolescence, lack of consciousness and powerlessness go hand in hand.) But unconsciousness was also rewarded; thinking about things deeply was not.

"Don't be too introspective!" my mother warned.

Consciousness was dangerous. I believe now that my mother spent most of her life pushing emotions and self-awareness deep down inside her. Because of Kathy's death, she had plenty of dangerous emotions to suppress, and I think she was afraid that her own feelings might drive her crazy.

Because both of my parents—but especially my mother—insisted that I get a college degree and have some way to support myself before following the traditional path into marriage and children, my behavior frightened them. They feared I would get pregnant before completing my education or get drunk one night and wrap their car around a telephone pole. My typically teenage response was to deny that I was doing anything I couldn't handle, which compounded my parents' frustration. They must also have been embarrassed that my "wild" behavior was widely known in our small town.

"God protects drunks, fools, and teenagers," my mother would sigh, hopefully and somewhat philosophically.

From the perspective of my more integrated, adult self, I real-

ize that my split teenage personality resulted from my insecurity: an ingrained, profound insecurity from which most
women in our culture do not escape. I embraced the external
formalities of femininity, its appearances, behaviors, look, and
feel. But I really wanted it both ways; I wanted the safety of
being a traditional girl *and* I wanted the dangerous adventures
of masculinity. My teenage behavior was a carryover from my
earlier tomboy identity. Even without the benefit of feminist
consciousness, it seemed ridiculous to me that this kind of acting out was expected of boys and was only "bad" when girls
did it. And I think that by pushing against the restrictions and
limitations of the day, I was able to develop the instinct to question authority—and luckily I never did crash the car.

Underneath all the rebelliousness, of course, I never envisioned anything but a conventional Valparaiso-like future for
myself. I would go on to college. But after that, like my mother
before me, I'd get a job for a while, then marry and have children. I would stay at home to raise them and live happily ever
after.

D on Anderson worked at Tony's Pizza Parlor. One year
older than I, a high school football player with dark hair
and beautiful eyes that reminded me of Roy Rogers, he came
from a hard-working farming family in nearby Morgan Town-
ship.

Don was quiet, charming but reserved—less overtly wild
than most of my other friends. In comparison with me, in fact
(since I tried hard never to see beneath the surface of anything),
he seemed downright sensitive. He was not intellectual or
scholarly, but nevertheless quite intelligent. In addition to being
handsome, Don had a car and could dance—important criteria
for a seventeen-year-old girl looking to take her next big step
in life without really knowing exactly what that might entail.
I found him intriguing. We dated. I fell in love.

Don attended Ball State. I graduated from high school and

went off to DePauw University for a year. During the following summer (which he spent working at a local steel mill, while I took a job as a candy clerk serving fudge and caramel popcorn at Fetla's Bargain Center) we decided to get married. My parents would have liked to forbid it. But they knew Don and I were probably having sex and therefore thought we should be married. I think they also feared that if they stepped in and took control of my burgeoning adulthood in such a way I would always blame them for whatever went wrong in my life. They were absolutely right.

So they helped plan our wedding instead.

At seventeen I was a year older than my mother had been when she married my father.

Before my wedding night, my mother accompanied me to the gynecologist's office. I wanted a prescription for the Pill.

Birth control was still illegal then in some states, even for married couples. It was legal in Indiana, but it certainly wasn't promoted or encouraged. In fact, the doctor we went to turned me down flat.

"Young lady, I don't even give the Pill to my own nurses." He chuckled. "Even though they're always asking for it."

My mother suggested a diaphragm.

"Come back after the ceremony."

I could feel myself flush with hot, painful embarrassment as he escorted us from his office. I felt a terrible shame, too, as if I'd done something wrong.

My mother's response was healthier. She was so angry by the time we got home that she called her bank to stop payment on the check she had written to pay for the visit. Wisely, perhaps, the good doctor never did try to collect.

The Irelands were prominent citizens in Valparaiso, and my wedding, right out of the pages of *Bride's* magazine, promised to be the social event of the summer season. Don and I had kept all our old high school friends. The guest list was huge.

Scheduled to take place at the First Presbyterian Church in August 1963, it would be a wedding in true fifties style: five bridesmaids and groomsmen, traditional music, flowers, photographers, first dance with my father, second dance with my new husband. I spent six weeks choosing the gown: a gigantic bouffant thing with train to match.

The planning phase was by no means idyllic for anyone. The tremendously serious, binding nature of this upcoming public ceremony and celebration of solemn vows, the seeming irrevocability of what I was about to do, sent me into an on-again, off-again panic. There were afternoons when, overwhelmed, I sat in my childhood bedroom sobbing, thinking that my life was over; all would soon be lost. I was half adult, half child; I confided every bit of fear and ambivalence to my parents. They listened, afraid to interfere. The result was a wild emotional roller-coaster ride for all of us. When the Big Hour arrived, my mother (who had understandably been on the edge of hysteria for days) nearly went to pieces because her stocking ran as we were leaving home for church. Turning to my sisters, my father said he'd pay them to elope.

Nevertheless, Don and I exchanged vows that day. We cut the enormous multilayered white wedding cake without incident and toasted our marriage with champagne. I had nervously practiced dancing the two traditional wedding waltzes, with Dad and Don, for weeks beforehand. At the reception both waltzes went smoothly, without a single bruised toe.

"What am I doing here?" I thought, in a tension-filled daze.

Only one traditional element was missing: Don and I did not rush off afterward in a hail of rice. Upon learning that the rice thrown at newlyweds was meant to symbolize fertility, my father banned it from the wedding. He threatened to throw himself in the line of fire should even a single grain be tossed. My parents already thought we were much too young to be married, and they were absolutely adamant that we both finish college before starting a family. My mother insisted that I "have something to fall back on" if my husband should die or leave me. It was clear to me that she thought it was terribly important for me to gain the sort of economic self-sufficiency that she herself lacked.

Apart from that, everything seemed picture perfect.

The truth is that it wasn't. My own feelings of discomfort and ambivalence had settled in as soon as we became engaged.

I sensed all along that Don felt differently. A quiet, stable person, he'd always seemed ready to settle down. I was holding on to some fanciful notion of marriage as a vehicle for independence. When it loomed as reality, though, I feared it would mean a dreaded closing-up of my life, the end of all future personal growth or full human development. But once set in motion, the enormous machinery of a traditional wedding had a life of its own. Stopping it or even pausing it would have caused terminal embarrassment for everyone involved. Marriage was a ritual celebrated—and strongly supported—by the entire community. A large, planned wedding like ours seemed to have its own momentum. I found myself carried along with the entire tidal wave of expectations. I would have found it very difficult to go against that tide.

In one of my many moments of tearful ambivalence, I remember thinking that if I canceled this wedding I would have to leave town and change my name. The image of Grandma Nell popped into my mind, admonishing me, as she had done so frequently while I was growing up, "Remember, your grandmother was a lady." I asked myself what, then, was wrong with me? How could I possibly countenance such thoughts? How could I even think of embarrassing my family? I wanted to rise to the world's expectations and to fulfill my parents'. I was too emotionally immature to ask myself what my *own* expectations might be. All I knew was that I loved Don, and marriage seemed to be the thing we were supposed to do about that. If there were other options, they never occurred to me. I wasn't about to set myself up against the weight of my entire culture.

Had I been honest with myself, I would have had to admit that married life, as defined at that time, didn't suit me. The prospect of continually adapting myself to my husband's views and needs was suffocating. Yet marriage still seemed to be the next required step, a sort of scout's badge signifying official passage from girlhood to womanhood.

D on and I transferred to the University of Tennessee that fall to continue our undergraduate educations, moving into a little one-room efficiency off campus. Our parents split the cost of our tuition and housing. I studied to be a teacher at the school of education. Don struggled with his business school coursework, trying hard to live up to someone's notion that he ought to study law.

Much of the campus social life revolved around fraternities and sororities, and as a married couple, Don and I found ourselves quite isolated. Nevertheless, from among the thirty thousand students attending the university, we managed to make a few off-beat, off-campus friends. Domestically, we were not badly suited. Don and I shared most household responsibilities. Neither of us did dishes, though; I woke one morning to find him eating cereal out of a saucepan. And despite the fact that we were clearly out of our element from the beginning, there was a lot of sweetness to our daily life: We shared more than just the chores.

Apart from these tender moments, however, I struggled to quell a pervasive sense of emptiness inside. Cinderella had gone to the ball; she had married the Prince. But she was not content. I hid my growing doubts about continuing in the conventional role I'd assumed. I tried hard every day to be the beaming young bride, the devoted new wife, but secretly I felt increasingly unhappy and I wondered what was wrong with me.

Don dropped out of school in June, dashing all hope of becoming a lawyer. He and I moved to his parents' farm for the summer. I wonder now if he sensed my confusion about our life together. For the most part, I was very unconscious of it myself. Instead, I searched everywhere for external clues to my feelings. Maybe Don's abandonment of school was a confirmation, in my own mind, that we were mismatched.

I left Don one morning, just after he came in off his tractor from the fields. I told him our marriage wasn't working for me, and it probably wasn't working for him, either. It would be best to end it early. I was sorry.

Stunned, he asked if anything could be changed to make it work. I told him I didn't think so. Then I drove off, with my clothes and without further explanation, to my parents' house. It was all quite sudden. I still remember the puzzled look on his mother's face as I left.

Our divorce was mutual, entirely uncontested. Because of the restrictive laws, I had to allege mental and physical cruelty, none of which was true. The real reasons remained unspoken. Don and I were probably never really suited to each other to begin with, and, after our year at Tennessee, it became clear that we were headed in different life directions. Nevertheless, we'd genuinely cared about each other. The breakup caused no lasting anger, but it did cause grief and tears. At one point, Don told me that he felt a sense of failure, that something important, yet unknowable, had gone wrong. I told him of my sense that something was indeed wrong—with *me*.

My mother came to court with me on the day our divorce was finalized. I had a terrible cold and spent much of the time blowing my nose. Everyone thought I was crying.

Don and I divvied up our belongings. We didn't have much. The only thing of real material value was a camera; he took it, but left the case.

Divorce wasn't part of the All-American Girl's Dream—not as I'd learned it. For the first time in my life, I had no clear role to audition for.

In school, I drifted. I was willing to go wherever fate seemed to lead, and while this made for a certain terrifying aimlessness in attitude, it also left me open to the adventures that I secretly yearned for. Between my junior and senior years I took a summer job as a cancan dancer at Six-Gun Territory, a Wild West theme park in Ocala, Florida. I lived there in a house with four other young dancers, dated a sword swallower and fire-eater, served root beer, and danced at the Palace Saloon, wearing a feather in my hair, a fringed halter top, a ruffled skirt, and tap shoes. (I muffled the taps to mask all my mistakes, though I can still do a pretty good soft-shoe rendition of "Tea for Two.")

Back in school in the fall, I buried my tremendous post-divorce insecurities by clinging to an earlier goal of becoming a teacher. It had always been touted as a suitable career for a woman—and here I was needing "something to fall back on." I imagined standing in front of a classroom leading discussions. That appealed to me. I would feel smart then, in control, as if I knew what I was doing.

But after I earned my bachelor's degree, an unhappy year in graduate school teaching German to Tennesseans at 8:30 A.M. three days a week convinced me that I wasn't meant to teach. During my second quarter in the master's program, I received incompletes in two of four required courses. I deserved worse; only the kindness of my professors, who had known me in better days, saved me from expulsion. It was 1967, and as a defense against my confusion, I'd taken to heart the credo of the times: Turn On, Tune In, Drop Out. By the third quarter I realized this self-fulfilling prophecy and dropped out for good.

Divorced, at loose ends, I moved back home to Valparaiso and got a waitressing job. It felt like dying.

Having jettisoned both marriage and future career, my choices now seemed quite limited. The other traditionally acceptable jobs for women—nursing and secretarial work—were out of the question; the only thing that chilled me more than the sight of other people's bodily fluids was the sight of a type-writer.

There was nothing like career counseling for women back then, either, although I do remember that in 1966 a game called

"What Shall I Be? The Exciting Career Game for Girls!" had hit the market. Game participants were supposed to draw Personality Cards and Subject Cards to aid them in searching out the right career path. Subject Cards gave scenarios like this: "You failed English. Bad for: Teacher and Actress." A Personality Card advised: "You are clumsy. Bad for: Airline Hostess, Ballet Dancer, Model, and Nurse." Six career choices. What clumsy girls who flunked English were supposed to do still remains a mystery.

Luckily for me, I wasn't *that* clumsy.

I decided that if I was going to serve drinks for a living, I'd rather do it on a plane to Rio than in a cocktail lounge in Valparaiso. Grandpa Ray offered to use his connections at United. Maybe he could get me a job there as a stewardess.

I liked that thought.

I remembered the old photo of Grandma Nell holding my five-year-old dad in that open-cockpit biplane. Flying, I told myself, was in the Ireland blood. And I remembered the first flight I'd ever taken by myself, when I was almost five. My own "solo" flight was from Indianapolis to Chicago to visit Grandma Nell and Grandpa Ray. Kathy had died only a few months before. My child's heart had shielded itself with a numbness and bravado that masked overwhelming grief. That must have been why, during that first flight, I felt responsible, fearless, powerful, just as I imagined real grown-ups would feel. It must have been rare to see such a young girl flying by herself in 1950. My career goal at the time was to become a tightrope walker, but that image of my grandmother had already been with me for years. Air seemed the only way to travel.

The deafening engine noise, the circular little port windows, the stewardesses with their winged hats, and the Chiclets gum they gave me all seemed part of a glorious adventure. And the occasional turbulence? Nothing but wonderful fun: a roller-coaster ride.

*　*　*

Now, at twenty-two, I was well aware that stewardess work balanced on the edge of social respectability. The book *Coffee, Tea or Me* would not be published for many years, but being a flight attendant already bore all the status and dignity of being a cocktail waitress—you were automatically assumed to have a low IQ and questionable morals. The airlines themselves exploited this image in much of their advertising.

None of it kept me from being excited about the prospect of becoming one myself. A job like that would provide me with a paycheck and a ticket out of Indiana. Anyway, the "bad girl" mystique appealed to me, probably a holdover from my childhood when I'd dreamed of being a saloon girl in the lawless Old West. (Of course, I would have preferred to lead a gun-toting outlaw gang. But the two choices for women—in the TV shows and movies I'd been raised on, anyway—seemed to be schoolmarm or saloon girl. Well, I'd enjoyed my stint as a dancer at the Palace Saloon. True, the saloon girl inevitably got killed off in the end while the schoolmarm was somehow rewarded for her chastity by marrying the hero. Despite her predictably unfortunate end, I identified with the saloon girl, who had an exciting, albeit brief, life. The schoolmarm's existence was so uneventful that living it would seem an eternity. Anyway, I'd tried to become a teacher and rejected it.)

Flying also promised the adventure of travel. My grandparents had been around the world. I remembered being fascinated as a child by the graceful brass statue of an African woman that adorned their coffee table; I remembered jangling the intricately carved elephant bells from a far-away marketplace in India that rested on their bookshelf. Fingering these bells, listening to their clanky sound, I would imagine them bouncing along the flanks of real elephants and yearn for the chance to see these things myself. Now, I might just get it.

So in the fall of 1967, I left Indiana in search of the friendly skies and headed to Chicago, where I began interviewing with different carriers.

TWO

It didn't take long to catch on to what the airlines expected of female employees. The stewardess interviews had a decidedly pimpish quality. The interviews generally included a weigh-in—like that for a professional boxer or prize steer—and a more than cursory head-to-toe once-over. Only TWA actually made me get on a scale before they would even talk to me, and only once was I actually ordered, politely, to stand and turn around, slowly, so the interviewers could get a good look. To me it all felt a little bit sleazy. One interview was conducted in a grimy old building where threadbare carpeting stretched over an industrial surface. The interviewer wore a short-sleeved white shirt and clip-on tie, which made him look like a used-car salesman. I still remember his blond crewcut and Slavic features with a bit of a jowl. One of my last interviews took place in a rented hotel room filled with cheap, nondescript tables. This time, a man and a woman interviewed me. I remember that the woman was dark-haired and a little older, maybe thirty-two. Her face was very pretty but severe; when she spoke, her voice seemed harsh. I wondered whether or not she'd been a stewardess once. Had she gained too many pounds, or years, and then been forced to retire? Was the edge in her voice a subtle way of passing on her bitterness?

Most interviewers did their jobs like judges at a beauty contest. If you were their "type," you had a much better chance of being hired.

All of this, by the way, was perfectly legal.

I eventually got a job with Pan Am.

"I'll bet you were hired out of Chicago," a training school instructor joked. "That guy likes his women tall. And brunette."

P an Am trained its fledgling stewardesses in Miami, Florida. All of the trainees stayed at the Miami Airways Motel just north of the airport. I shared a room with three others. There was a pool and beautiful warm weather, but with the racket of planes taking off above us, cars honking away on Thirty-sixth Street, and the smell of pollution, chlorine, and mildew all around, it was hardly paradise. A new class of trainees started every Monday. Men prowled the motel like packs of wolves searching out easy prey.

The training school itself was more pleasant, with its big, clean, reflecting pool and colorful flags representing all the countries Pan Am visited. We called it the Taj Mahal. It was in this comparatively palatial setting that our trainer welcomed us to our new life.

"First of all," she said, "we expect you to use your heads. This is South Florida. Getting sunburned is a sign of irresponsibility and will result in your immediate dismissal."

The privilege of being chosen by Pan Am, she told us, carried with it certain obligations. "Please remember that your behavior reflects on the company wherever you are. We expect you to be pleasant at all times, attentive to the needs of those around you, and compliant with company requirements. Bursting into tears at the sight of your new haircut, for example, would demonstrate an unacceptably bad attitude."

She didn't laugh—or even smile. But I assumed she was joking. How bad could a haircut be?

I would learn later that week, after each trainee had been

looked at separately, from every angle, by one of the trainers whose job it was to assess us—and who then decided exactly how our hair would be cut and worn. Of course, the airline's mandated coiffures were, like the shaved heads of army recruits, a way to strip us of our individual identities in order to assume control over us. And it worked. That shearing had a deep effect. I often caught myself staring into a mirror, wondering who that was staring back.

One woman from Norway actually *did* burst into tears after her gorgeous long auburn hair was chopped off. Apparently, the beautician didn't report her.

The trainers never missed an opportunity to remind us that we were expendable. We could be sent away at any time and replaced immediately by scores of other eager young women waiting to work their way out of dead-end little towns—not just in the United States, but all over the world. We became so paranoid that we began to believe Pan Am spies had been planted up and down Thirty-sixth Street, carefully watching us at the uniform shop or the beauty salon, waiting for one of us to slip up and act unpleasant, inattentive, or noncompliant.

Throughout training, we were constantly told that the job offered wonderful preparation for fulfillment of marital duties, too: learning how to make your husband comfortable, how to serve him scotch on the rocks, how to diplomatically handle dinner conversation with his new boss. It was understood that working on an airplane (especially in first class) was a dandy way to catch a man.

The day I started training school—December 18, 1967—the morning paper carried a story about simultaneous demonstrations that had occurred the week before at the Equal Employment Opportunity Commission offices in New York, San Francisco, Chicago, Atlanta, and Washington, D.C. The protests had been staged by the National Organization for Women, a group formed the year before to advocate for women's rights.

The actions were part of an attempt by NOW to make the EEOC enforce Title VII of the 1964 Civil Rights Act, which requires equal employment opportunity for women. Waiting nervously for my first day of training to begin, I read about it as I sat in the coffee shop at the Miami Airways Motel. Years later, I would remember the story.

There was a saving grace in all this for me: James.

I met James Humble during my year in graduate school at the University of Tennessee. James attended school sporadically, interrupting his studies to earn money doing factory and agricultural work periodically. A big, handsome, fiercely individualistic and intelligent man, he stayed on the edges of the crowd I hung out with; we got to know each other through mutual friends. (My divorce had predetermined that I would find my friends among a fringe crowd of social outsiders.) On weekends, some of us would travel into the Smoky Mountains, swim in streams, take hallucinogens, rappel down the sides of caves.

James wasn't like any of the men I'd dated before. He was a thoughtful, serious skeptic—a talented painter and artist who wasn't afraid or ashamed to make a living doing manual labor. (It was James who first told me that most of our hippie friends of the sixties were going to wind up wearing three-piece suits one day. I remember that whenever I run into some old friend who sells insurance or is a stockbroker.) He enjoyed challenging all assumptions. He would play devil's advocate with anyone; arguing with him, I quickly learned how to stay on my toes. I also loved the fact that he took me seriously. He came from a family of strong, successful, highly educated women; he expected the other women in his life to be that way, too, and was most comfortable around women who knew what they wanted and went after it. James was also tremendously loyal to people he cared about, and in him I found a true friend. He visited me in Indiana while I was waitressing, and our relationship grew.

Later he showed up in Miami near the end of my stint at training school, and he never really left. We moved in together when I finished training.

From the beginning, James hated the way stewardesses were treated by the airlines. His ability to articulate his feelings about the disrespect we were subjected to on the job eventually allowed me to look at work—especially women's work—in a whole new way. Years of discussion with him would help me to express my own growing dissatisfaction.

Not everyone survived stewardess training. Those of us who did took off for our assigned bases. Mine was Miami.

I soon found that practically everyone had authority over the lowly stewardess. This was true both in the air and on the ground. When we weren't working a flight, the men in charge of scheduling—they were all men—could exercise almost complete control over our lives. In the air, the all-male flight crew ruled. Navigators and second officers were our superiors, never to be disobeyed. Captains had dictatorial power; some used it more benevolently than others.

Some pilots used to joke that, like ships' captains at sea, ours could perform marriages that were valid—at least for the duration of the trip. This, of course, suggested to us in a not-so-subtle way that we were there to provide service—and entertainment—on layovers, too. In the years to come, as fewer and fewer stewardesses were willing to play that game, one pilot moaned that "because of all you women's libbers" no one would go out to dinner with him anymore. "The only evidence that you're even here," he added, "is the picked-over chicken bones on those room service trays outside your doors!" I couldn't help but smile, pleased that so many of us had found better things to do.

Next in rank after pilots came the pursers. Pursers had direct control over all the tasks and activities of stewardesses during a flight. Several women, including me, had taken the additional training required for this post, and I eventually gained the necessary seniority to get the promotion. But when I began working as a stewardess, the majority of the pursers were men who'd been hired long before Pan Am decided that all-female cabin crews made for better advertising. In addition to being our supervisors in the air, they competed with pilots for our attentions on the ground. At the beginning of a ten-day trip, one guy actually asked me whether I was "a pursers' girl" or "a pilots' girl"—apparently he didn't want to waste his time on me if I was the latter. I laughed this off with an unresponsive comment about the arrogance of the cockpit crew, hoping to feed his purser's ego and at the same time deflect his question. When the flight began, I busied myself handing out magazines to first-class passengers.

It was more difficult to laugh it off later, though, when the same purser brushed against me too enthusiastically in the narrow galley. My skin crawled; anger flushed my neck and cheeks. Then my internal defenses kicked in: Anger was suppressed by shame when I realized that my earlier comment had probably emboldened him. The reality was that I was afraid to confront him and risk being stuck in the economy-class galley for the rest of the trip. So I let him get away with it.

Of course, I also took pains not to give offense to another group of people who had the power directly to affect my job: passengers. In training school, we'd been told the apocryphal story of a rich woman who, upon boarding in New York, disdainfully dropped her fur coat at the feet of the stewardess working first class. What did our long-suffering paragon of good grace do? She simply picked up the coat with a smile and hung it in a closet. The message was clear: No matter how surly or insulting passengers became, we weren't supposed to do anything but grin and bear it. I learned a similar lesson in the value of a good sense of humor on my first flight. During take-off, one passenger began frantically ringing her call button.

From my jumpseat at the rear of the plane, I could see her, and I remembered she had two small children. Since most passengers don't expect service during takeoff, I figured it must be an emergency. Filled with adrenaline at the thought of performing some heroic deed on my very first assignment, I swiftly unbuckled my shoulder harness, clambered up the steeply inclined length of the plane, and arrived breathlessly at her seat, fully prepared to administer mouth-to-mouth resuscitation.

But she was calmly reading. Without looking up she said, "I'd like a Coke. No ice."

I was supposed to smile sweetly. To tell her there was no drink service at that time, but I'd be glad to help her once we leveled off. But I was afraid that if I opened my mouth fire would leap out. I slid back down to the jumpseat instead. Now that I knew she wasn't dying, I wanted to kill her myself. Back in my seat, I shared my homicidal impulse with the other stewardesses, and we worked ourselves into a state of happy hysteria debating the ideal place to hide the body and imagining the maintenance worker who would someday find the mummified remains wrapped up in the inflatable life raft. The camaraderie was a psychic lifesaver.

The work of a stewardess is physically very demanding. In those days we served hot meals to everyone on each flight. We were constantly on our feet: running up and down aisles serving soft drinks and food, rushing to bring hundreds of trays and glasses back to the galley before landing. And there was, of course, the mental pressure of continually being at everyone's beck and call for hours on end. The easiest target for every passenger's frustration—whether they'd lost their luggage, missed a connecting flight, or been bumped from another—was the friendly stewardess. I had a college education and was fluent in German and Spanish. In fact, well-educated, multilingual women from many different countries worked as international stewardesses. Ironically, the passengers usually treated us as if we were invisible, the lowliest of servants.

Sometimes invisibility would have been preferable. We stewardesses had to deal with everything from whistles to virtual molestation by men all along the way—airline employees and passengers alike. I remember feeling the bold touch on the back of my thigh while serving food; looking around, I saw a guy grinning crudely, daringly, across the aisle. "Watch out for the guy in 3C," I warned everyone back in the galley. "He's a grabber."

The passengers weren't the only problem. Twice a year, flight attendants were required to undergo a review of emergency and first-aid procedures. To get to the training area at our base airport, we had to walk the length of a huge hangar where most of the mechanics worked. These fellows—and they were all fellows—always raised a ruckus as we passed through. Sometimes I'd try to ignore the hoots and maintain a little dignity. Far too often, though, I'd wave back, acting as if it were a great compliment to be treated like a rack of meat.

Complaining would have done no good. It would have shown someone higher up that I had a decidedly "negative" attitude, one unbecoming the perfect Pan Am stewardess. Our jobs were always at risk. And it wasn't as if there were scores of great employment options for women in those days. Many women, myself included, viewed sexual harassment as the price of admission into the workplace. Since I felt powerless to stop it, I simply resigned myself to paying the entrance fee. If this was what it took to have the economic independence denied to our mothers and grandmothers, so be it.

Our job brought us in contact with hazards other than those posed by demeaning behavior. Dealing with drunks in flight was a common danger. And, of course, some places on the ground were dangerous for an unaccompanied woman: Tehran, Bogotá, Rio de Janeiro. In these cities, in countries and cultures so far from my own, I began to get a picture of just how restricted women's lives were. I knew better than to walk through the marketplace in Tehran without a pilot by my side; local women, their angry eyes peering over the top of their chadors, would throw tomatoes at an unaccompanied woman or one with bare arms and a short skirt.

On the ground at our Florida base, we were all subject to the ironfisted rule of the grooming supervisor, a kind of homegrown equivalent of the tomato-throwers. This civilian drill sergeant—always a woman—was in charge of seeing to it that every flight attendant followed all the personal grooming regulations mandated by the company.

Of course, as in Tehran, these regulations may have been enforced by women, but they were usually mandated by men (although it was rumored that the wife of Pan Am's president had a say in selecting our getup). In any case, the specifications pointed to a man's image of the stereotypically ideal woman (an ideal that, in reality, few women can ever achieve, although many waste tremendous amounts of energy trying).

We stewardesses had to wear red lipstick and fingernail polish—no other color was acceptable. On the ground, our black high heels had to measure at least three inches. White gloves and a pillbox hat were absolute necessities. As in training school, hair was strictly regulated: Not one strand could drop below the jawline, and the style had to "look good in the rain" (or, by extension, during an emergency evacuation at sea). Pan Am even interested itself in our underwear. Brassieres and slips were required at all times. So was the iron maiden of women's wear: the girdle.

Our grooming supervisor also kept a sharp lookout for the forbidden: glasses, false eyelashes, dangly earrings, clanky bracelets, and too many rings on our fingers or pounds on our hips. If she thought we looked a little heavy, she had the right to stick us on a scale—and suspend us if our weight surpassed company-designated limits.

Before each trip we passed by this woman's office on our way to the preflight briefing room. It was nearly impossible to sneak by without getting the once-over (especially if you looked guilty).

"Patricia, you're not wearing your girdle!" she'd yell from behind her desk. I'd stop to listen to her lecture on the importance of not jiggling when I walked.

In fact, I conveniently "forgot" to wear my girdle whenever possible. Though not as bad as the whalebone corsets foisted on women in earlier centuries (Victorian ladies were always swooning because their internal organs had been crushed together), the elastic contraptions were no picnic. They cut off circulation, made it harder to breathe during altitude changes, and wreaked havoc on varicose veins.

For its part, Pan Am must have viewed the girdle as a kind of modern-day chastity belt. Our supervisors wanted us to be friendly and flirtatious with male passengers, but they certainly didn't want *their* girls looking like hookers. As long as we wore those magical girdles, it must have signified to them that our supposedly wild sexual urges could be kept safely under control. We were mythological whores; we were also mythological virgins. As a result, Mr. So-and-So in 16A could leer or call me "honey" without feeling unfaithful to his wife.

The truth is that most of us would wear our girdles only until takeoff. Then we'd sneak into the bathroom and stash them in our flight bags. Those damned things hurt.

That I could get through the flights themselves in relatively good humor was due in no small part to the other stewardesses. When those plane doors closed behind us, we needed each other's support. What bound us together was an us-against-the-world mentality and a determination to retain the very sense of individuality that everyone around us—especially the company—was trying to stamp out.

In spite of all this, flying remained a tremendous thrill for me. During takeoff, I loved the overwhelming rumble of the plane revving up; the release of brakes made me feel as if I were catapulted through space from a giant slingshot. Then came the rush, the hint of weightlessness, of being freed from gravity. Even the thought of it made me giddy. And there were those glorious sunrises in flight, breaking through the clouds. I was never afraid. In fact, part of the pleasure was feeling fearless—especially in situations that made others nervous.

Most of the time I could convince myself that the girdles and the obnoxious pilots and pursers and passengers were just the downside of an exciting job. Nothing about the work was routine, including my schedule. I loved getting paid to fly to Barbados for dinner, or spending hours exploring Mexico City's museums. My ever-changing schedule meant that I could drive across the Rickenbacker Causeway to Key Biscayne and tan on the beach or slide into an air-conditioned movie house without fighting weekend crowds. Above all I loved the feeling of great mobility, of continually heading off to new and different places. Part of the yearning to be somewhere else, of course, was a desire to be someone else, without all the pressures of conforming to any particular community. And off the job—away from the pressures of company-imposed uniformity—I keenly felt the possibility of growing into a different woman: from Patty to Pat to Patricia. I could shed parts of my old persona and really start to *be* who I was becoming.

"Hey, Patricia. Fix me a steak while we wait this one out." The captain emerged from the cockpit, adjusting his hat to a jaunty angle, and turned into the jetway. "Make it medium rare."

In training school I'd been taught that the captain was, if not God Himself, at least a minor deity. I moved into the galley and fired up the grill.

Pan Am had received another bomb threat that day, and our flight from Miami International to Piarco Airport in Trinidad had been temporarily grounded. This wasn't anything out of the ordinary at the time; bomb scares and skyjackings—especially from Miami—had become relatively routine. Armed

U.S. sky marshals were a common sight on our flights; we stewardesses could always spot them by the pained looks on their faces (their concealed guns and holsters made it difficult for them to sit comfortably in the cramped economy seats). This time, after herding a lot of unhappy passengers back to the safety of the terminal, I returned to gather my own belongings. That's when the captain emerged, ordering dinner.

So a future president of the National Organization for Women found herself alone in the galley of an evacuated 727 that might blow up at any moment, cooking this guy a filet. Medium rare.

As blasé as I'd become about bomb threats, it suddenly occurred to me that this one might just be the real thing. I had resigned myself to the other hazards of a lowly flight attendant's role: the long hours, low pay, leering passengers, groping copilots. But in that moment I realized that I had no real obligation to lay my own life on the line for our captain's dinner. If he didn't feel obliged to risk going down with the ship, why should I? I turned off the grill. I left the plane.

He was sitting comfortably in the crew lounge, reading a newspaper. I approached, smiling.

"Captain?"

"Hmmm?"

"Cook your own steak."

Ever the cordial flight attendant, I refrained from telling him where he could stick it.

I n retrospect, that incident was a turning point. A small thing, really, just a moment of rebellion. It didn't feel important at the time; after all, I told myself, I was just expressing aggravation. It didn't immediately change my career, my relationships, or anyone's attitude about me. But it was a first step toward taking some real control over my own life. No matter where we are in life, it's important to seize these moments of opportunity and take the next step—whatever that may be—to gain more control. It doesn't matter if the step seems small. No change is insignificant. It *does* make a difference.

Individuals don't act in a vacuum. We're part of history—of the world events happening around us, all the time. We reflect and mirror and react to them daily.

While I was wandering up and down aisles serving coffee, tea, and a tightly packaged version of my stewardess persona to passengers on either side, the 1960s were happening, too, and it was much more than sex, drugs, and rock 'n' roll. The civil rights movement, the antiwar movement, the gay rights movement, and a newly revived feminist movement all were gaining strength and visibility. There was the sense, shared by many people of many different backgrounds, that the limits of anyone's role could be expanded—exploded—and that this was the right thing to do.

Even those stewardesses who didn't identify with the burgeoning feminist movement, or with *any* of the other political movements of the sixties, were affected by the atmosphere. Oh, some still clung to the fantasy of meeting her knight in shining armor: an oil baron, perhaps (sitting in first class), who would sweep that lucky stewardess off her feet and into a Bel Air mansion. Personally, I never witnessed such an event. But most of us, like so many other women in our country, were starting to look at ourselves in a different light, to value ourselves more, to demand more respect from others.

Despite all the loud turmoil, social experimentation, and exploration and expression of individual freedom going on in our country in the late 1960s, the airline industry remained rooted in the past. The industry still presented fifties-style advertising schemes to the public, like Continental's "We Really Move Our Tails For You!" and National's "I'm Cheryl—Fly Me!" Painfully oblivious to the social upheaval of the day, all the major airlines gleefully perpetuated the notion that flight attendants were pretty bimbos, there to service men.

Because it was difficult at best to develop a sense of self-worth working as stewardesses, many of us looked elsewhere.

I worked with flight attendants who were Girl Scout troop leaders, church choir directors, and volunteers at rape crisis centers and county courthouses in their spare time. Many flight attendants had a second job, not just for the money but to ensure their primary identity would be based on more than running up and down airplane aisles. Of course, whether we did it for pay or not, women's work continued to be service work, caretaking work. The doors leading into the halls of real political and economic power and influence were still shut tight against us.

Working as a stewardess continued to be a never-ending struggle to maintain some kind of identity apart from the care-taker/seductress persona that the airline insisted we constantly wear: In defending its women-only hiring policy regarding flight attendants (*Pan Am* v. *Diaz*, 1967), the company hypocritically argued that passengers preferred women attendants, because our "maternal" presence had a calming influence on them. But if the airline considered you overweight, all respect for the "maternal" image went out the window—you were gone. In fact, motherhood was grounds for dismissal.

This extraordinary double message that we were given about motherhood is still prevalent in our culture today. Motherhood is good, beautiful, necessary, and important, we are told; but it is treated as unattractive, irresponsible, and worthless. Mothers deserve to be put on a pedestal, begifted and adored; but mothers are second-class citizens, undeserving of society's practical support.

Though I never suffered the indignity of choosing between a child and a job, slowly but surely I began to feel the need for a lot more respect—in the air and on the ground. Here I was: a highly skilled employee who could rattle off emergency instructions in three languages, deliver a baby at thirty thousand feet, and evacuate a 747 in ninety seconds upside down, underwater, in the dark—and I was being sold for my smile! It was getting harder and harder to stay in character as the Ever-

Pleasant Flight Attendant. How could I respect myself if I couldn't respect the way I acted in uniform twenty days or more each month?

I had started to see the countries we visited as more than just exotic places to get a tan. During layovers I spent less time lounging by the pool and more time exploring. The devastating poverty in Nicaragua and El Salvador and the tin and cardboard shacks of Mexico City—where people also lived under plastic sheets on the rooftops of buildings, where tiny children sold Chiclets on the corner and fire-eaters destroyed their throats and lungs to earn a few pesos—made a crushing impression. I'd seen rural poverty in Indiana, but nothing like this. Whenever possible I devoured local newspapers, trying to get a feel for the politics and social conditions of each place. I began to think more globally and more politically.

Nor was I blind to what was going on back home. It was virtually impossible to live in the United States in the late 1960s without being exposed to the growing antiwar movement. For most of my life I'd been pretty apolitical. But any ambiguity on my part about the Vietnam War evaporated when, in early 1968, the Viet Cong overran the U.S. Embassy in Saigon. Television footage and press coverage of the Tet Offensive showed me the extent to which our own government had been lying about our "success" in this war. It also brought home the grim reality of what was really going on in Southeast Asia. *Life* magazine's bloody spread on the seventy-seven-day bombing of Khe Sanh cut through any last belief I might have had in some cryptic domino theory. Like others my age, I found that I could no longer accept a foreign policy based on destroying people in order to save them from Communism.

So there I was in a Pan Am stewardess uniform several days each week—heels, hat, lipstick, and all; the rest of the time I was hanging out with James and our friends, wearing love beads and patchouli oil and worrying about the war. I had dealt with the job by treating it as a role, as though, on duty, I were playing someone else, but as the differences between my private life and life at work became more pronounced, I found that what had once been a pretty good internal coping mechanism had started to crumble. My day-to-day existence began to feel schizophrenic.

James and I got married around this time.

We'd been pretty happy living together up until that point, without religious or official sanction. But after Grandpa Ray passed away, my mother called and offered us his big blue Rambler. We'd have to fly up to North Carolina to pick it up.

"You know," she mentioned, "there's only a one-day waiting period to get married in North Carolina."

Thinking it over, I realized I'd feel more comfortable if James and I were married, too. I was crazy about him, sure—we had a wonderful relationship—but, in retrospect, I realize there was more to my desire for marriage than that. I wanted to hold on to him somehow, because I felt incomplete and insecure about us, about myself. Oh, I liked the facade of being a free spirit well enough. But the traditional part of me felt I needed a man as a sort of legitimizing credential in the world and wanted the security of a legal tie.

Anyway, matrimony carried an added bonus: travel benefits. As an Eastern mechanic I once knew joked, "Marry me, and fly for free!" If James became my legal spouse, he'd be able to share in the one part of my job that I truly loved—the freedom to fly almost anywhere in the world.

I also assumed that as my husband he would be covered by my health insurance plan. This was no minor consideration. I earned barely ten thousand dollars a year, and James was still in college. With so little money between us, I often worried about what would happen if he ever became ill.

We got married in a minister's study in Hendersonville, North Carolina. My parents were the only guests.

Afterward we drove Grandpa Ray's blue Rambler back down to Miami. A month later, we had to sell it for rent money.

* * *

James and I began spending more and more time in Miami's Coconut Grove, a longstanding community of artists and hippies. The area has changed since the sixties: Now a series of large, expensive shopping malls and exclusive little boutiques line all the streets, but, at the time, it was the Southeast's answer to Haight-Ashbury. As a painter, James fit right in. And, in Coconut Grove, I always underwent a dramatic transformation from nail-polishing stewardess to a freer, more questioning self. At the same time that my airline job constricted my personality, it also allowed me the free time to spend with our crowd of Grove friends, who were not nine-to-fivers. We found ourselves happily entrenched in a vibrant subculture of writers, artists, and poets. Although this community imposed its own brand of conformity in many ways, individual expression was valued highly.

Stimulated by James's creativity, and by the comparative freedom of the Grove, I began to chafe at the cookie-cutter image Pan Am had designed for me. My acts of rebellion at work, however small, did not go unnoticed.

At first my growing dissatisfaction manifested itself in rather unproductive activity. I still had one thing in common with many of my coworkers: the will and the way to get knee-walking drunk. I don't even remember how many layovers were spent partying and drinking in hotel rooms, taking the party—complete with glasses and rapidly emptying bottles—out into lobbies, skinny-dipping in pools, laughing at the irate complaints of the hotel managers. I used the booze to keep from having to deal with my life. That way I didn't have to face the question, What's wrong and what would I rather be doing?

But just because we were drinking buddies didn't mean that I wasn't starting to alienate some of my coworkers. I had been reading Simone de Beauvoir's The Second Sex and articles by feminists in this country, and these writings spoke to me. Inevitably, I tried out my new ideas on the people closest at hand: Some were more receptive than others. In a swelteringly hot crew van on the way from the airport to the hotel in Buenos

Aires, exhausted at the end of a sixteen-hour shift, I was engaged in an interesting discussion with the copilot about how women's work—especially housework—was undervalued and underpaid, when the captain turned around and interjected, "I think my wife's got a good deal, a damned good deal. We have a maid for the housework, so she really doesn't do anything all day. But *I* come home after a long flight, and she's got this list of demands . . ."

All conversation in the van stopped dead, and everyone looked at me to see if I'd explode. I obliged them.

"Isn't that the ultimate sign of wealth!" I snapped. "To be able to afford a slave who doesn't *do* anything?"

I was a little shocked at myself after saying this. I hadn't been aware of thinking anything like that. But it came from somewhere inside me, somewhere real.

After a few moments of stunned silence, he started to laugh. "Boy, Patricia. You really *have* gone off the deep end!"

End of conversation. True, by letting my anger and sarcasm get the best of me, I'd blown my chance to have a persuasive conversation; then again, I thought I'd made a pretty snappy comeback, and I felt pretty good about it. Years of experience with political leadership would later teach me that I can make my arguments passionately and still be persuasive—if I don't let indignant rage get in the way; but I wasn't quite there yet!

My anger (and all my futile attempts to bury it) was symptomatic of something that was happening inside me. I was at another real turning point in my life: Willing, and *almost* ready, for change, I didn't yet possess the tools to make that change on my own. This is the most frustrating phase in the process of change: The beginnings of consciousness, awareness of self, painful dissatisfaction with self and world, and the desire for great change in both are the first unsettling glimmerings that tell us a turning point has been reached—when you *know*, but don't have the slightest idea yet what to *do* about it all.

As a budding feminist, I hadn't left my armchair (or jumpseat, as the case may be). Mouthing off in crew buses hardly made me a political activist. When getting drunk or belligerent became too exhausting, I went out exploring on layovers. Once, I got lost hiking in El Salvador. I wandered through a poverty-stricken village in the countryside, flies swarming over me under a baking sun. Women and children stared. I felt ugly, odd: a tall, pale woman from some other world who did not belong here at all. I felt I had absolutely nothing of use to give or to share. Somehow, I imagined, they knew that. An old farmer, speaking an Indian dialect that I could not understand, finally pointed me toward a road with a bus stop. Saved from further introspection and terror—about myself, my future, the world—for another day.

It was in El Salvador, too, that I ran into a British film crew making a political documentary; I spent several hours with them in a little café, doing what I now loved best—talking politics. At the end of the day they offered me a job. I don't know whether they were serious, but I do know that on the flight home, I realized that something *had* to change in my life—and soon. Yet, everywhere I turned, change seemed unfeasible. I spent a depressing few hours wondering about what might have been. But as a way of avoiding these difficult issues I told myself that climbing into the mountains to search out hidden villages or to interview the campesinos about their annual income, documenting economic disparity and terrible social inequity, couldn't pay the rent.

James and I traveled together whenever we could to out-of-the-way places that few people we knew outside the airline had seen. In Latin America, the Middle East, and Asia poverty was gruesomely overt, signaled by tremendously high infant mortality rates and high incidences of illness and chronic health problems that one rarely saw in the industrialized West. In pre-revolutionary Nicaragua, I saw how a devastating earthquake had intensified the misery of the abject poor. Everywhere, men, women, and children suffered horribly. But the extreme suffering of women and their children stabbed at my heart. I was perilously close to being touched once and for all. So much of women's suffering seemed avoidable. Too much of it was the result of a lack of just a little bit of education, of a little more freedom of mobility, of the most basic resources that any society owes its members: clean water, sanitation, sufficient protein for newborns, respect and humane treatment from families and spouses.

In many places, women seemed beaten down and resigned to their second-class status. In Mexico City, where I often had layovers, I could no longer ignore the innumerable women and children everywhere who clung to life in wretched poverty. These women were old and toothless at a young age, their eyes bereft of hope. But I was always keenly aware that these women, as pummeled as they were, yearned for their children to have a better life, and I saw firsthand the desperate measures to which this yearning led. As long as I live, I will not forget the day in rural India when a young woman tried to give James the infant she held in her arms.

But I remained protectively detached in the face of my first real encounters with the worldwide suffering of women. It was as if it represented something that did not, and could not possibly, have anything to do with me at all. This was part of my lifelong, increasingly futile attempt to keep things that really moved me at arm's length. Yet despite my best efforts and my early training I couldn't help but begin struggling to deal with my own emotions. My first response (a distinctly unproductive one) was guilt. If people all over the world were suffering so much, I told myself, I ought to stop being such an ingrate, complaining about things like housework and girdles. My second response was a feeling of wanting to help all these suffering others, as if I was some white Lady Bountiful.

Then I realized that if I was going to change anything, the first thing I had to change was myself. I wasn't sure how, but I began to believe that if I changed myself, then maybe I would be able to do something for other women.

For the time being, this decision to change took place on a

purely internal level. Nevertheless, my consciousness was permanently aroused; it felt like an awakening. I began to consistently ally myself, in my heart and mind, with the progressive side of political movements. While James worked on a film crew for CBS News at the 1968 National Democratic Convention in Chicago—the front line of the antiwar movement—I was in my stewardess uniform getting ready to fly to San Juan. Walking through the Miami airport, I passed a bar and saw on its TV screens the violence unleashed by Mayor Richard Daley and the Chicago police on the protesters. I went cold with fear. It was obvious that the last thing Daley would want was for the world to see the carnage going on in his city, and I was terrified that James, whose job it was to take fresh footage from the camera crew and run it in for broadcasting, would be an obvious target for the police. And the police were out of control. James was stopped by a cop who confiscated the film he was carrying and hurled James's motorcycle into a crowd of demonstrators for good measure, but luckily, he escaped unharmed. To this day, I believe the only thing that saved him from a beating was his short hair. He had always kept it close-cropped; occasional sideburns were his sole concession to the style of the hippie era.

Besides fear for James's safety and anger at the danger he found himself in, I felt shame for having taken no risks for the cause I'd come to believe in. Of course, I didn't consider myself much of a revolutionary. I knew that the world wasn't exactly a perfect place, but I also felt powerless to do much about that. So I continued to race up and down airplane aisles in a state of inner turbulence and discontent, serving champagne to rich people. Some radical.

My first tepid foray into activism was the Pillbox Hat Incident.

Although it had already fallen out of fashion by the late 1960s, this annoying bit of once high-fashion headgear, popularized by Jacqueline Kennedy, was required wearing for stewardesses whenever we were on the ground in uniform. The utterly useless hats invariably mashed our hair into a rat's nest of tangles. As soon as we were airborne we'd tear them off, then run to the tiny bathrooms and try desperately to comb ourselves back into some semblance of presentability. It wasn't just vanity: Our coiffure had been legally mandated to look perfect; nobody wanted any bad-hair reports to get back to the grooming supervisor.

The compulsory wearing of pillbox hats may not seem like a burning human rights issue, but it was a source of real stress and a general waste of energy. We might land and take off several times a day, traveling up and down Central America or the Caribbean on flights that lasted little more than half an hour. With 125 passengers on board waiting for magazines and Bloody Marys, we really didn't have time to be beauticians on each leg of the trip.

Finally, ten of us sent a letter to our base manager, John Lorenz, complaining that the pillbox hat requirement constituted discrimination against female flight attendants. After all, none of Pan Am's male pursers had to deal with this moronic bit of millinery.

Lorenz's response dripped sarcasm. Men and women at Pan Am had always worn different uniforms, he wrote, and always would. Would we be satisfied, he asked, if the company required men to wear brassieres and skirts? (We might have been, but we knew he'd say no if we decided to take him up on it.) The message was clear: Decisions about how we dressed, like everything else about us, would continue to be made by men in a corporate boardroom; if we didn't like it, tough.

Such humbling experiences tended to kill any enthusiasm for activism among the stewardess ranks, but for some reason, Lorenz's discouraging response had a different effect on me. It made me mad to be treated that way. It made me feel small and foolish and helpless. But it also made me determined to start fighting back against some of the systematically demeaning elements of my job. Although our letter had brought us nothing but sarcasm, it was a first step of sorts. I'd had a tiny taste of activism. And regardless of the outcome, I liked it! In some small but essential way, I was inspired.

If I was going to stand up for my rights again, though, I needed a better issue—a more clear-cut incident of discrimination, one in which we stewardesses had much more of a direct *economic* stake. The opportunity soon came in the form of James's impacted wisdom teeth.

We had no large appliances left to pawn off for quick cash when his teeth began to really hurt him, so I breathed a sigh of relief at the thought of Pan Am's medical coverage. His benefits as the spouse of an airline employee would be a lifesaver. Dutifully, I headed down to the company insurance offices to fill out paperwork. I was probably a bit naive—this being my first experience with major medical costs of any sort—but I certainly didn't expect problems. Imagine my surprise upon being told that Pan Am's insurance didn't cover my husband, even though it covered my fellow employees' wives. This was like a splash of ice water right in my face. If I'd been a man, my family would have been protected. Because I was a woman, my family was not.

I shouldn't have been so shocked. The airline and its competitors were much more interested in their bottom lines than in anything as esoteric as equal rights. Short-shrifting stewardesses was easy, relatively risk-free, and a sure way to show higher profits. Up until 1966, stewardesses faced mandatory retirement at age thirty-two or upon marriage—whichever came first. And, even after that policy fell, it would be another decade before flight attendants could become pregnant without getting fired.

What a great deal for the airlines! The entire operation was geared to ensure that we female flight attendants didn't take too big a chunk out of profits. (Stewardesses are still paid so little that, in many cases, new hires qualify for food stamps.) The industry could get away with it, even after the collapse of the mandatory retirement policy, because stewardesses generally didn't stay on the job long, and very few of us were active in the union or held union posts. If the airlines could keep moving us out at a relatively young age, they didn't have to worry about providing pensions or long-term health care benefits, not to mention maternity leave or child care. Ultimately, they were assured of a cheap and exploitable labor force through the constant turnover of young, female employees.

I didn't think about any of this at the time. Instead, I assumed there had been some kind of mistake. So I went to my supervisor and told him what had happened. "That's just the way it is," he said. And finally, something inside me snapped.

My anger—and a newfound sense of confidence—was fed by the certainty that this double standard was blatantly unfair; there was no way Pan Am could get away with it. The role of ditsy stewardess who could be counted on to keep her mouth shut was no longer one I was willing to play. Anyway, I had no choice. Neither James nor I had the money to cover his oral surgery. I decided to fight.

Had I tried to take on insurance practices in the airline industry ten years earlier, I would have been in trouble. But after the explosion of civil rights activities in the sixties, I knew that a lot of groundwork had already been laid for this case. I had never in my life been to a political meeting or demonstration organized by the revitalized feminist movement. But I identified with the movement from a distance, and instinctively felt that, in some way, I was a part of it. Help was out there; I just had to figure out who to call.

I looked up the local chapter of the National Organization for Women in a phone book and left a message on their answering machine.

Elaine Gordon, then chair of the Employment Discrimination Committee for Dade County NOW, returned my call the next day. I explained my situation.

She asked me if Pan Am did any federal contract work that I knew of. They did. "Pan Am flies military air command charters taking soldiers from Vietnam for R and R in Hawaii," I told her. "I think they also do maintenance work at Cape Canaveral. Is that what you mean?"

"Call the Department of Labor," she advised. "Any company doing federal contract work is absolutely bound by affirmative action requirements and equal employment laws to cover you. If Pan Am doesn't deal up front with your complaint, they could face losing all their government business."

Affirmative action for federal contractors had been ordered by Lyndon Johnson just a couple of years earlier; he had extended the affirmative action requirements in 1967 to cover women less than twenty-four months before my call to NOW. No company had yet lost government business for failure to comply, but the law was on the books. The National Organization for Women had initially been founded for the specific purpose of pressuring the government to enforce equal opportunity laws on behalf of women, Elaine reminded me. She wished me luck.

I listened carefully and followed her advice.

The response was astounding.

I never even had to file an official complaint. I placed the call to the Labor Department and told my story. I can only assume that they called Pan Am, because the next thing I knew, the same supervisor who had told me "that's just the way it is" was telling me that the entire episode had been a "misunderstanding." Family coverage was only for heads of household, he said, and women were automatically assumed not to qualify. But if I *was* the head of my household—which I was because James was a student at the time—then of course they would cover his dental surgery.

My initial reaction was relief: We had averted another financial crisis. Eventually, though, it hit me: *I had won!* Patricia Ireland, the pillbox hat–wearing, scotch-pouring servant, had taken on the big boys and come out ahead. For once, I didn't feel like a helpless pawn.

I had buried the tough little tomboy part of my nature so

deep inside that I'd begun to see myself the way the rest of society did: as a little girl, too well mannered and weak to fight back. My long-established pattern—the socially ingrained pattern of many women's lives—had been to blame myself for every slight, every perceived injustice—and to keep my mouth shut. To refrain from rocking the boat. But the liberation I felt at finally taking matters into my own hands, taking action, taking on the power establishment and winning, can't be expressed in words.

For his part, James had always had more confidence in me than I did. He didn't parade a brass band through the living room to celebrate. But, unbeknownst to me, ice pack pressed to his face, he did call my mother to brag about it. The following day I received a telephone call from her that put the frosting on the cake.

"James told me what happened. Congratulations!"

"Uh—great. About what?"

"What do you mean, 'About what?' He told me how you went right in there and convinced them to give you the insurance money. He says that you just let them *have* it! Oh, honey, I'm so proud of you!"

I couldn't take all the credit for my victory. The laws were there and NOW was there to tell me how they applied to me. And since equal employment laws were in their infancy, corporations weren't quite sure how the game was going to be played; in other words, they were taking the rules seriously. My bet is that the airline had just been temporarily frightened. Pan Am wasn't about to risk losing its business with the Pentagon or NASA over some guy's impacted wisdom teeth.

Of course, it was more than wisdom teeth they were going to be forced to cover. The issue here was family medical coverage—potentially for every woman employee's family. That's why they tried to hide behind the "head of household" rubric in the first place, rather than deal with it as a straightforward matter of equal compensation. Their first move was to change the coverage to include the families of women who could prove that they were heads of household. This did cost them something extra. But the families of *all* male employees were still automatically covered—without having to prove anything.

Nevertheless, some real gains came out of it. I immediately spread the good tidings among my married colleagues. I know that many of them were able to take advantage of the victory. One stewardess came up and hugged me, saying, "I can't believe it! We won!" That word—*we*—had a potent effect. I'd essentially fought the battle for personal benefit; yet, the ripple effect would improve the lives of hundreds of other flight attendants. "We" had won, indeed. And, for the first time since I'd been at Pan Am, I realized that "we" were far from powerless.

Years later, in 1973, the U.S. Supreme Court gave its own stamp of approval to the requirement that all women employees, not just heads of household, are entitled to the same fringe benefits as men. In *Frontiero* v. *Richardson*, a lawyer named Ruth Bader Ginsburg—who would later be appointed to the Supreme Court—won her argument that military women had a constitutional right to receive benefits for their families on the same basis as men.

For me, NOW's assistance had quite an impact. Elaine's voice over the phone had conveyed to me the strength, knowledge, and confidence that I felt so sorely lacking in myself. I'd called because I had a problem. And she had convinced me that I could do something about it—*myself*. NOW didn't step in and take action on my behalf. They did something much better: They empowered me; they gave me the information and encouragement that I needed to fight for myself. In doing so, they planted seeds for my activist future.

Armed with the right ammunition and convinced that I wasn't alone, I was also irrevocably changed. I'd won. We'd won. It felt great.

Oh, and here's the postscript: Elaine Gordon went into politics and before retiring in 1994 became the most powerful woman in the Florida legislature. I went on to become the president of NOW.

And Pan Am went bankrupt. Bringing business down is not a goal of the feminist movement, but there did seem to be a certain poetic justice at work there.

I found it incredible that none of the women employed by Pan Am had challenged the insurance discrimination before me. After all, the Civil Rights Act had taken effect five years earlier, making these kinds of inequities illegal. That legislation was a cultural and political watershed; our country was still deluged with headline news detailing the ongoing struggle.

Of course, some political awareness had begun to reach the airline industry, with its enormous numbers of women employees. Flight attendants at other carriers had filed various complaints with the EEOC, successfully challenging rules that required them to quit when they got married or reached the age of thirty-two. TWA "hostesses" (as their company's female flight attendants were called) had claimed the right to be promoted to higher-paying purser positions, previously open only to men. And a man had gone to court to force Pan Am to hire men as stewards.

Because of all this activity going on in the industry, before James's wisdom teeth became impacted I'd assumed that much of the pioneering civil rights work for employees at Pan Am had already been done; I was shocked to find that such blatant disparity in benefits still existed. How many other laws, I wondered, were being ignored? One thing was obvious: If I wanted to avoid being taken advantage of in the future, I needed a better understanding of the corporate process and of the law. Those antidiscrimination laws meant that my rights and the rights of others were supposed to be protected by the federal government. We could turn to the law for justice rather than depend on the mercurial whims of some benevolent or dictatorial boss.

Another thing was obvious, too: The law alone had not saved the day. Just as essential as the law was the movement that pressed for enforcement of the law and an individual (in this case, me) who was willing to challenge the status quo. A personal need had led to my actions, and the movement and the law had gotten the results.

Although my initial incentive in challenging Pan Am's insurance policy had been personal, I also felt a profound satisfaction knowing that my actions would benefit *all* of the company's women employees. I began to see myself as someone who could actually be part of making a difference—not just for myself, but for other women as well.

For the first time in my adult life, I had played a role that really satisfied me. I'd been true to myself, putting all my long-suppressed anger and frustration into something constructive. This had been my first and only real incursion into the legal battlefield, but I was hooked. The adrenaline rush that came from winning was addictive. I needed another fix.

But I couldn't see where I'd get it from next. Was I supposed to sit idly by until I, or someone I knew, encountered more job discrimination? Oh, it probably wouldn't have been a very long wait—but I didn't want to wait at all.

Then my sister-in-law Cheryl, a lawyer who worked for Legal Services in Knoxville, Tennessee, came down to Miami for a visit.

It's hard to imagine now, but even as recently as the early 1970s, law was not considered a realistic profession for a woman. (In fact, many of the top law schools had only just begun to admit women.) Becoming a lawyer was a brass ring of sorts; only men were encouraged to grab it. A tiny 4 or 5 percent of all lawyers in the United States were women. I was twenty-five years old. Cheryl was the first woman lawyer I'd ever laid eyes on.

She quickly became my role model. When she talked about her work, she shone with enthusiasm. She loved being able to stand in front of a judge in court, she said, armed with credentials and knowledge, helping people who'd been cheated out of wages, or illegally thrown out of their apartments, or who weren't getting heat in the winter. Her stories of courtroom drama had a strong effect. I began to fantasize about becoming a lawyer myself. If I were a lawyer, I'd be able to fight back against corporations, like Pan Am, that continued to get away with blatant discrimination simply because nobody had bothered to step forward and challenge them. Part of my own former sense of powerlessness had come from the fact that I didn't have the tools to work my way successfully through the system. Lawyers had special knowledge; they owned those invaluable, powerful tools.

If I became a lawyer, I could fight discrimination daily. If I fought, I knew I could win. And as I knew, winning felt wonderful.

Cheryl, James's brother Randy (also a lawyer), and James all encouraged me to go to law school. By now, of course, it was impossible to hide the unhappiness I felt working at Pan Am. James pushed me to make a change even though it would mean sacrificing our ability to fly anywhere in the world together for next to nothing. The women in his family had a tradition of breaking through restrictive female stereotypes. His great-aunt Mary had graduated from Barnard in 1913, his great-aunt Grace from Virginia Polytechnic Institute that same year. Mary became a painter, Grace a mathematician. His aunt Jo, born deaf, became a doctor and managed a medical mission in Africa during the 1950s. James's father had died when he was young; his own mother had raised five children by herself—and she still found time to get a master's in education. James wasn't merely at ease with the idea of being married to a strong woman following a purposeful career; he wanted it. He would feel more comfortable being married to a lawyer than to a flight attendant.

Of course, it didn't take much to convince me. Once the thought of going to law school entered my head, my heart latched tenaciously onto it. A pep talk was all it took.

While passing out trays of airline food or sitting quietly in a crew car listening to pilots talk about football, my dreams of adventure changed. I imagined being a powerful lawyer, a woman everyone would finally have to take seriously, a woman willing *and* able to change the world for herself, and for others.

Not that the profession was necessarily going to welcome me into the fold with open arms. Many lawyers, teachers, and students of law still didn't think women had any business whatsoever on a law school campus. And they weren't shy about voicing these opinions.

At the University of Florida Law School in Gainesville, the male law students had carried on a tradition of loudly shuffling their feet whenever an unknown woman entered—and they'd keep the noise going until she left. In 1967, though, one woman who either didn't know the rules or didn't care entered the law library and decided she would not be intimidated. When she entered, the shuffling began. When she stayed put, the men began pounding their fists on the tables as well. When she refused to leave, the male students' frenzy escalated until they were on their feet, pushing over tables and bookshelves. Eventually, the campus cops came and removed the *woman* from the library; no punishment or sanctions of any kind were meted out to the "boys," who had done more than forty thousand dollars' worth of damage to books and furnishings.

Institutional resistance wasn't just from male students angry at the possibility of having to face additional competition. When my friend, past Dade NOW president and former state senator, Roberta Fox entered the University of Florida Law School that same year, she and the twelve other women in her class were called to the dean's office, where he informed them that they'd be serving coffee at meetings of the board of regents and the trustees, and at homecoming—a job ordinarily reserved for the Law Dames, the wives of male students.

And the parents of many women in my generation would never have considered supporting their daughters' dreams of becoming lawyers, doctors, or politicians. My graduate school roommate's father, who gladly paid for his daughter to become a teacher, flatly refused to spend his hard-earned money sending her to law school. Though it was what she desired most, he considered it a waste.

I got a personal taste of this kind of thinking when, in the process of applying to law schools, I asked our longtime family attorney for a letter of recommendation. He refused. "Girls don't belong in law school," he told my mother by way of explanation. "They belong at home—not taking some man's place in the system!" I was shocked; he'd always seemed like such a nice person.

The truth is that, had he been sitting on the admissions board of any law school in the land, he would have been within his rights to reject me simply because I was a woman. Until 1972—my first year in law school—this kind of discrimination against women was *not* illegal. Finally that year, thanks to the leadership of Edith Green and Patsy Mink in Congress, equal educational opportunity became the law, if not the practice, of the land.

I was very fortunate to have the support of my family (if not all their friends). My father, who had always expected me to excel, stood firmly behind whatever I did, as long as I worked hard at it.

My mother was even more emphatically supportive. I'd gotten the idea of going to law school late in the year and rushed to get all my applications out. Although my aptitude test scores were high, I hadn't had time to pull together the right recommendations or mount a campaign to get into any of the Ivy League schools. Florida State University Law School had sent me a recruiting letter because I'd checked a box on the LSATs inviting schools with affirmative action programs to send me information, and had already accepted me. But I considered putting everything off for a year, during which time, I thought,

I would devote my energy to packaging myself, schmooze some of my father's friends from the University of Michigan, draw on family contacts in Chicago, and try to talk my way into an elite program. But my mother became frantic. She begged me not to wait, to go immediately to Florida State. A lot could happen in a year, she said, to throw me off course; she didn't want this window of opportunity to close—as she'd once seen it close for herself.

It dawned on me that my mother may have suffered in ways that I had never understood from not having a college degree and the opportunities a degree afforded—life opportunities as well as economic ones. At the same time, I saw a kind of irony in this: I *had* a degree and a job, but I suffered the same feelings of inferiority that I now imagined she had always had. In the end, I knew, what my mother really wanted me to have was self-confidence, economic independence, and a career that offered more than travel benefits—all the things men of her generation had that women did not.

So, in the fall of 1972, James and I packed up ourselves and our three cats and moved to Tallahassee. There, I began law school at Florida State.

THREE

Learning the material that would lead to passing the bar didn't begin until classes started on day two, but what I think of as my real legal education began on my very first day at Florida State University Law School. Within minutes of arriving, I was confronted with a registration form that asked me for my wife's name. (This led some of us to joke that we hadn't realized acceptance to law school entitled one to a wife. Someone to cook and clean while we studied and attended classes—not a bad deal! Where could we sign up?)

Within the hour, I had to find a bathroom—which turned out to be easier said than done. FSU's law school building was only six years old when I arrived, but there were no women's bathrooms on the first two floors. We had to climb three flights to the administrative offices, where architects had been kind enough to provide a ladies' room for the secretaries.

And then, the big moment, when all the other first-year students and I gathered to be welcomed officially to FSU by the distinguished B. K. Roberts, Chief Justice of the Florida Supreme Court. After some cursory opening remarks on the sanctity of law, Roberts turned to the subject of ethics.

"One of the most difficult parts of my job," he intoned in his booming bass, "is to disbar or discipline attorneys. And the most frequent reason I have for doing so is that some lawyers can't seem to stop stealing from their clients! Since I'd hate to have to discipline any of you some day, please remember this: If you find yourself overcome with an irresistible urge to take something from a client, *don't* steal his money." He paused for effect. Then, with a Cheshire-cat grin: *"Steal his wife!"*

Most of the audience laughed.

Now, feminists are often accused of having no sense of humor. As one of the few females sitting in the audience that day, I confess that I lived up to the stereotype. I wondered how he could assume that all attorneys are men, all clients are men, and a wife is a possession that one can simply steal. This was the chief justice of the state supreme court! With these sorts of ingrained prejudices, how would he treat me—or another woman lawyer—if we ever wound up arguing a case before him?

Several months later, FSU imported another outside specialist to remind us that the world of law was a man's world. This fellow had come to Professor Ray McGuire's class to lecture on the art of jury selection. He began seriously enough, stressing the importance of putting one's self in the shoes of a potential juror, sitting there in a large pool of other potential jurors, in an intimidating courtroom setting. Then: "By the way, most women are very ill at ease when you call them out from the jury pool. They've got to get up, walk across the entire length of the room with everybody's eyes on them. They're going to be a lot more nervous than most guys. So you have to be extra smooth with the ladies—make sure they trust you."

Okay, I told myself, maybe this wasn't *so* bad. It certainly was plausible to speculate that women, in general, might be more concerned than most men about their personal appearance; as a stewardess, I knew all too well that looks are often the strongest measure of a woman's value.

But the speaker didn't quit while he was ahead. Women, he told us, being more sensitive by nature, were desirable as jurors if you were trying to win an acquittal on criminal charges; likewise, they made undesirable jurors if you were prosecuting. Finally, he said, other considerations came into play when selecting women for a jury.

"There *are* advantages to choosing your jury by looks. Some of my best dates have come from my juries."

I was out of my seat and out of the lecture hall before he could finish laughing at his own joke. Thankfully (proof to me that, in fact, I was not being totally unreasonable), a handful of other women also took an early exit.

I was proud of myself for this little bit of nonviolent protest. It had never been easy for me intentionally to create social tension of any kind and, if I'd thought too hard about walking out, I probably wouldn't have done it. But the move had come instinctively, almost as a reflex. Not all of my fellow students were as pleased with me, though. One male classmate cornered me later in the student lounge.

"Patricia, that stunt you pulled was totally uncalled for."

Stunt? I thought. I stared at him blankly, not prepared for a lecture on etiquette from a peer.

"I'm not saying you didn't have reason to be upset. I'm not saying his joke was funny. But he was a guest of the law school, and you made us *all* look bad by being rude to him."

"Well, what about *him* being rude to *us*?"

"So what? These older guys don't think the way we do. You've got to put yourself in his place. Anyway, you really should have just taken the useful tips from his lecture and let the rest slide. There are plenty of *important* things in the world to get upset about—don't sweat the small stuff," was his condescending finish.

I thought of walking out on this guy, too, but decided against it.

I knew that stereotypes are not trivial. But almost as disturbing to me as Mr. Jury Expert's pickup tips was my classmate's response to my action. He had unconsciously been paraphrasing the age-old mantra for socially constraining women: Don't make people uncomfortable; if you're going to disagree with someone, do it so nobody knows about it—or at least do it in some magical way that isn't at all threatening. In other words: Shut up. Don't rock the boat! Well, I was still working weekends as a stewardess in order to put myself through law school; walking up and down those aisles, I still found myself in the position of having to be agreeable and nonthreatening, and I certainly wasn't going to let that be my style as a law student during the week. Here I was, face-to-face with a struggle that was both personal and political, because it applied not just to me but to so many women: that deeply ingrained yearning to be liked and to keep the peace inevitably conflicted with the need to live honestly.

So I certainly wasn't going to shut up, but I still had no real intention to act up on a regular basis, either.

For one thing, with the taste of failure in graduate school at Tennessee still fresh, I was determined to prove myself at FSU: no partying, no movies, no dancing—no fun for Patricia Ireland, law student. I was going to become a serious, powerful lawyer! And the little time I had outside of school was taken up with weekend and holiday work for Pan Am, which was absolutely necessary to James and me. It gave us medical coverage and helped cover our living expenses.

Between work and school, I didn't have much time for extracurricular activities like becoming the campus radical. I planned to maintain a single-minded focus on my studies, to get through and excel—with blinders on.

Then I came across a line in my property law textbook that nearly knocked me out of my seat. I must have stared at it for a good five minutes, in shock that it even existed in this day and age.

"Land, like a woman, is meant to be possessed."

Not only was this bad law—historically, women were considered "chattel," or personal property, *not* real estate—but it was written *as if fact* by a prominent Columbia University Law School professor, in one of the more widely used texts of the day.

I decided on the spot that I would just have to step out of my self-assigned role as single-minded student. I drafted a letter to the publisher, complaining about the offending sentence. And I was about to mail it when I hesitated. One thing I'd learned from being a curious bystander to the various social and political movements of the sixties was that collective action was often the key to success. My lone signature probably wouldn't change anyone's mind. If I could convince some of the other students to co-sign, the letter would have much more of an impact. After all, we were the law professors of the future.

Unfortunately, this plan involved doing something I'd never done before: public speaking. Rounding up a large number of signatures person by person would take too long. I'd have to address a large group and ask people to sign all at once. So, hands shaking and voice trembling, I called the hundred or so members of my property law class to order one day before our professor arrived and read them my statement. Seeing all those tired pairs of eyes centered on me—expecting me to come up with a very good reason for interrupting their pre-class gossip or study—nearly ended my public speaking career on the spot. Luckily, I had a script; I was able to turn away from all the staring faces and simply read my letter.

The message itself was truly naive: This country fought a Civil War, I read, to ensure that no human being could ever again be treated as property. (Of course, neither the Civil War nor any of the constitutional amendments that followed did anything to change the legal status of nineteenth-century *women* per se; but that wasn't the sort of history we were learning in law school in the early seventies.) Youthful idealism aside, the message worked. About two-thirds of the students in my property law class signed that petition.

I can't be sure what effect my petition had, since I never did receive any reply from the publishing company. But I do know

that later editions of that same textbook were free of the offending sentence. Several factors probably went into the editorial decision to delete such an antiquated phrase. Knowing that
the letter might have been one of them continues to give me
great satisfaction.

And other signs helped convince me that I was on the right
track. At the end of our first year, Professor McGuire gave us a
farewell speech. He mentioned how proud he was of his students—especially of those who'd walked out of the jury selection lecture in protest.

"Conviction is rare in this world," he said. "It was nice to see
some in action."

Nevertheless, what dominates my memories of that first
year of law school was the burgeoning gap between my
newfound, enthusiastic political idealism on the one hand and
the law's stone-cold reality on the other. Newly converted to
feminism, I assumed that the law would become my High
Church, providing all answers, illuminating every patch of
darkness in an unjust world. These expectations—and a lot of
the ensuing disappointments—were heightened and exacerbated by my own deep-rooted impatience. Upon arriving in
Tallahassee, I'd secretly anticipated being immediately (and
somewhat magically) transformed from flight attendant to respected lawyer. If my disappointment was deep it also taught
me something important: Although the desire for radical
change sometimes seems to happen overnight, the change itself
never does. Every positive transformation—of an individual or
of an entire society—takes plenty of time. Upon close examina-
tion even those transformations that appear to happen as if in
a thunderclap reveal themselves to have been percolating for
many years. Any time we set out to change our lives or the
world, we have to take the long view.

* * *

M y first year of law school—1972—was also the year that Congress finally sent the Equal Rights Amendment on to state legislatures for ratification, forty-nine years after it was introduced in Congress by Representative Daniel Anthony and Senator Charles Curtis, both Republicans. The amendment to the U.S. Constitution, proposed right after women won the right to vote by Alice Paul, head of the National Women's Party, had been around Congress in some form since 1923. The version that passed was modeled on the suffrage amendment. It would become very familiar to me over the next decade.

Section 1. Equality of rights under the law shall not be denied or abridged by the United States or by any State on account of sex.
Section 2. The Congress shall have the power to enforce, by appropriate legislation, the provisions of this Article.
Section 3. The Amendment shall take effect two years after the date of ratification.

Through the efforts of Alice Paul, the Equal Rights Amendment had been introduced in every session of Congress from 1923 to 1970, but remained locked up in committee for forty-seven years. Extraordinary action was required to get the amendment to the floor for a vote. NOW members disrupted Senate Judiciary Committee hearings in a successful demand for hearings on the Equal Rights Amendment. On the House side, Rep. Martha Griffiths used a discharge petition to get the ERA out of committee, only the eighth time in twenty years this unusual parliamentary tactic had been successful. In 1971, the Equal Rights Amendment was approved by the House of Representatives, 354–24. On March 22, 1972, the Senate voted for the amendment, 84–8, and sent it to the states for ratification by three-fourths or thirty-eight of the states, as required to amend the U.S. Constitution. For no discernible constitutional reason, the Equal Rights Amendment was encumbered with an arbitrary seven-year deadline for ratification.

I learned about the Equal Rights Amendment, which was in

the newspapers regularly, at the same time that I was learning how much discrimination against women had been accepted by the courts as constitutional. As I studied the cases in law school, I realized that for the first two hundred years of our nation's history, the Supreme Court never saw a discriminatory law against women it didn't like. Illinois wanted to keep women from practicing law? No problem! The court in 1873 cited "the law of the Creator" as a good enough reason to protect these delicate creatures from being sullied by the corruption of legal and business practices.

The justices in 1908 articulated as constitutionally sufficient reasons for Oregon's limitation on the number of hours women could work, both that women must "rest upon and look to [men] for protection" and the seemingly contradictory view that the law was needed "to protect [women] from the greed as well as the passion of man."

Again, in 1948, the Supreme Court found no equal-protection problem with a Michigan law that allowed women to work as waitresses in taverns but prohibited them from the higher-paid bartender job; "protecting" women from making too much money just didn't seem unconstitutional to the justices.

The court's willingness to wear blinders against the harsh glare of reality is nowhere better illustrated than in a 1961 case. The justices upheld Florida's virtual exclusion of women from juries because "women are the center of home and family life." Unfortunately, the "center of home and family life" in this case, Mrs. Hoyt, had just bludgeoned her husband to death and wanted women on the jury who might understand how a wife could be driven to such a deed.

Finally in 1971, attorney Ruth Bader Ginsburg made the first breakthrough in the court's historic "anything goes" attitude toward sex discrimination. She convinced the court to throw out an Idaho law that gave an automatic preference to a man over an equally qualified woman to serve as an executor of an estate.

I was also beginning to understand how thoroughly the concept of women as property, first of their fathers and then of their husbands, was woven into the very fiber of our legal tradition. I studied the legal implications of the old maxim "husband and wife are one and that one is the husband." I had my first case law encounters with "head and master" laws, still in force in many states, that allowed a husband to mortgage the family home over his wife's objections and denied a married woman the right to her own earnings.

As my understanding of women's second-class legal status in the United States grew, my point of view about the contract of marriage itself changed dramatically. I couldn't believe the state could impose terms on our relationship that made me unequal to James, without our consent and against our beliefs. I stopped wearing my wedding ring. When Don and I were married I had taken his last name and become Patricia Anderson; when James and I were married I had taken his last name and become Patricia Humble. Now that I knew that the loss of a woman's name at marriage signified the loss of her very existence as a person under the law, I took back my family name: Ireland.

Consciousness is a funny thing: Once you become conscious, you can't just regress. In fact, the opposite happens: You find yourself becoming conscious of more and more. And consciousness is the predecessor of transformation.

So the Equal Rights Amendment had come to Florida, and living in Tallahassee, the seat of Florida's state government, I found myself in the thick of things. Patricia Dorr, a professor of constitutional law at FSU, called some of us together to form a women law students' group (the school's first), and we decided to cut our activist teeth lobbying legislators to pass the ERA. Being law students, with pertinent legal facts at our fingertips and all the right textbook arguments lodged firmly in our brains, we thought ourselves just right for the job.

It appeared to be a simple enough challenge. The ERA hardly seemed radical to me; it provided a Constitutional requirement to protect legal equality between men and women. Who could possibly oppose it? Like my insurance complaint against Pan Am, the entire issue seemed free of any frightening gray areas, any moral or political ambiguities.

As our group walked the few blocks to the capitol building on a cold wintry day, my biggest concern was how to address the politicians: Should I call them "Mister Senator" or "sir"?

After we entered the rotunda, though, I came face-to-face with the real politics of activism, which, I quickly realized, had nothing to do with my textbooks and case studies. Anti-ERA groups had rounded up hundreds of supporters from rural communities all across the Florida panhandle and bused them to the capitol. These people were mad as hell. At first, it all looked to me like a human zoo. A lot of them had megaphones. They screamed; they shook raised fists; they brandished signs with slogans like YOU CAN'T FOOL MOTHER NATURE! One woman, enraged at my pro-ERA button, bellowed, "If you loved your mother, you wouldn't support the ERA!" I began to understand that my lobbying efforts might not have as much impact as I'd imagined.

That day, I learned the difference between informing and persuading. While our group attempted to convey real information—in other words, hard facts about court cases and legal standards of review in constitutional cases—to politicians and voters alike, hoping this would help them make a logical decision about the ERA, our opponents were attempting to steamroll these same people with the threat that the ERA would change their lives—and the lives of all of us—forever . . . and for the worse.

In a perfect world, many of the arguments used against the ERA would not have stood up to logic. We had to chuckle at some of the opposition's scare tactics: If the ERA was passed, they said, husbands would no longer have to support their wives; daughters would be drafted into the military and thrown into foxholes in steamy Third World countries; gays would be allowed to get married; all public bathrooms would become unisex. But it wasn't really funny. We stopped laughing when we discovered that the votes to pass the ERA simply weren't there.

I was stunned. While I'd been making abstract points about equality and self-actualization, my opponents had been successfully playing on fears rooted deeply in the heart of the conventional family. They had been raising questions about basic survival. I had been mistaken to believe that a mere laying on of facts could make lame (and lamebrain) senators walk. This lobbying day was my first direct contact with politics and the legislative process, and I had come with a junior high–level, civics-class view. It was a shock. I didn't even know yet about the campaign contributors and anti-ERA business interests whose dollars were shaping the legislators' agenda behind the scenes, but I saw that logic and legal arguments alone weren't going to do the trick.

With my introduction to the Equal Rights Amendment, I began to think about the difference between making structural change—in the Constitution, in society itself—and taking on individual cases as I'd done on my own behalf at Pan Am. The old-boy system would have to change, really change, for women in our country to ever approach equality in fact and in the eyes of the law. I also committed myself to finding ways to work for passage of the ERA.

After a year at FSU, I transferred to law school at the University of Miami. We made the move primarily for financial reasons. I was still employed by Pan Am, but having to come down to Miami from the state capital meant that I couldn't work enough flights to earn a paycheck that would cover law school expenses and ensure basic survival. Tallahassee was teeming with students and students' spouses, all willing to work for pitifully low wages, and the competition was overwhelming. While he continued to paint, James had taken a low-paying job at an animal shelter. This got us another cat, but it didn't do much to keep food on the table. (Once, I had to use all of my newfound powers of persuasion to induce a skeptical county caseworker to give us an emergency issue of food stamps.) The Tallahassee banks were too cash poor to give me a student loan; anyway, in true small-town fashion, any available funds went to the locals.

Although my tuition skyrocketed in Miami, our financial situation improved. James got a well-paying construction job. I worked more flights. And the banks there had plenty of loan money—enough so that we'd still be paying them back more than a decade later.

At Miami, too, I decided not to take any vows about keeping out of politics. My experiences at FSU had taught me that learning about the politics of activism was as important to me as learning about the law, and in Miami I stumbled across several strategies I'd use years later against presidents and congressmen—to powerful effect.

Shortly after I arrived, I found out that the National Council of Jewish Women was giving training in public speaking in order to develop teams who could address various women's groups about the ERA. I signed up. For someone whose knees shook when she tried to read a letter to her classmates, the training was more than useful. So was the speaking experience. I also admired and learned from the careful thought that this organization had put into their program. One tactic in particular that I remember was the way they created the teams of speakers: a law student was paired with a nurse's aide, a young, single banker was paired with a middle-aged housewife and mother. The idea was to show that the Equal Rights Amendment was of concern to, was relevant to, and was supported by a full range of women. They wanted our audiences to listen to us, and they also wanted them to identify with us.

Some additional lessons in my education came at the expense of Professor Phil Heckerling, a highly respected scholar in the field of trusts and estate planning. Heckerling was short, round, a little jowly, his movements measured; at first appearance he seemed quite serious and scholarly, and because of this he was somewhat intimidating to students. The truth is that he was open and friendly—and startlingly, refreshingly nondefensive—but I didn't know that at first. Heckerling taught one of those courses all law students dread: a class right out of *The Paper Chase*, in which we were routinely called upon to analyze real and hypothetical cases and felt humiliated if we didn't know the specifics of a particular statute or case. During one lecture, Heckerling addressed the issue of establishing financial security for the widows of deceased clients.

"Of course, it's your job to advise your client to make sure that she'll be taken care of after his death." But, he cautioned, we should not simply hand the estate over to the bereaved woman. The best course of action would be to leave it in trust for the little lady, so that "your client won't have to worry about her running off to Rio with the man with a waxed mustache."

According to this logic, all of our future clients would be men; a married couple's estate belonged to the man, not to the couple; and no woman could be trusted with any significant amount of money, because, given the chance, she'd naturally elope with the first attractive villain who presented himself.

Two other students, Linda Wolf and Christine Ashcraft, sat around with me afterward talking about it. Eventually we worked ourselves into such a state that we knew we had to do something. The next day we marched into Heckerling's office and announced that we were a "delegation" from his trusts and estates class. (Of course, no one else in the class had any idea that we were doing this; but we figured what he didn't know wouldn't hurt him—or us.)

Heckerling wasn't defensive at all when we told him we were there to complain about him teaching sexist law. He was quite gracious instead, thanking us for taking the trouble to discuss our grievances with him. I was relieved and surprised at this reaction. We left satisfied, expecting nothing further.

But he began the next trusts and estates class by announcing to a hundred or more perplexed law students that he had received their "delegation," and wanted to apologize if he'd offended anybody with his last lecture. He went on to explain that he had been speaking from his own personal experience with the wealthy men who'd been his clients; we certainly shouldn't assume that he thought all women were helpless dolts. He recognized that many wives already managed the couple's finances, and some had earned the bulk or entirety of their family's income in the first place.

Heckerling spent the rest of that semester calling on Linda, Christine, and me to cite precedent and answer his questions at every opportunity. Maybe he did this to prove that he respected the intelligence of women. Maybe it was a subtle form of retaliation. Maybe, in such a large class, ours were the only names he knew. In any event, I wound up knowing much more about probate law and estate planning than I'd ever really wanted to. And I grew to have a tremendous liking and respect for Phil Heckerling.

But my political clashes with him weren't quite over.

Iron Arrow is the University of Miami's version of Yale's Skull and Bones Club. It's a society for the movers and shakers of the Miami community. Membership in it is considered "the highest honor the university bestows." Once accepted into the club, you're in it for life. Of course, the practical perks of belonging to an elite group like that are considerable; the personal connections can lead to financial gain as well as influence and power.

The Iron Arrow "tapping ceremony," which designates new inductees, is a goofy piece of theater. The ritualistic trappings— like those of groups led by modern men's movement guru Robert Bly—draw on Native American culture for inspiration. In practice this meant that, once a year, a group of paunchy, middle-aged white guys dressed up as Seminole chiefs marched onto campus banging away at ceremonial drums, strutted around for a while looking solemn, and caused quite a scene. When they happened upon one of that year's lucky inductees, they "tapped" him with an iron arrow. Then the new member had to beat a drum himself. For hours.

By 1973 people in the university community were beginning to question the club's all-male status. In a major victory for NOW and other women's rights groups, Congress had voted for Title IX of the Education Amendments of 1972, prohibiting sex discrimination in federally funded schools at all levels. Less than a year later, Tom McGuigan, editor-in-chief of the law review, created quite a stir by rejecting an offer of Iron Arrow membership on the grounds that the organization discriminated against women.

And some of us decided to do a send-up of Iron Arrow. Linda, Christine, and I, along with a small group of regular coconspirators, founded a new club. We called it "Broken Arrow." Our first inductees were McGuigan and Professor Minnette Massey, one of the first tenured women on the law school faculty. Deserving honorees if ever there were any.

Both agreed to take part in Broken Arrow's first induction ceremony, which (of course) was planned to coincide with Iron Arrow's. We had no intentions of disrupting theirs, though, and arranged to hold ours separately. Our protest was meant to be purely symbolic. It would take place in the student lounge at high noon, when we could be guaranteed a large lunchtime audience. All participants would be clad in mock Native American garb, with a few extra accoutrements.

But nothing turned out as planned.

Christine later blamed our actions on the power of the drums. The truth is that the University of Miami had survived the 1960s without hosting so much as a single student demonstration; it was high time for one. Whatever the cause, we gave Iron Arrow—and ourselves—quite a day.

From inside the student lounge, where we sat in our ridiculous outfits waiting for our fun to begin, we could hear the Iron Arrow delegation pounding away on their tom-toms. As the pounding got louder and louder, suddenly Christine snapped. She jumped to her feet. "This is so ridiculous! We've got to do something!" Then she raced out.

The rest of us froze, but just for a moment. Linda and I soon charged after her. I experienced a flash of sheer terror, born of embarrassment: I had absolutely no desire to run around campus dressed in phony Indian garb; I'd really never planned on a direct confrontation with such a hallowed institution—especially when dressed like a Seminole princess. But Christine was our sister in crime; we couldn't let her take on Iron Arrow all by herself.

Ironically, the Iron Arrow participants were heading for the offices of Professor Heckerling, whom they planned to induct that day.

Led by Christine, we waylaid and encircled them in the courtyard, letting out evil-sounding war whoops, brandishing homemade tomahawks, squirt guns, toy bow-and-arrow sets. I shot a miniature toilet plunger at Iron Arrow's chief.

And though I was enjoying the adrenaline rush, I feared we'd gone too far. Spoofing a discriminatory club was one thing. But we were about to embarrass one of the preeminent members of the law school faculty—a man I personally liked. Nevertheless, I swallowed my fears. We followed the men of Iron Arrow up three flights to the balcony outside Heckerling's office door. His secretary flew out, screaming at us to get lost. This was her boss's big moment; she wasn't about to let a bunch of upstart feminists ruin it.

"You're spoiling his day! It isn't fair!"

She threw a right cross that nearly knocked me over the railing.

Having made our point, we retreated, and held the Broken Arrow "tapping" rites for McGuigan and Massey out in the open air. Our ceremony took place just as morning classes were ending. Happily, the combination of spectacle and timing meant that a large crowd gathered to watch. Television news crews, which had been on campus that day to cover the Iron

Arrow ceremony, immediately changed plans and turned the cameras on us. (All in all, we were a lot more colorful.) At the sight of TV cameras, even more people stopped to watch. The day's lesson: Nothing attracts a camera like a crowd; and nothing attracts an even bigger crowd like a camera. That night thousands of south Floridians saw what looked like a huge campus protest against the sexism of Iron Arrow on their local TV stations.

The aftermath was surprisingly constructive. Iron Arrow eventually found itself dragged kicking and screaming into the twentieth century. Of course, the muscle wasn't provided by Broken Arrow alone. When Soia Menschekoff became the first woman dean of the law school in the fall of 1974, she informed the group that they would not be allowed on her campus until they accepted women members. Additional pressure was brought to bear when women on campus began filing complaints with the federal Office of Civil Rights against the university's financial support of an all-male honor society. The complaints alleged that the University of Miami was directly violating Title IX.

When OCR investigators showed up on campus and began interviewing students, faculty, and staff, including members of the Broken Arrow conspiracy, word spread, and the administration got nervous. Finally, the university was threatened with loss of federal funding over Iron Arrow's discriminatory policies. They got the message and ordered Iron Arrow to begin accepting women. In a fit of self-righteousness, the group left campus and did not return until the fall of 1985, when they agreed to admit women.

Silly though it may have seemed at first, these all-male secret societies are bastions of extraordinary power and influence. When Ronald Reagan came to Washington, he brought four of his cabinet members from his all-male secret society, the Bohemian Club.

Too, this series of events showed me clearly that the combination of a woman in a position of power and authority, a willing contingent of activists, and an equal opportunity law just waiting to be enforced can be a powerful one indeed.

There were happy endings all around. The school didn't discipline us. Nevertheless, the fear of reprisal was a personal demon for me, one which I constantly struggled with throughout my legal career. Every time I took an activist step, I experienced a moment of true panic. What would happen to me if I went through with it? Would I get thrown out of school? What would my friends and family think? In each case, though, I knew I was doing the right thing, and most of my worries turned out to be unfounded. I decided that any doors that were closed to me as a result of my activism probably wouldn't lead anywhere I really wanted to go, anyway. And in retrospect, when I look back at the smallness—the silliness, really—of the Broken Arrow incident, I'm amazed at how afraid I was of the consequences, especially when I compare it to the demonstrations I've taken part in since and the genuine risks I've run. But I also realize that it was my first demonstration, my very first foray into protest politics. No matter how small, it was another important step without which I might never have gone forward at all.

Part of my good fortune in those years, of course, was due to the relatively protected nature of the college campus. The real world would not be so forgiving. But I began developing a consequences-be-damned mentality during my law school days that would carry me through many difficult years in the future.

Incidentally, I never was invited into the new, improved Iron Arrow. But one of the first women to be invited into the club, Dr. Janet Canterbury, would later become my closest friend. To give the old boys some credit, they couldn't have made a wiser choice. Of course, they still may not know that—in addition to being deputy dean for medical education at the University of Miami School of Medicine—Janet is my strongest ally in NOW.

*   *   *

The juxtaposition of weekend flight-attendant work and studies during this three-year period was exciting, if also frustrating. I wanted control over my life and I was working hard to get it, but I wasn't there yet. On the other hand, I felt myself growing, becoming more and more of the woman I wanted to be with each passing day. Law school and my work on behalf of the ERA were helping me to create a new blueprint for my life—a far better blueprint for me, I knew, than the one that had been lost after I left my earlier, more conventional plans behind. In these final stewardess years, I began to take a real interest in passengers. I talked to them, garnering many letters of praise to my administrative supervisor, but more importantly learning about the great complexity of other people's lives and struggles in a much less voyeuristic way than I ever had before. Unable to deny the frustrations and complexities of human existence, I had to stop shying away from my own strong emotions and passions, too. During these difficult years, despite the frustration and struggle, I found that my life was tremendously enriched.

I made law review at Miami and graduated, with high honors, in 1975.

It was a boom time for women joining the bar; the number of us earning law degrees doubled between 1970 and 1976. This burgeoning female presence in such a traditionally male venue was beginning to shake up the entire profession. I saw all these new women lawyers as a potentially powerful support base for effective feminist activism.

Also in 1975, North Dakota became the thirty-fourth state to ratify the Equal Rights Amendment. Two years later, Indiana would bring the total to thirty-five. But these victories were marked with a sense of urgency. Under the deadline imposed by Congress, at least three more states would have to ratify by March 22, 1979, for the amendment to become part of the Constitution.

FOUR

Women lawyers were still a rarity in 1975. We were also twice as likely as male lawyers to go into public interest law or legal services for the poor. Some of this was by choice. But it was also true that private firms were far less willing to hire us.

Even when we did make it into the private sector, we often found ourselves saddled with a disproportionate amount of probate and divorce work. These were areas of the law where, many old-time senior partners believed, we could best put our "womanly virtues"—compassion, patience, conciliation—to use.

Personally, I appreciated the importance of being able to empathize with a newly widowed or soon-to-be-divorced client. But I also recognized that this allocation of work based on stereotypes of feminine virtues had the not-so-coincidental effect of freeing men from having to compete with us in the more lucrative kinds of practice.

Finding a job that wouldn't pigeonhole me because of my sex was part of the reason I did not follow a more obviously idealistic route after law school. Many of my friends (female *and* male), shaped by the social turmoil of the late 1960s, had decided to help the poor and downtrodden of the world by becoming public defenders and legal services attorneys. I shared their sensibilities, and when I started law school, I had no intention of jumping into a three-piece suit to go to work for Big, Big & Pig after graduation. But by the time I graduated, I also recognized that I wasn't really suited to follow that path. Helping impoverished clients with domestic problems, fighting to stop landlords from throwing poor families onto the streets, or battling the state to keep it from strapping their sons into Old Sparky (as Florida's electric chair was called) was noble work, but I could see that it would burn me out in no time. I admired the role these lawyers played; like the work my mother had done all her life as a homemaker, their work was undervalued and economically risky. But I'd come to a greater understanding of myself over the past few years. My new self-knowledge told me that my personality, goals, and skills were best suited to the political arena. There I could flourish as an insider—with an outsider's progressive sensibilities.

I wanted to change the system that caused so much suffering, and one way of doing it—a way that might just be best for me—was to run for elected office. During my years in law school, I'd come to believe that if women were ever going to gain real equality in the United States we'd have to elect more of us to office; it was the most direct way we could make and influence policy. But I've always been practical. I knew full well that the road to a successful political career needs to be paved with much more than good intentions. Corporate and commercial law seemed a pragmatic choice, an important place to start. That's what I decided to aim for.

My game plan was simple, really: Get a good job in the private sector, go as far as I could go there, then make a lateral move into public service. With the money and influence I hoped to access as a lawyer, I'd be able to tap the necessary financial resources and personal connections—the "cash and bash"—to get elected.

This rationalization was both practical and true. But some

other personal factors were also at work. I'd turned to law in part to purge myself of the humiliation and disrespect I'd so often experienced in my stewardess uniform. I was personally insecure. I wanted very much to succeed. All this had propelled me to excel as a student; now, it drove me to seek work that was financially rewarding *and* prestigious. I wanted to prove myself by competing with the big boys. Cloaking my ambition with what I thought was a more socially acceptable notion—to break barriers for women—I headed out into the world determined to gain all the power and privilege a lawyer could possibly have. This goal put me in the position of testing potential employers as much as they'd test me.

One of my mentors, Professor Alan Swan, steered me in the direction of Paul, Landy & Beiley, one of Miami's leading international law firms. He felt that my language skills, my interest in inter-American culture, and the knowledge of corporate politics and political advocacy I'd gained (albeit without meaning to) at Pan Am would all serve me well there. Burt Landy, one of the firm's senior partners, was the city's leading inter-American law specialist by far. With a single phone call from Swan, the door of the old-boy club opened for Patricia Ireland, Esq., new feminist lawyer in the making.

Burt was a slight man with a trim mustache and a runner's slender physique, meticulous in his appearance and his work. He spoke impeccable English and Spanish, appeared infallibly calm and reasonable when negotiating, and—even when correcting my first-year lawyer's mistakes—he was always respectfully polite. I liked him immediately.

After a good first meeting with Burt, I was convinced I'd be able to put my experiences and skills to good use at the firm. I wasn't so confident, however, that my feminist politics would serve me well during the hiring process. I'd listed all of my political activities prominently on my résumé, figuring the firm should know exactly where I stood. None of it seemed to faze him.

My next interview was with Landy's partner, Bob Paul. In contrast to Burt, Bob was a big man whose height and girth substantiated his forceful, dominant personality. Ferocious in his work, his saving grace was a terrific sense of humor about everything—including the ability to laugh at himself.

Five minutes into our interview he asked, "What does your husband do?"

"James is a painter. What does your wife do?"

He seemed thrown for a second. Nevertheless, he recovered quickly and began describing, with enthusiasm, the fund-raising work his wife Christa did for the Miami Philharmonic.

I tried hard not to be paranoid; maybe I was wrong to think that he would never have asked the same question of a male prospect. On the other hand, maybe he wanted to see whether or not my feminism would cloud my better judgment. It might have been a test to see how I'd respond to clients who asked such things. At any rate, the interview was a success.

That little bit of table-turning on Bob had been an instinctive response. But I liked the result so much that I began asking all the lawyers at Paul, Landy about their wives, and listening carefully to each reply. Did they speak respectfully or dismissively of their wives' activities? I didn't want to work with any-one whose attitude toward women even approximated the misogynistic one I had experienced so often at Pan Am. In the end, I sensed that Paul, Landy would be a good place for me to practice. Even though I'd be the only woman lawyer at the firm, I felt increasingly at ease there as the interviews pro-gressed. And I grew so comfortable with Bob that I began to grill him a bit myself. During our final interview, I asked him just what he thought women lawyers couldn't do as well as their male counterparts.

This was obviously a subject he didn't want to touch. But, after I'd prodded him a little, he responded reluctantly.

"Sometimes I wonder whether or not women can be effective

litigators. Litigation's a brutal business. And not that many women really feel comfortable going for the jugular. Also, they have to deal with the prejudices juries and judges have against women lawyers.'' He went on to say that he believed women did have an advantage in deal making, because of our social skills.

I disagreed with Bob about the issue of litigation, but I liked his honesty. And, although I hated to admit it, I couldn't really say he was wrong about the existence of prejudiced judges and juries. All in all, I enjoyed feeling comfortable enough to have such a discussion. When he made me a job offer, I accepted. But I did promise myself to get involved in litigation—and to be good at it.

First, of course, I'd have to deal with being low lawyer in the Paul, Landy food chain. My dreams of playing the female Perry Mason would have to wait. Every new associate—male or female—was assigned a lot of dirty work. During my first year at the firm, though, I *did* sometimes wonder whether or not some of these assignments were sex specific. And I'll never forget one new client I found waiting for me in the conference room. I walked in expectantly.

"Could you get me some coffee, hon?" he said, barely looking up.

My stewardess persona saved me—and him. Reminding myself that part of the job was to keep our clients happy, I went and got coffee without a word, and I presented it to him in the exact same way I would have done for some malcontented passenger in 12E. When I sat at the head of the table and pulled out legal documents I'd drafted for his review, he turned beet red. That was worth every second of service.

Most situations were more subtle. I was sitting in my new office on my very first day trying to figure out how the phones worked, when another, more senior associate walked in pushing a cart stacked three feet high with case files.

"I just talked with Bob. He said you should take over the Juan Martinez estate."

This was the first I'd heard of Juan Martinez or his estate. The look of relief on my colleague's face belied all his attempts to convince me that this was going to be lots of fun. Before leaving, he hesitated.

"One more thing. Juan's son is on the phone. You'd better take the call."

For a second, I wondered if he and the other associates had decided to play some sort of first-day prank on me.

I pressed a blinking phone button. The angry voice of Jose Martinez, calling from Spain, quickly convinced me that he was no figment of anyone's playful imagination. Jose was very displeased that his father's estate had been passed on to a new, inexperienced lawyer.

"What the hell is going on there! After four years we've got to start all over with someone new? This is ridiculous! I want to speak to Burt Landy—right now!"

I didn't yet know, however, which button would transfer him to Burt's office or disconnect his call. So I decided I would have to deal with him myself. Using my best flight-attendant skills, I managed to calm him down (doing everything but offering him a free drink in the process). I wasn't all that pleased with the situation myself; it seemed as if the partners at Paul, Landy had really wanted a woman professional in the fold just so they could throw probate cases on her lap. But when this dark thought had passed and I'd calmed my*self* down a bit, I realized that, as one of Professor Heckerling's star pupils, I was entirely up to date on all the recent changes in Florida's probate laws—and probably the best lawyer for the job, male or female, in the firm. An excellent working relationship with Jose Martinez and constructive resolution of the problems with his father's estate proved entirely possible.

Learning to practice law in Miami was a trial by fire in the mid to late 1970s. The city was quickly becoming a center of big money and business, both legal and illegal. People were armed on all sides. I got a taste of this at one of my first face-to-face meetings with a client. It was just a few weeks after I'd joined Paul, Landy. The meeting had been scheduled early that morning at the client's Coral Gables office. Eager to make a good first impression, I arrived half an hour before anyone else. As I sat in the lobby waiting, I pulled some documents out of my embarrassingly new briefcase and decided to review them once more (even though I'd practically memorized them the night before). Maybe it was my imagination, but when the client finally arrived he seemed more amused than impressed by my obvious dedication.

"Come on in," he chuckled. My heart nearly stopped. What if he asked me something about this deal before Burt got there? I hurried to gather the papers together, dropping them all over the floor. When I finally did retrieve them and walked into his office disheveled, clutching messy folders to my breast, my heart nearly stopped again. There was our client—a Bay of Pigs veteran—calmly removing a dark pistol from his shoulder holster. He placed it nonchalantly in a desk drawer.

"Let's get to work."

I nodded numbly and sat down. Like Dorothy in *The Wizard of Oz*, I knew I wasn't in Kansas anymore.

Throughout my years of practicing law, I found my feminist views repeatedly challenged and tested against reality. In retrospect, I realize that this strengthened my ability to become an effective leader. But coming to a fuller understanding of the complexities of real-life human behavior wasn't always pleasant.

Although I was the only woman associate at Paul, Landy (in those days, the term was "lady lawyer"), I wasn't the first. Unfortunately, my female predecessor had helped convince other members of the firm that the negative expectations about professional women were true: She'd gotten married shortly after she was hired, and when her husband began to complain about her hanging around with a bunch of men all day, she quit. Whenever her name came up, I did my best to remind my colleagues of all the male lawyers who'd come and gone, too. But the impression that women somehow weren't serious about maintaining a career (except insofar as it allowed them to catch and keep a man) was lasting; nothing I could say would change that.

Being the sole woman lawyer there could sometimes be difficult. Obviously, I *wasn't* one of the boys. While I worked hard to fit in at the firm, I also spent increasing time with the growing ranks of women lawyers and the few young women hired as summer associates at other downtown law offices. I got to know their problems, at home and on the job.

One of the summer associates in another firm told me that a partner there had proved a real lightning rod for trouble. She said he saw himself as a kind of Don Juan. But among many of the women in the office he'd gained a reputation for being something of a lout. A couple of weeks before the firm's annual June jaunt to a resort in Jupiter, Mr. Personality burst in on the summer associate while she was alone in the library doing research. As she later related the story to me, he got right to the point.

"How'd you like to spend the weekend with me?"

Stunned, she stared dumbly at him. This lothario had probably expected either a sly yes or an indignant no; he obviously wasn't prepared for a total nonresponse.

"I mean," he sputtered, his face reddening, "what I mean is that, um, the firm's spending the weekend—I mean, my wife and I are going to be in Jupiter, so—ah, if you want to join us for a drink, or, I mean, dinner, we'd really love it."

Then, without waiting for yes, no, or another bout of silence, he backed quickly out of the library.

The summer associate and I had a good laugh later, at his expense.

I decided we might have stumbled onto something. If women respond to these kinds of presumptive advances by giggling or smiling (a common reaction when one is nervous, or trying to pacify someone more powerful), the man might think of it as encouragement. Even if a woman gave an immediate negative response, he might still feel encouraged to continue; *any* kind of response was reinforcement. Maybe *no* response was best.

Later, though, the same partner chose a different, more vulnerable target. This time his female employee of choice was a paralegal. I knew her a little; our firms had handled some business together for our respective clients, and she and I had talked about her young son and the difficulties she had raising him as a single mother. One morning, months later, she called me at my office, distraught.

"Can I talk to you, Patricia?"

"Sure. What's up?"

She told me. "He keeps coming on to me. He sneaks up behind me and whispers in my ear, saying stuff about how the two of us should just go out for a 'quickie.' I tell him to stop, but he won't. When I get mad, he acts all innocent and says he's just joking. But I'm afraid to even get in the elevator with him."

Given what I already knew about this guy, I wasn't exactly shocked. But I *was* surprised that he'd be so blatant, crude, and persistent in the face of resistance.

"Okay," I said, "what would you like me to do?"

"Well, could you talk to him? Ask him to stop?"

My heart sank. I was in a difficult position; although I clearly had a lot more power than she did, I was only an associate. He was a partner in a major firm and a friend of the partners in mine. Who knew what kind of effect my barging into this guy's office making accusations would have on my own career?

On the other hand, what kind of feminist would I be if I let it slide?

This woman obviously believed I could help her. And the guy's behavior was at least as embarrassing, I thought, as if he'd been caught smiling at a client with spinach stuck in his front teeth. I'd warn him about that, wouldn't I?

So I screwed up my courage, made an appointment to go see

him in his office, walked in resolutely, and let him know what I'd heard. His defensive statements were true classics:

"She's crazy!"

"She's lying to get attention!"

"She's the one who flirts with *me!*"

Standing there, I had the same eerie feeling I'd had back at Pan Am when Base Manager Lorenz sent us his patronizing, dismissive response to the pillbox hat complaint.

My goal had been to make him realize that *I* knew what he was up to. I'd raised the issue with him face-to-face in real hopes of changing his behavior. But he honestly didn't think he'd done anything wrong. Obviously, he still thought he was just having a little harmless fun. He hadn't a clue that what was fun to him as a man in a position of power might be terrifying to a comparatively powerless woman.

Less than a month later, all of us found ourselves in Orlando at a party during the annual Florida Bar convention. There was plenty of dancing and drinking. I stood on one side of the room in a pleasant buzz of my own. Then I saw something that sobered me up fast. Right in the center of the dance floor, the paralegal and her harasser were in the middle of a deep soul kiss. As I watched in amazement, the partner gazed over her shoulder and gave me a big, mocking, self-satisfied wink.

My first response was to be angry with the woman. I'd gone out on a limb—at her request—and this was my reward.

Then, I redirected my anger toward the partner. I'd been wrong to think that he didn't have a clue. His was the smug look of a man who knew he was in total control and liked it that way. There was no doubt in my mind that what he'd done constituted an abuse of power. If I felt helpless to change his outlook or behavior, the paralegal truly was helpless. She occupied a lowly rung on her firm's ladder, and she was a single mother who desperately needed the job, who could be replaced at a moment's notice without any loss to the business. Who was she, really, to resist a powerful partner—a man who could easily have her fired? Even if she felt that her willingness to be sexual with him gave her a firmer grip on the job, it didn't make what she'd said in our earlier conversation any less valid. I realized that the enthusiastic kisser I saw on the dance floor did not in the least cancel out the distraught woman who had called me in my office.

If I'd needed a thorough introduction to some of the gray areas surrounding the issue of sexual harassment, that kiss at the bar convention party was it.

I had my own personal boundaries to define at work, too.
Sometimes, my paranoia over being professionally slighted just because I was a woman—and the ensuing inner struggles I had to sort out—put my coworkers in a difficult position. During one marathon meeting that went on far into the night, some copies of documents had to be made. Being the junior attorney in the room, I should have been the one rushing out to the copy machine. But Rene Murai, a partner, didn't even look my way before heading out to do it himself.

After the meeting, Rene took me aside.

"Look, Patricia, I understand you're sensitive about being treated fairly here. But in that situation you should have made the copies, and the next time I expect you to do so."

"Wrong," I shot back. "I wasn't hired to work the copy machine. Next time, if we're going to need clerical help, you can get a secretary to stay late."

To his credit, Rene didn't snap at me. But he did hold his ground. After some negotiating, we made a deal: In an emergency, I'd do the photocopying, but under no circumstances would I ever serve coffee.

Rene and I became good friends. Nevertheless, he was a continual reminder to me of the comparatively late start I'd gotten in the legal profession. Only six months older, Rene was six years ahead of me career-wise. He was already a partner. While I had no reason to resent the man, I did resent his power over me. All of it made me that much more determined to succeed.

* * *

I n my case work, as well as in my relationships with my colleagues, I was learning lessons in the terrible circumstances
of some women's lives. In school, I'd studied our English common law heritage, learning about spousal unity ("husband and
wife are one, and that one is the husband") and the rule of
thumb (which considered it "reasonable" for a man to beat his
wife, as long as he used a stick no thicker than his thumb). Out
of school, I began to understand firsthand the truly devastating
impact these outworn concepts—still encoded in the law—had
on women's lives.

Roberta Fox, a state legislator I knew through my ERA work,
brought one such case to my attention. The facts were grim.
The woman's husband had beaten her savagely on many occasions, sending her to the hospital more than once. This time,
though, his behavior had reached a new, chilling level: He pur-
posely hit her with the family car in the driveway of their
home. The force of the blow had thrown her up onto the hood.
Not finished, he slammed into reverse so quickly that she fell to
the ground. Then he proceeded to hit her again. From inside the
car, their two children watched in horror.

Under these circumstances, it wouldn't seem as though any
seasoned attorney would have had much difficulty helping the
client recover money for her medical expenses, pain, suffering,
and all the other damages resulting from her injuries. After all,
the man had hit her twice—on purpose—with a car. But a doctrine called interspousal tort immunity, a remnant of law
blending the rule of thumb and the concept of spousal unity,
stood in the way. In effect, it meant that a wife could not sue
her husband in civil court to compensate for injuries he caused,
whether intentionally or through negligence. It meant that
even after a man had blackened his wife's eyes, bloodied her
nose, or hit her with his car, he could hide behind interspousal
tort immunity and legally deny her compensation—all because
he had once promised to honor and cherish her. In other words,
if a thug beat you up on the street, you could sue him; but if

the thug in your bedroom beat you up, he was protected by law.

The doctrine had a far-reaching, devastating impact. Similar cases were working their way to the Florida Supreme Court. At Roberta's urging, I helped draft a friend-of-the-court brief, urging the Third District Court of Appeals and the Florida Supreme Court to overturn the doctrine. We convinced six women's rights and women lawyers' associations to sign on to the brief. Legal Services filed a separate, concurring brief of their own.

Despite all our efforts, the Florida Supreme Court refused to overturn the doctrine on the grounds of "protecting family unity and resources." In other words: better a broken woman than a broken family.

This was a legal battle that would go on for years. In the meantime, this woman—and many like her—would just have to wait.

Paul, Landy didn't normally handle domestic abuse or divorce cases, which suited me just fine. Professionally, I had some idea of what to expect in the world of business, but there'd been no classes in law school on affairs of the human heart. Of course, I also feared that the firm would be more likely to pass such cases on to me. So I didn't exactly volunteer for any that came our way. In the end, I worked on only a handful of them in my twelve-year career. One of the first was the case of Ling Lo, a Taiwanese woman who worked in the library at the University of Miami. Her husband, who was from Hong Kong, was a student there.

When he assigned me the case, the partner shrugged it off.

"Don't worry, Patricia! They've already agreed how they're going to divvy up their property—it isn't much. A little hand-holding, a little paper-pushing. It'll be a piece of cake."

After meeting with Ling Lo a few times to discuss the particulars of the settlement, though, I was worried. She was so far from home, and she seemed so isolated. I wondered if she'd be able to find the kind of support that someone in her situation really needs. At our final meeting, after the divorce had gone through, I asked her about her future. The concern in my voice must have been obvious; she immediately tried to reassure me.

"Please don't concern yourself about me. I'll apply to graduate school to get a master's degree in library science, and I already have my library job. Really, I will be fine."

She almost had me convinced. Then I asked whether or not she had any family in the States to help her through the next couple of months. Maybe, I suggested, she'd want to invite a relative down to Miami for a while; it would take the edge off being so alone.

"My family does not know." The confidence in her voice leaked out suddenly, like air from a deflated balloon. "I cannot tell them."

"Would you like me to help explain it to them?"

She flinched. "You cannot imagine the shame a divorce brings to my family. I will never tell them. I cannot."

Her eyes never met mine when we talked. At this moment they were directed straight into her lap, where her tiny hands were clenched in anguish.

I tried to convince her that this wasn't such a great idea; her family was bound to find out sooner or later. But her mind was made up. And I didn't feel well versed enough in Taiwanese culture to play therapist, so I let the matter drop. Obviously, Ling Lo was afraid of her new life; but who isn't, after a divorce? And she had been able to articulate concrete, practical plans for her future. So I convinced myself she'd land on her own two feet.

When she left I quickly immersed myself in the safer, less emotional facts and figures of a real estate deal. I spent the next couple of weeks trying to forget Ling Lo and her problems. But I found I couldn't get her out of my mind. Something about our last meeting hadn't seemed quite right. In retrospect, it grew more and more apparent that she'd been trying to persuade herself, as well as me, that she was going to be okay. She hadn't really convinced me; had she convinced herself?

A few weeks later I received a phone call about the case from a lawyer at the university where Ling Lo and her husband lived in married student housing.

"Hi, Patricia. What should we do with the guns?"

I was perplexed, trying to remember whether or not some cache of firearms had been part of the divorce settlement.

"What guns?"

"Mr. Wu had quite a collection. There's a whole mess of paperwork you'll have to take care of, if you want them shipped back to Hong Kong. Do you want to try that? Or just keep the guns here and put them up for auction?"

"I don't really know what you're talking about."

There was silence on the line. Then: "You mean you haven't heard?"

"Heard what?" I managed and began to feel sick.

"His wife shot him, then turned the gun on herself."

I hung up.

The news was devastating. It forced me to confront a messy tangle of emotions. Sorrow: Ling Lo had seen no hope after her marriage ended. Guilt: If I had probed more, I might have been able to help her. I would never know what really went into the creation of this tragedy; but I believe in my heart that it was related to Ling Lo's role as a woman. Had she felt unbearably humiliated by the divorce? Faced violence from him? Had some deeply rooted shame kept her from telling me what was really going on? Years later, I'd wonder if her immigration status had depended on her husband. I'd failed to press her about any of these important issues, all of which had legal as well as emotional ramifications. I'd failed to convince her that it would be okay to tell the truth about her life, to reach out for help.

I was overwhelmed by my feelings of inadequacy. How could I change the world for all women, I asked myself, if I hadn't even been able to provide this one woman with a little of the help she really needed?

On top of my agony over these needless violent deaths, I was angry. I believed that the case had come to me in the first place because I was the firm's only woman lawyer. It wasn't long before I marched angrily into the office of the partner who'd assured me that Ling Lo's case would require a little paper-pushing, nothing more, and announced that I wanted to insert a new, nonnegotiable clause in my contract: no more divorce cases—not ever.

But I didn't really try to avoid trouble and strife for long. Throughout my early years at Paul, Landy, I dropped hints (whenever a partner was in earshot) about how much I'd like to get involved in litigation. Eventually, they gave me my shot.

All I can say is, be careful what you wish for; you just might get it.

My first case involved a claim against officers' and directors' insurance, and it was as boring as it sounds. Far from being *L.A. Law*–type action—in which every exciting case is solved after an hour of sex, tears, and style—my first litigation assignment proved to be mostly sweat and grind. I would sit, hour after hour, in a room filled from floor to ceiling with documents, sifting through every single piece of paper, trying to figure out all the different ways a particular corporate officer had managed to defraud his company. This was no small task; the man hadn't missed a trick. He'd done everything from sending flowers each week, at company expense, to his wife, his girlfriend, and his mother (which I thought was kind of sweet, actually) to building a house in the Bahamas using company equipment, employees, and supplies. Of course—after months and months of work—we settled out of court, as happens in nine out of ten cases.

This single experience cured me of thinking that litigation was exciting and business transactions were boring. It also convinced me that just because someone slaps up a sign somewhere reading NO GIRLS ALLOWED doesn't automatically mean that it's a terrific place to be. It would be years before I chose to do litigation again.

By the time I returned to it during my last years of practice, I knew that litigation work could be as interesting or as dull as the client, the issues, and the skill of opposing counsel made it. Of course, much of it would always be tedious. But that's why they called it "work" and paid me to do it.

Luckily, I was really enjoying my work in international law. My urban surroundings only added to the excitement. A good decade before *Miami Vice* hit the airwaves, south Florida was already a bit like a modern version of the old Wild West. The drug trade was starting to kick into high gear. The Everglades had become home to an odd assortment of heavily armed paramilitary groups: Cubans who'd fled Castro's revolution, Nicaraguans pledged to fight the Sandinistas, Haitians dedicated to the overthrow of Papa Doc and Baby Doc. And all of them trained in the same swamps crisscrossed by cocaine cowboys. Some of that high adventure found its way into the big downtown Miami law firms. We could predict which Central American government was going to collapse by which wealthy families were sending their sons and money to Miami. Bidding wars for cash-rich Florida banks began. Real estate was booming.

In law school, I hadn't given much thought to international business and finance. But I quickly became engaged by the challenge of it. I was also fascinated by many of my clients: most of them high-energy types who could do things like bring capital into Florida from some wealthy Middle Eastern oil sheik through a series of offshore companies and invest it in Texas real estate. It wasn't exactly socially redeeming, and I worried occasionally about embodying Bob Paul's stereotype of "lady lawyers" being good at deal making, but mostly I was having too much fun to care. For the first time in my life, I enjoyed the work I did from morning to night. Taking pride and joy in my work had seemed just a dream to me once. I now understood some of the privilege and confidence of men.

During the years that my corporate legal career was developing, I also became increasingly involved in working for passage of the Equal Rights Amendment. Through my own practice and the network of lawyers in other states with whom I became acquainted, I heard the disturbing stories of women's lives, and those stories fired my commitment to work for constitutional change.

From Charlotte, North Carolina, came this: "My husband and I own our home. It's in both our names. We rent out one of the rooms for seventy-five dollars a month. But North Carolina law says I have no right to the money, because I'm a woman."

From Missouri: "I run a crafts business from home. According to Missouri law, all my earnings belong to my husband."

From Utah: "A speeding car hit and injured our child. As a wife and mother I cannot sue, because I'm a woman."

From Philadelphia, Pennsylvania: Susan Vorchheimer, a bright eighth-grader who'd won science awards in junior high, wanted to attend the all-boys Central High, an academically superior public school. The Philadelphia school board ordered the Vorchheimers to send Susan to Girls High instead, even though the board admitted that Girls High had inferior science facilities. The Vorchheimers fought back—all the way to the U.S. Supreme Court. But in 1977 the Court upheld Central High's exclusion of Susan solely because she was a girl.

You didn't have to read between any lines to understand what it meant to women that, under the fundamental law of the land, we still did not have the same rights as men and in some ways were still barely more than their property. Horror stories surfaced under Louisiana's head and master law. In 1978 the state supreme court ruled four to three that Salina Martin's unemployed husband had the right to take out a second mortgage on their home over her objection, even though she was the family's breadwinner. Joan Feenstra and her daughter also faced foreclosure on their home after her husband pledged it as security for fees to the lawyer he'd hired to defend him on criminal charges of molesting the daughter.

I saw the ERA as a bread-and-butter issue. One year, I reviewed Dade County's dismal record of employment discrimination the same week I paid my property taxes. Women constituted nearly a third of all Metro Dade employees at the time, but more than 90 percent of the jobs paying twenty-five thousand dollars or more per year went to men. I was equally angry when I learned that the federal work incentive program was mandated *by law* to give priority for job training and placement to unemployed fathers. What about all the unemployed mothers who were trying to keep their families together, their heads above water? I was furious. Both county and federal governments were taking tax dollars out of my pocket and using them to discriminate against other women.

As I heard story after story, the Equal Rights Amendment became my passion. It was so obvious to me that the lack of a clear constitutional guarantee of equality under the law continued to make progress for women all over the country incredibly slow, difficult, and easy to reverse. My work for the Equal Rights Amendment led to an ever-closer involvement with NOW, the largest and most visible national organization working for ratification, and NOW's national campaign to make the ERA part of the U.S. Constitution became a perfect vehicle for my ongoing political education.

The Florida Bar Association had endorsed the Equal Rights Amendment. So had the American Bar Association. Through the ERA work I met lawyers like Pat Seitz. A few years ahead of me in her career, Pat worked at a prestigious Miami firm and was active in the Florida Bar. She'd gotten some funding from the bar for an educational program on the ERA. Along with Pat and Martha Barnett (who was well placed in a powerful firm that had offices throughout the state), I helped organize pro-

ERA speakers' training for lawyers in Tallahassee, Tampa, Palm Beach, and Miami. Pat and Martha were wonderful to work with. Pat, a slender woman with thin features and a ready smile, was a strong and effective litigator with an assertive, direct style; Martha appeared softer, more subtle and low-key, but (as is the case with many Southern women) anyone who underestimated her intelligence or will was in for a big surprise.

We must have been doing something right: Opposition surfaced almost immediately. The wife of a member of the Florida Bar's board of governors caught our act in Tampa and, as an ERA opponent, became highly incensed that our educational program, paid for by her husband's bar dues, was promoting the ERA.

"Hey, can we help it if an objective presentation of the law and the facts comes out sounding pro-ERA?" I asked Pat when she called to tell me about the controversy. After a fight, in the end the board of governors withdrew their endorsement of the ERA, retreating to what they said was a "neutral" position. We countered with a successful campaign to convince the young lawyers section to take a pro-ERA stance.

Pat and Martha decided that the best way to change the bar was to work from within. And both women eventually attained positions of power inside the traditional structure: Pat became the first woman president of the Florida Bar Association in 1993, Martha the first woman chair of the American Bar Association's House of Delegates in 1994. Personally, I just didn't have the patience or desire to work my way up in *either* organization. I began to focus my energies on the Florida Association for Women Lawyers.

FAWL had been started in 1951 as an independent women's bar association. But by 1975, the organization was in rough shape. During my final year of law school, their annual meeting consisted of five women in the bar of a hotel that was hosting the robustly attended Florida Bar Association convention. After this pathetic showing, Meredith Sparks—one of the pioneer women lawyers in Miami (a patent attorney with a graduate degree in chemistry) and an FAWL stalwart—invited a group of us law students to her home to talk about how we might build a strong organization, one that would monitor women's law issues throughout the state.

As accomplished a woman as Meredith was, she once expressed frustration to me that people seemed to patronize her, because she was in her seventies, white-haired, and wore glasses. But Meredith inspired me. I took a major role in helping to revitalize FAWL. As I'd hoped, my position at Paul, Landy provided concrete resources for mailing newsletters and carrying on other practical activities. Having the firm's name as a return address also helped draw in new members. Within the hierarchy of the local legal community, FAWL gained a certain cache and legitimacy.

Our small cadre of feminist lawyers played FAWL and the Florida Bar like accordions, pushing and pulling to advance a women's rights agenda. Knowing that women lawyers could turn to an increasingly vigorous FAWL as an alternative bar, the Florida Bar promoted more women into leadership within its ranks. When we convinced our FAWL membership to open the organization up to any lawyer, male or female, who supported our issues, the response was overwhelming: men who were running for office in the bar, on the bench, or in the legislature joined FAWL immediately, as did plenty of other male lawyers who simply supported women's rights issues. All this additional competition encouraged the Florida Bar to increase the number of programs it offered for professional women; and, to some extent, it increased its advocacy of women's rights legislation in Tallahassee.

Nevertheless, FAWL did not turn out to be my dream organization. Its big annual event in Dade County, a banquet honoring the judiciary, just made me impatient. Members would escort local judges to a fancy dinner at a fancy hotel; they'd spend the evening socializing. I knew how important this kind of access could be for women—we were traditionally shut out of the business lunch clubs and golf courses where such contacts are often made—but I still couldn't stand it. I wanted live action, not polite conversation and chicken cordon bleu. And I wanted women, all women, to have more real power in the world without having to kiss anybody's ring. FAWL raised tens of thousands of desperately needed dollars for a local battered women's shelter, and even though I understood how urgently necessary these services were, I wanted to be out there pushing the state and county to fund such shelters adequately as an essential responsibility of government. So, while I stayed involved with the organization, I also began to look for other activist possibilities.

In 1978, I got a call at my office from Chris Drennan, the chapter president of Dade County NOW. She knew of my work with the Florida Feminist Credit Union. (I served on their audit committee. I was also the recipient of a tractor loan.) She was calling to ask if I'd consider becoming the chapter's pro bono legal counsel. I remembered how NOW had helped tremendously during my battle with Pan Am over medical insurance benefits. I also knew NOW as an effective political group deeply involved in the ERA struggle I cared so much about. I said yes.

But I couldn't figure out why I should provide free legal assistance *and* pay for the privilege of doing it, so I didn't actually pay dues to join the country's largest feminist organization for years.

I ronically, most of my early work for Dade County NOW consisted of taking hot line phone calls much like the one I'd placed eight years earlier. These calls were referred to me only if the callers needed legal help. The women I spoke to asked my advice for a variety of problems, most of which were a lot more serious than needing money to cover a spouse's dental work and harder to solve, too. It was sobering to pick up the phone and listen to a woman who was afraid to leave her abusive husband, or to a mother who couldn't get her ex to pay child support for three hungry children, or to a secretary who had been fired for getting pregnant.

Talking with these women made me more committed than ever to the ERA. But it also frustrated me. These women couldn't wait for long-term political solutions; they needed help right now.

Handling cases that might set new precedent appealed to many more lawyers than handling cases that were critically important to an individual woman but involved more run-of-the-mill legal issues. Setting precedent is the stuff careers are built on. This made it difficult to get legal assistance for many of the women who called NOW. My reputation as an asker of favors spread quickly; lawyers I knew started avoiding my calls, and when I managed to get people on the phone, they did their best not to make any promises. They had a hard time turning me down, but they also knew that most of the clients I brought their way would be slow-pay or no-pay. I wasn't the most popular lawyer in town! But I took great satisfaction in being able to coax and cajole my colleagues into doing their share of pro bono work, so that a lot of women in desperate need were provided with legal counsel they'd never have been able to afford otherwise.

Sometimes I handled a case myself. When a woman named Judy called about job discrimination in the Miami Beach Building and Zoning Office, I seized the chance to combine NOW's political clout with my legal skills. NOW was urging organizations all over the country to boycott Florida as a convention center until the state ratified the Equal Rights Amendment. This was a powerful weapon that would cost Miami Beach millions in projected revenues annually. "How can I recommend to the national board that NOW stop boycotting Miami Beach, when not a single woman works as a municipal zoning officer?" I complained to city officials. Judy won a job as the city's first female code enforcement officer—with back pay.

NOW's boycott of Florida was part of an overall national strategy. Throughout the country, the ERA had become a victim of political monkey business and outright deceit. In Nevada, eleven state legislators had been elected on pro-ERA platforms in the 1976 elections, but when the time came to push the button each of them voted against it. Eight of these legislators had taken campaign contributions from ERA proponents. Key vote switches in Florida and North Carolina confirmed that ERA had become an item for political horse trading.

Two years before the original ratification deadline, NOW had taken decisive action. In April 1977, national leaders called for a boycott of tourist and convention facilities in the fifteen states that hadn't ratified. Some four hundred groups ultimately joined the effort nationwide.

In the first two and a half years of the boycott, four major organizations canceled conventions that had been scheduled on Miami Beach. (The largest, a 2,200-member AFL-CIO convention, would have brought an estimated two million dollars into the city.) The Miami Beach Visitors and Convention Authority estimated that about thirteen million dollars in convention revenue had been lost by the fall of 1979; projected future losses hovered in the neighborhood of two hundred million dollars. Needless to say, the Beach's business and political leaders were incensed. They were also desperate to stop the boycott.

The boycott made me nervous, too. I had no law firm clients in the hospitality industry who would be directly affected by a boycott, but as an activist, I had real questions about its value as a strategy. I was skeptical about whether it would gain us a single vote (and in fact it never did); on the other hand, I did like the idea of flexing our economic muscle. But I wanted a strategy that would show that we could turn the money on as well as off. In other words, to promote our cause, we needed a carrot as well as a stick.

In October 1978, Congress extended the deadline for ERA ratification to June 30, 1982. The extension was only half of the seven years NOW had sought, a compromise made in the Congress that spelled defeat for the ERA. NOW president Eleanor

Smeal had initiated a nationwide extension campaign, inspired by an original legal argument constructed by two law students whose ideas a less astute leader might have dismissed.

In December 1978, federal district judge Marion Callister ruled that the extension was unconstitutional. Furthermore, he ruled that individual states were not bound by any previous pro-ERA ratification votes, but could *rescind* their original action at any point before the thirty-eighth state voted to ratify. It wasn't until January 1979, when the Ninth Circuit Court of Appeals overruled Callister's extraordinary decision, that we knew the ERA was still alive and well. Faced with the prospect of another three and a half years of the boycott, Miami Beach political and business interests started scrambling for some relief.

In late August 1979, some of the ERA supporters from Miami Beach called me to find out whether Dade County NOW would consider helping them get an exemption from the boycott. They argued their community was doing everything it could to pass the ERA. They deluged us with papers documenting lobbying meetings, letters, proclamations, and trips to Tallahassee on behalf of ERA. I spoke to the chapter officers, and we began negotiations to see what could be gained.

NOW's national conference was coming up in October. In light of their strong efforts to promote ERA ratification, Miami Beach boosters urged us to approach the organization's national officers for some relief from the boycott. For our part, we offered to publicize Miami Beach as the only area in the state that had elected an entirely pro-ERA delegation to the state legislature. (The chief sponsors of the ERA in the state capital, Representative Elaine Gordon, who'd taken my original call to NOW, and Senator Jack Gordon, no relation, both represented the Beach.) We would recommend the Beach as the only appropriate place in Florida for pro-ERA organizations to hold state meetings, and we would try to convince Florida NOW to schedule its spring 1980 state conference there. Although we couldn't guarantee the outcome, we'd also introduce a resolution at the upcoming national conference, asking for some reciprocation of the Miami Beach area's commitment to the ERA.

In exchange, we wanted the city to pass their proposed "Little ERA" ordinance, which would ban sex discrimination in the city of Miami Beach, and strategize with us on plans for the ERA campaign. I convinced an initially skeptical city attorney that the little ERA was legal and appropriate, and in September 1979, the Miami Beach City Council passed the ordinance with great fanfare. Hiring the first woman building and zoning enforcement officer was added as a show of good faith.

Being active in more than one organization—being both an "insider" in a big corporate law firm and an "outsider" in NOW—was tremendously effective when it came to getting things done. My connection to a politically active national organization had strengthened my hand immeasurably. When it came to opening doors for women, being involved with NOW afforded me real power to make changes—well beyond any power I had as an individual lawyer.

It was while working on the negotiations with Miami Beach leaders over the boycott in late summer of 1979, that I first met Janet Canterbury.

It was a little unusual for me to attend the chapter's board meetings (although, as legal counsel, I was supposed to). I found them long, tedious affairs: Minutes, treasurer's reports, and discussions of planned programs and fund-raising events dragged on while I sat fretting about all the work I had waiting for me at home or piled up on my office desk. But since we were going to strategize for a formal meeting with the Miami Beach bigshots later that week and also to plan for the Dade County chapter's participation in NOW's upcoming National Conference, I decided to attend.

The breakfast meeting took place in a Denny's restaurant on Dixie Highway in Coral Gables—right across from the University of Miami. I was preparing myself mentally for another series of dreary discussions when a large, very determined woman of obvious substance and power, wearing a white lab coat, burst into the half-empty dining area, sat at the end of the three tables we'd pushed together, and, after listening for a few minutes, abruptly said, "Look, I don't want to be rude, but I really don't have much time—let's cut to the chase. What can these guys from the Beach do *to* us or *for* us? What exactly do we have to decide here?"

Hurray! I thought. A practical woman of purpose!

She proceeded to take over the meeting, which easily became the most efficient and interesting one I'd ever attended. Afterward, while she was rushing back out the door, I managed to grab hold of her and introduce myself. In a brusque but not unfriendly style that I'd soon become familiar with, she gave me her card and told me to call.

That was my introduction to Janet. She was a full professor and associate dean of student affairs at the University of Miami Medical School, and a respected endocrinologist. I learned that she'd been recruited to run as Dade County NOW chapter president (the current president's term would expire soon). My interest in getting to know her was definitely piqued. Here was another ambitious professional getting ahead in a fiercely competitive field, and at the same time making no bones about the fact that she was a lesbian and a feminist. I immediately sensed I'd learn a lot from her.

Whether because she's a doctor or a Texan, Janet has a confident physical presence and is at home in her body in a way that encompasses her sexuality. It's this confidence, along with her determination to defy the conventional limits placed on women, that made her decide she could make it in the cutthroat world of academic medicine as an open lesbian. That, and her Lone Star native's love of a good fight—one that would be worthy of her extraordinary intelligence and fierce drive—spurred her on to succeed. (Janet has occasionally joked about running for political office as Florida's first radical feminist lesbian-

Republican candidate. I'm forced to remind her that the Republican stuff would kill her chances.)

In truth, her openness about her sexuality has made her life and career tremendously difficult. She has needed every ounce of the inner toughness that I came to rely on politically for her own success and survival. Because she's a talented teacher and a successful researcher, Janet won full professorship and tenure before she turned forty—an unusually fast-track career for medical school. Because she's also a brilliant political strategist and an artful administrator, she quickly rose in the school administration to deputy dean for medical education, making her one of the handful or two of women in the United States to reach the highest ranks in academic medicine.

Jealous colleagues have sometimes attempted to use Janet's sexuality as a weapon against her. Most of the time, when someone tries to discredit Janet by "outing" her to the dean (who, of course, already knows she's a lesbian), he valiantly ignores them. Janet has described him as one of the truly good guys, a really fair man. While he might not always approve, he always respects others' choices. "But every once in a while," Janet says, "he calls me in and we have a chat about working on 'all those women's issues.' I ask him if he's unhappy with my work and he says, 'No, no, that's not it,' but doesn't really say what 'it' is. Then I know that someone's been filling his head again with fears that some major donor or state legislator might cut off money to the med school because he has a lesbian dean in his administration—and a feminist activist, at that."

From the beginning, when we worked together on the ERA campaign, to the present, as we lobby to get more women elected or appointed to public office, Janet has challenged the status quo and the balance of power in highly visible ways. And she has more than once found herself targeted for that. Once, after a particularly grueling period organizing for a big abortion rights march, she called me, terribly unhappy.

"Damn it, Patricia, it's happening again. I've got a coup attempt on my hands here at school."

"How many are coming after you?"

"As far as I can tell, eight or nine of 'em."

"Well," I responded with the only answer I could think of that might cheer her up, "at least it will be a fair fight."

I was right about the odds. Janet survived that one, as she has survived everything before and since. She remains one of the most powerful women in academic medicine and in the feminist movement. She's also been a tremendous source of inspiration to me in my own career as an activist. She takes risks that other successful women on the inside wouldn't dare. And frankly, as activists, she and I egg each other on.

Our working styles meshed perfectly. One of the other Dade County activists called us "the brains and the brawn" of Florida NOW. But, she added, she wasn't sure who was which. Neither were we, most of the time. Both Janet and I tend to be sure we're always right; both of us like to be in charge; and neither of us likes to back down.

At first, she and I had legendary shouting matches over tactics and strategies: out-and-out verbal blood baths that left other activists cowering. Then, because Janet and I also have tremendous respect for each other, we'd back off, go home (where each of us would reconsider her position in light of the other's arguments), come back the next day . . . and, having switched sides by then, start the fight all over.

In her zeal to change the world and further NOW's agenda, Janet was always willing to consider outrageous tactics. Cheesecake posters of voluptuous women romping in the surf off Miami Beach had long been a staple of the city's tourist promotion. But these posters had been in storage for several years when the new Visitors and Convention Authority director, desperate to get business going during the ERA boycott, decided to start using them again. Of course, the board of Dade County NOW had a lively discussion on how to kill off these female-only advertisements, which we thought were distinctly out of step with the Beach's ostensible support for women's equality. Janet suggested that we threaten to create—and widely distribute—counter-publicity posters. Ours would highlight women whose physical appearance represented a keen departure from the stereotypical bathing beauties: winners of hairy leg contests; the very large, or very pregnant, in minimalist bikinis. Janet, an imposing figure herself, volunteered to lead a group of models down to the water. I dubbed this action "T and A for the ERA" and leaked our plans to the press at the city council hearing where I was testifying in favor of the Little ERA. To Janet's disappointment and my relief, the VCA did not call our bluff; otherwise, we would have had to carry out our threat and actually schedule a photo shoot. In the end, they decided that their old cheesecake posters really were out of style, after all.

As Janet and I began working together, my commitment to NOW deepened. I realized that NOW could be the outlet I'd been seeking for my political activism. It was exciting to think of all the possibilities that strong, effective leadership like Janet's presented to the organization. Privileged to observe her style from a close working perspective, I learned from her successes as well as her mistakes—and, of course, my own!—as we struggled to fulfill NOW's agenda in the Dade County area.

In the past, Dade County NOW had placed little importance on participating at the national level. Due to a limited agenda and even more limited funding, the chapter's delegates to NOW's annual national conference had always been chosen on the basis of who could pay her own way. But in 1979, Eleanor Smeal was running for reelection as NOW president, Florida NOW wanted the national organization to allocate more resources to our state for the ERA ratification drive, and our chapter's agenda also called for some sort of resolution to the boycott of Miami Beach. At the chapter meeting, Janet suggested it would be smarter to base delegate selection not on who could afford to go, but on who would be the best advocates for our agenda. She raised the issue with seeming innocence at first. But she became increasingly forceful as the meeting progressed, insisting that Elaine Gordon and I should be included as official representatives of the Dade County chapter. Of course, I thought it a wonderfully wise and inspired decision!

Several weeks later I found myself on a plane to LAX. My introduction to politics on the national level had begun, and I was about to discover that place where my politics and emotions would intersect—a state of mind and of being, really, that I'd been searching for all my life—where my own wants and needs, and my ongoing struggle to fulfill them, made me ready to advocate for others, too.

The Los Angeles conference really cinched it for me; I'd never been with so many dynamic feminists before from so many parts of the country, gathered together in one place. The energy and power was palpable; you simply couldn't help but feel inspired and invigorated. And it was wonderful to watch NOW's president, Ellie Smeal, in action. An olive-skinned woman whose dark hair was, at the time, just touched by gray, Ellie is a woman of ferocious intelligence, a powerful speaker with a flair for the dramatic. Her appearance at the podium was preceded by the L.A. NOW marching band playing a spirited song written specifically for the occasion; Ellie appeared on stage to a standing ovation. After I got to know her better, I was impressed by her genuine desire to reach out and solicit opinions on strategy from absolutely everyone she came in contact with: taxi drivers, waitresses, and hotel housekeepers, as well as NOW activists, feminist leaders, and recognized experts. It was Ellie who, in her graduate work in political science at the University of Florida, first projected the possibility of a "gender gap" in voting patterns between men and women; this was finally documented in the mainstream press in 1980. The *New York Times*/CBS News Poll reported that 8% fewer women (46%) voted for Reagan than did men (54%). Ellie's special capacity for inspirational and intelligent leadership comes partly from her uncanny ability to perceive patterns and draw accurate conclusions from what others see as isolated, unrelated facts. (The only drawback to this is that she sometimes comes up with analyses that initially seem paranoid. But having seen so many of her hypotheses borne out in reality, I've learned never to dismiss them out of hand.)

Our ability to fulfill the Dade County agenda at that Los Angeles conference was limited, and our results mixed. In fact, it would take our home chapter another two years to convince the national board to exempt Miami Beach from NOW's boycott. In L.A. we settled for a resolution that, in effect, added a carrot (though not the one I'd been hoping for) to the stick: It promised to steer the many hundreds of boycotting groups' national convention dollars immediately to the next state that ratified the ERA.

Back home, Janet was turning Dade County NOW into one of the most exciting and powerful chapters in the country. When she first came to office, the group had about forty members—and about forty dollars in the bank. Shortly after her election, the local board met to discuss goals and strategies for the year. Janet listened, uncharacteristically silent. Then, leaning back in her chair, she announced that it sounded as if we needed at least a few hundred working members and a budget of eight to ten thousand dollars. Everyone absorbed this quietly for a moment. Then a chuckle of disbelief sounded around the room. This didn't please her one bit.

"You'd better not think I'm kidding!" She glowered as she pointed the end of her gavel around the table, assigning each of us specific tasks, pushing, pulling, driving us all.

By the time she left office two years later, Dade County NOW would have more than one thousand members, and so much cash in the bank—with an annual income of more than twenty-five thousand dollars—that we'd pique the interest of the IRS. Under her leadership, our chapter also became a major player on the local political scene.

We learned early on that Dr. Canterbury didn't understand

the word *can't*. She also had no grasp of the concept *volunteer*. If you said you would get work done, she expected you to go ahead and do it—immediately—with all your heart and soul. And she was ready to test us.

The 1980 elections were critical. We had only one more chance to change the composition of the state legislatures, in many of which passage of the ERA was being blocked by a mere handful of votes. In Florida, we weren't about to give up hope. Our state house of representatives had voted to pass the Equal Rights Amendment three times, but in each case the state senate had voted it down—the last time by only two heartbreaking votes, as three key senators switched sides.

One of those no votes had been cast by Vernon Holloway, a turncoat from Miami. Holloway had pledged to follow the results of a straw poll in his district. His constituents responded in favor of ERA by two to one, but Holloway voted against it when the amendment hit the floor. We decided that Holloway would have to go. He was a fourteen-year incumbent with influential friends throughout the state; but we believed that we could help defeat him this time around. Under Janet's leadership, we already had a greatly increased number of activists looking for a good fight. This would be an excellent way to test and continue to build our chapter's strength. Personally, I was excited at the prospect of participating in a real blood-and-guts battle against a prohibitive odds-on favorite.

We convinced Ellie Smeal that Holloway could be defeated, but we told her she'd have to send us some reinforcements to make it happen. So Molly Yard, an experienced field organizer and political director of NOW, came down to Miami. With her help, we set up and staffed phone banks, calling many thousands of voters in Holloway's district. We held roadside demonstrations, passed out flyers, got thousands of petitions signed as a way to target voters, raised money, and hounded our opponent. In the end our candidate, Dick Renick, defeated Holloway in an upset victory. A number of our other local candidates won as well, and we were invigorated.

* * *

Nevertheless, on the national level 1980 turned out to be a politically devastating year. The Republican platform withdrew support of the ERA. Republican presidential candidate Ronald Reagan, an archconservative dedicated to the defeat of the ERA and to abolishing many reproductive and other rights for women, lurked in the wings.

In Florida we had suffered some organizational problems inside the NOW ranks due to a lack of effective communication between the southeast region's national board members and our state's local activists. I'll never forget the furious call we received at the beginning of the presidential campaign from Elayne Weisburd, one of the Democratic city council members we'd been working with on Miami Beach. Janet answered the phone.

"What the *hell* is going on over there!?"

"What the hell are you talking about?"

"NOW's *non*endorsement of Carter! What the hell do you think!?"

Janet told Elayne she'd get back to her. Then she called me at my office and proceeded to curse the way only an angry Texan can. I became pretty upset and threw in a few invectives myself—aimed mostly at national NOW.

Not that we necessarily wanted NOW to endorse President Carter. We understood all the arguments the national board had made: Carter gave the Equal Rights Amendment a lot of lip service, but he'd never really made it a priority and hadn't been willing to spend political capital on it. Like the early suffragists, we agreed that we ought to hold the party in power accountable. What bothered Janet and me was that our representatives on the national board had not bothered to inform *us* of the organization's decision! We'd been caught behind the knees in a situation that directly impacted our work. On a purely practical level, this put us in a difficult position with our political friends and allies in south Florida—most of whom were Democrats. They felt betrayed; and we hadn't been given time to figure out how to handle the situation.

"That's never going to happen to us again," Janet said, when the storm had died down.

"Easy to say. But if the national board members don't want to tell us what they're up to, we're never going to know."

There was a gleam in Janet's eye as she turned to me.

"That's why we're going to get *you* on the national board."

That year, NOW's regional elections for the national board were in Columbia, South Carolina. There were three seats in our region, the Southeast. Janet started a mailing and telephone campaign urging members of our chapter who could to get themselves up there for the vote. We planned to arrive in Columbia with a specific agenda: to get more effective representation for the Southeast region at the national level. We figured the Equal Rights Amendment was at stake. Janet arranged for inexpensive transportation to the event: cheap airfare to Jacksonville, Florida, where travelers would be met by rented passenger vans for a drive up the coast.

The fifty or so who showed up were probably surprised: The "vans" turned out to be station wagons that would hold up to nine people each—if three passengers, with knees tucked under their chins, rode backward in low-slung pull-out seats. The trip to Columbia was over five hours long. Tension over smoking was compounded by several insistent, off-key singing voices. But there was enough esprit de corps among our group to overcome this discomfort with a minimum amount of grumbling.

The women in Columbia were shocked, to say the least. No one there had expected a contested election. But Dade County NOW blew into town, struck an alliance with one of the candidates from South Carolina, overwhelmed the conference, and managed to get me and another chapter member, Maria Saiz, elected by a comfortable margin. Our South Carolina ally, Sandy Damon, was elected, too, completing the three-member delegation that would represent the Southeast region on the national board.

This experience confirmed to me how unique NOW is. As an organization it is member-driven. And those members are grass roots all the way. NOW's democratically elected representatives operate with a strong practical and financial commitment to this all-important grassroots constituency—even if they can't carry a tune.

The 1980 election results devastated feminists and progressives across the nation. Everyone involved in supporting these agendas had to stop and reassess. A conservative majority had been elected to the U.S. Senate and, at the state level, conservative Republicans everywhere swept into legislatures on Reagan's coattails. In states that had not ratified the ERA, relatively few gains were made. The question of whether we could realistically continue to devote so many of the organization's resources to fighting for the Equal Rights Amendment dominated NOW's national board meeting in April 1981.

"The Equal Rights Amendment is no icing on a cake," Ellie Smeal argued. "It means billions of dollars to American industry, and of course billions of dollars to American females. When we say women make fifty-nine cents on the dollar, some companies are profiting dearly because of this—they're making forty-one cents on the dollar for every hour a female works rather than a male!"

Meanwhile, the specific threats posed by the new Reagan administration were very real. In fact, they were similar to the threats we're facing now, in that they involved assaults on women's gains, women's equality, and women's freedom at every level.

Wherever we turned we saw another burgeoning political threat to women's rights. Hearings to consider a proposed constitutional amendment outlawing affirmative action were scheduled. Anti-abortion House and Senate members began a drive to give full citizenship to fertilized eggs through the Human Life Amendment. Proposed budget cuts would hit women hardest of all, affecting, as they did, all social service programs for women, infants, and children, including child-care and nutrition programs. Equal educational opportunities were threatened when funding for programs under the Women's Educational Equity Act was severely slashed. Federal funding to the states for similar programs was reduced, and provided in the form of lump-sum block grants. And a federal district court judge (in an opinion subsequently upheld by the U.S. Supreme Court) ruled that Title IX—the federal law to end sex discrimination in education—could only be enforced if federal funding was linked to a particular school program. Under the block-grant funding system, this was an almost impossible task.

But even in the face of these manifold and imminent threats, NOW leaders came to the conclusion that it was important not to roll over and play dead on the ERA, even if we lost the fight. We had to go on; otherwise, our opposition would smell blood, and that would make them too eager to take us on in future battles. If we quit before the campaign was over, we would not only lose the ERA, but risk never being taken seriously again as a political force. But if we fought all out, even in the face of daunting odds, we could rally our supporters and our opponents would know we were a formidable enemy on all of their efforts to roll back women's rights. I believed that our chances of winning were slim, but I too was convinced that the fight was still worth waging. The national board voted to intensify the ERA campaign and to launch massive ratification campaigns in several key states.

Florida, like the other states targeted for a final ratification drive, had a Democratic state legislature, a Democratic governor, and a strong base of ERA activists. (The unratified states were basically a map of the old Confederacy, plus Utah and the surrounding states that were impacted by the strong anti-ERA stance of the Mormon Church. Illinois, which required a three-fifths vote to pass a constitutional amendment, was the only unratified northern state.) We knew our state would need more of the national organization's resources, so we sent a large delegation to the next national meeting. After we'd lobbied Ellie Smeal intensively, Florida—along with North Carolina, Illinois, and Oklahoma—became the beneficiary of hundreds of new volunteer activists and staff. And hundreds of thousands of dollars were directed our way for an all-out grassroots organizing drive.

The decision to continue campaigning for the ERA wasn't just based on moral imperatives; there were very practical reasons as well. Extremely strong, effective, tenacious, and powerful political networks can be built when you fight losing battles as well as when you win. Some campaigns are not worth waging if you can't win; others have to be fought on grounds of principle regardless of the chances for success. But in any grassroots campaign, building an ongoing base of support is as important as winning the immediate goal. So NOW's decision to continue with the ERA campaign was a wise one: It would contribute immeasurably to the foundation and development of a strong, enduring women's rights movement regardless of the final results.

Ironically, since Reagan's election, NOW's membership and financial resources had increased substantially. A lot of people had been scared into recognizing that they needed a strong women's rights movement. Polls showed that a vast majority of women agreed with our goal. Win or lose, an intensified ERA campaign would strengthen our forces on all of our issues.

For the first time since the suffrage movement, large numbers of women massed behind a single women's rights issue. For many it was their first foray into politics. Networks were strengthened and expanded. (A decade down the road, the power of these networks would become apparent nationwide when, in 1992, the "Year of the Woman," an unprecedented number of women candidates were swept into local, state, and national political office. That was no fluke—it was the result of a long-term strategy.)

The power of NOW's call to arms for the ERA campaign was undeniable. Give us everything you've got for the next twelve months, we urged members during volunteer drives. After one year you can get back to your job, save your marriage, get to know your kids, get your teeth fixed. But if we don't push this through now, you and your daughters might never have equal protection under the law.

We placed an ad in the *National NOW Times:*

> HELP WANTED. EQUAL RIGHTS AMENDMENT
> MISSIONARIES—IMMEDIATE OPENINGS FOR
> VOLUNTEERS. NO EXPERIENCE NECESSARY.
> TRAINING AVAILABLE. WORK IN UNRATIFIED
> STATES, IN CHALLENGING ENVIRONMENT.
> LOTS OF PUBLIC CONTACT. EXCELLENT
> BENEFITS.

It was a lot to ask; the excellent benefits were primarily spiritual in nature. But the response was incredible. The *New York Times* on November 8, 1981, reported that "Hundreds of so-called missionaries have left homes, husbands, children, jobs and schools to work in distant states." That same article went on to profile Lillian Ciarrochi, who left her high-paying job at an established Philadelphia accounting firm to work for a year full-time as an ERA organizer in Florida, as part of what she called "a memorial to my mother," who had died the year before.

"I suppose I should worry about financial security," Ciarrochi said. "I'm single, and I'm forty-nine, and when all this is over I'll be looking for another job and facing another problem: age discrimination. It's nice to have money in your old age. But it's also important to like yourself. If I hadn't taken this job, I wouldn't like myself."

I couldn't have said it better. For the first time in my career, feminist work took absolute precedence over law.

And my life changed dramatically. While still carrying a full load at my firm, I was also working far into the night and all through the weekends for the ERA. Whatever remaining good health habits I had went completely by the wayside: no more exercise, no more softball—only door-to-door canvassing, waving picket signs at highway entrance ramps, marching on the state capitol. Having proudly given up eating sugar and red meat in the late sixties, I found myself existing on whatever fast food I could grab at all-night Burger Kings on Dixie Highway. I got no more than five hours of sleep a night. Yet, I'd never experienced such a sense of invigoration or fulfillment.

NOW's strength was growing exponentially. Hundreds of women and men in Dade County would turn out at 5:30 A.M. to distribute doorhangers; dozens of us were busy with fundraising, organizing, media contact, public speaking, lobbying. In addition to gaining new skills and confidence, I also felt, for the first time in my life, the satisfaction of knowing that I was really a part of making history. I was improving the lives of women; I was continuing to help move our country forward toward a "more perfect union."

To get the campaign started, NOW opened ERA Countdown Campaign offices in Tallahassee, Broward County, and Dade County, and a lot of high-powered activists from Washington and across the country came down to help. Janet and I fought hard to become more fully a part of the leadership at the statewide level; we ended up taking over the Dade County office, implementing grassroots organizing from Miami to Key West. All along, we held regular telephone conferences with Ellie Smeal and other national and state leaders to discuss strategy.

No sooner had Janet and I wrested control of the Dade County office away from Ellie's national staff than Janet, my best friend and comrade-in-arms, said "good luck," and left to write a medical research grant! I didn't see her for six weeks.

The anti-ERA legislators didn't know it yet, but they were in for a wild time. After years of lobbying and letter writing, the full force of our fury would be directed against them during this final, intensive campaign. Dick Anderson was one of the first politicians to experience the full range of our efforts.

Before his election to the Florida state senate, Anderson had been a popular player for the Miami Dolphins; he had two Super Bowl rings to show for it. As far as most mainstream residents of Miami were concerned, Anderson was The Man. But in Tallahassee he was known as Dempsey Barron's boy. Barron, the ERA's chief opponent in the legislature, was dean of the Florida Senate and ruled it with an iron hand. Dempsey Barron was also a lawyer whose firm represented a score or more insurance companies, and Anderson, his protégé, owned his own insurance agency and sponsored insurance legislation in the Senate. All this explains, at least partly, why Anderson was the only representative from Dade County who opposed the ERA, this despite the fact that his constituents overwhelmingly supported the amendment.

There are several crucial reasons why the insurance industry was so opposed to the Equal Rights Amendment nationwide.

First, the insurance industry employs vast numbers of women and pays them even less than comparable jobs in other industries. In the early eighties, insurance companies employed 1.9 million workers, 60 percent of them women. While the average employed woman in that period was paid 59 cents for every dollar paid to a man, women managers in the financial and insurance industries were paid only 50 cents to the man's dollar. In addition to its dismal record of employment discrimination, the insurance industry relies on pricing structures that discriminate on the basis of sex, charging women higher premiums for lower benefits. Of course, industry lobbyists argued that the ERA would end the "young women's discount" on auto insurance. (The discount supposedly excuses ripping women off on health, disability, whole life insurance and annuities.) But most people pay unisex adult rates, charged by year rather than by odometer mile. The more you drive, the less you pay for each mile of insurance protection used. This favors men as a group because they drive more miles and have more accidents than women. A strong ERA would stop this sex (and income) discrimination by making insurers use cents-per-mile rates. Savings for women would average several hundred dollars per year.

Finally, insurance is one of the only major industries that's regulated at the state level. Put it all together and you have an industry with a major stake in ensuring that no federal law or constitutional amendment banning sex discrimination takes effect and that's invested a great deal in its state legislators.

NOW tried to lobby Anderson at first. We inundated him with petitions, cards, letters, phone calls, and visits. We met with him, his staff, his friends—anybody we thought might influence him, including one of my neighbors in Homestead, a man who was reputed to be a hunting buddy of Anderson's.

"What about your daughter?" I'd say, whenever I ran into my neighbor. "Don't you want her to have the same rights as your sons do, when she becomes an adult?"

He stared back at me suspiciously. "We don't need the federal government to take care of our women. My daughter'll be just fine, thanks—don't you worry."

Over time, it became clear that Anderson wasn't going to change his mind on this issue either. We'd have to make an example of him.

Throughout the campaign we had made signs—this one was my brainchild—patterned after the old Burma Shave ad campaign I'd seen growing up in the Midwest. Anywhere from a handful to several hundred of us would hold them up by the side of Dixie Highway during rush-hour traffic, for all to see: EQUAL RIGHTS. EQUAL PAY. RATIFY THE ERA. We started adding new groups of signs targeting Anderson. SOCIAL SECURITY CHEATS WOMEN. DICK ANDERSON DOESN'T CARE. It didn't rhyme, but made the point.

As our frustration with Anderson grew, so did the intensity of our messages. The "clincher" series read: WHO OPPOSES THE ERA? THE KU KLUX KLAN. THE AMERICAN NAZI PARTY. AND DICK ANDERSON.

This got us a call from Ellie Smeal.

"Could you please *stop* this nonsense? We don't really want to go the McCarthy route just yet!"

"But Ellie, we've lobbied the man to absolutely no avail. He's not going to change his vote! The only possible use he is to us now is as a bad example—if we can show other politicians the consequences of being anti-ERA, they might change their minds."

"No," she snapped. "There's got to be a better way."

Grudgingly, I pulled the Klan series off the highway—and auctioned it off at a later ERA fund-raiser.

I turned next to researching Anderson's voting record. The results became a convenient doorhanger that portrayed his pro-business voting record as anti-consumer and anti-woman. More than a hundred NOW volunteers fanned out before dawn one morning to distribute thousands of doorhangers in Anderson's district. One of our activists hung one on Anderson's front doorknob and it made the TV news. Of course, most of Anderson's votes were great for people like my clients! But that doorhanger came from my heart as a NOW activist.

Fuming, Dick called Janet, accusing her of twisting his record. "I really think you're being unfair, Janet. I've been good on other women's issues."

"We're not talking about other issues, Dick. We're talking about the ERA."

"Come on. Reasonable people can have reasonable disagreements without pulling the kinds of sick stunts you folks have. Why can't you take your cue from someone with class, like Patricia Ireland? She's a feminist! But she would never stoop so low."

With great relish, Janet asked him just *who* he thought was in charge of the campaign against him.

I was a little upset at being "outed" like that. I'd had a good lobbying relationship with Anderson until then. After his conversation with Janet, we never spoke again.

He still had Barron in his corner and plenty of insurance dollars in his coffers, and he wouldn't budge. On the other hand, our organizing proved successful; he didn't even stand for reelection when his term was up in 1982. My old friend Roberta Fox won his seat in the state senate.

Trying to bring down targeted politicians was only one NOW strategy. I also did a lot of traveling around the state of Florida, willing to speak to any group, anytime, anywhere. I spoke to the Greater Miami Chamber of Commerce and the Homestead Ham Radio Operators. I had twenty-minute, ten-minute, and three-minute speeches and thirty-second sound bites. (How luxurious that thirty seconds sounds now, when we need to do eight- to twelve-second sound bites for network news these days!) For a while I did what I called Talking to the Animals: organizations like the Elks, the Moose, the Lions—and any other stag clubs that would listen.

I also spent many days training NOW volunteers in groups called action teams. These teams organized in their own communities to help build pro-ERA visibility and momentum at the grass roots. It was a good way for people to take part in the campaign close to home. The action teams sponsored forums, spoke at clubs, schools, and churches, wrote letters to the editors of local newspapers, called in to radio talk shows, visited legislators in their local district offices, and collected signatures on petitions. They were the heart of our organizing campaign.

After simulations and role plays, I'd take new action teams into the field for some hands-on experience.

"Ask everyone you see to sign up for the campaign," I counseled. "It doesn't matter what they look like! Don't let stereotypes scare you away. Just walk up and ask if they support the ERA. If they say no, don't waste time arguing; just thank them and move on to the next person."

I wanted them to ask everyone because I knew that, if they did, they'd see that a majority of people supported us. I wanted them to understand that strength. I wanted them to *mobilize* it.

During one trip to Homestead I led a group out to a local shopping center. The first person to cross my path could have been a stunt double for Dolly Parton: She wore easily five layers of makeup and sported a big, big hairdo that couldn't have been broken with a sledgehammer.

Great, I thought to myself, just my luck. She'll probably take one look at me and pull out a shotgun.

After the lecture I'd given, though, I had to approach her. So I walked up meekly. "Hello. Are you a supporter of the ERA?"

A smile lit her face. "Where the hell you gals been!?" she bellowed. "I thought you'd never get out this way!"

Within seconds, she had snatched up every piece of pro-ERA paraphernalia I had on me. She promised to try and rile up some of the other locals, too.

Sometimes the pressure we were under clouded our judgment. While most of our meetings were open to the public, some strategy sessions were invitation-only. At the very first meeting of the Florida campaign, held in my law firm's conference room—in which state and local organizers met with national staff prior to kicking off the Countdown—a woman none of us knew came in and sat at the end of our large table. We eyeballed her suspiciously, and a hostile buzz went around the room; clearly, she was some sort of spy. Finally Pat Kennedy, the Florida NOW president, walked over and, very politely, informed her that this was a closed meeting; she would have to leave. Looking slightly insulted, she nevertheless left without putting up any fuss. We sighed with relief, congratulating ourselves on our vigilance.

The sense of relief dissipated when we found out that the woman was Katherine Kelly—a bigwig in the state Democratic party and a longtime friend of Molly Yard—who had come that day to give us a check for a thousand dollars. Eventually, she sent the donation to national NOW, but it was years before she gave anything to the state organization.

M eanwhile, the absolute deadline of June 30, 1982, loomed on the horizon.

Throughout the months and years of fighting for the ERA, spending untold hours canvassing, giving speeches, chasing politicians through airports, and organizing rallies, I had feared deep down inside that we could not win. The signs were all against us. Too many wealthy, influential corporate lobbies, who stood to lose if they had to treat women equally, had too many important legislators in their pockets. The votes in the state legislature weren't there, and every time we'd win a new vote, Dempsey Barron would call in a chit and we'd come up short again. This despite the fact that nationwide and Florida polls showed people supported passage of the ERA by a two-to-one margin. If this had been a plebiscite, we would have won in a landslide.

Initially I agonized over whether to share my pessimism with other activists. I knew that as an organizer it was important to have as positive an outlook as possible. It's not particularly inspiring to people to go around urging them to bang their heads against a wall. On the other hand, honesty is an absolutely necessary policy as a matter of principle and also credibility. As early as 1978, I'd given a speech to members of Dade County NOW, in which I tried to lay out the reality as I saw it. I ended my remarks by paraphrasing Susan B. Anthony, who in her last public words, had said of the woman's suffrage drive, "failure is impossible." (She was right, although she didn't live to see success.) Failure was *not* impossible, I said; unless we had activists of Anthony's courage and conviction and unless we picked up our pace. The local chapter leaders waiting in the wings seemed upset. When I finished speaking, the applause was notably restrained. Immediately, chapter officer Ingrid Hunter rushed up to the front of the room and tried to revive the crowd's flagging spirits.

"We *can't* lose! We won't let that happen!"

The audience perked up. People started to applaud. By the time Ingrid had finished they were fired up again, ready to do whatever was necessary.

I had tried to do what I thought was the right thing. A leader needs always to hold out hope for success, but I knew we had to make our plans in the face of reality. I had wanted to shake people out of any illusion that the ERA would be ratified without *all* of us making a very major commitment to it, and becoming intensely involved in electoral politics. During the final, intense year of the ERA Countdown Campaign I began to learn how to be honest about reality while still inspiring others.

As we focused on grassroots organizing and lobbying, I began to understand that all of our work would result in NOW becoming a stronger, more effective political organization whether or not it resulted in ratification. And we had other important reasons for pressing on: For one year, we focused the attention of the entire nation on the extent of discrimination against women and on what equality—enshrined in the Constitution—could mean. We spread the discussion about equality for women through every community in the nation. We raised the country's consciousness, changed and mobilized public opinion, and gained lots of legislative victories along the way. (We called it "guilt legislation.") We won rape law reform, equal credit protection, and the repeal of the hated head and master laws in many states, to name just a few of our gains.

On June 10 we had our final rallies for the Equal Rights Amendment in the capitals of the targeted states: Raleigh, North Carolina; Oklahoma City, Oklahoma; Springfield, Illinois; and Tallahassee, Florida. We sent bus after bus off to the state capital from Miami, starting at 6:00 A.M. the day before, with great press and fanfare. But the personal photos I have from that morning are telling. Janet and I look half dead. Too many sleepless nights, too many days spent running from jobs to NOW headquarters to rally sites with hardly any rest, too many McBurgers, McFries, McShakes, McMeals had taken their toll. But by the time the march stepped off the next day, even though we knew we were going to lose, the photos show us standing proudly arm in arm, our heads held high. Being with the ten thousand supporters who came to Tallahassee, the fire started to burn in our tired bellies again, and we were out there chanting and hollering like everybody else.

In the end, none of it was enough.

The Florida house passed the Equal Rights Amendment 60–58. But it was doomed in the state senate by Dempsey Barron, Dick Anderson, and friends: 22–16. With that vote, it was all over. Since only the Illinois legislature was still actively considering the measure, it would be impossible to get ratification by the three additional states we needed for ERA passage. This was the end; we had lost.

When the vote was announced, all the anti-ERA constituents broke into cheers. The rest of us sat in a daze. Even though I'd prepared myself for this moment, I hadn't realized to what extent a small part of me had hoped against hope. As the antis' applause rang around us, a shared kind of rage and determination spread among ERA supporters in the room. It was hard to believe that, after everything we'd done, this was the way it ended: in a room, in a building, with a bunch of politicians congratulating themselves on having reinserted their boots in the small of our backs. Within seconds, someone yelled, "Vote them *out!*" The shout swiftly became a group chant, drowning out the polite applause with some powerful emotion. "Vote them *out!* Vote them *out!* Vote them *out!*"

We poured out of the capitol building to a rally outside, where the chanting continued and grew. "We'll remember in November" echoed our determination never to give up, never to give in. Eventually Roberta Fox managed to quiet everyone down.

"We have nothing to be ashamed of today! Everyone understands that the senate is a dark place, a secret place, a place not unlike a cesspool! You must now give everything you have—and *send in reinforcements!*"

The energy of that rally got me through the night. But by the following morning I could have used a little reinforcing myself. Out of habit more than anything, I dragged myself down

to the local NOW office. There I found Janet sitting by herself
in the conference room, staring at a hole in the wall.

"Hey."

"Hey."

I sat and stared too for a while. Finally I said, quietly, "You
didn't really think we were going to win, did you?"

She waited before answering. "You know, I think I really *did*.
I needed to convince myself that we had a fighting chance—I
couldn't give it up."

L ater, with the help of other activists at the National Action
Center in D.C., we analyzed the causes of our defeat. The
Republican Party hadn't just deserted women's rights; it had
led the attack against them. Nor were women's rights high on
the Democratic Party's agenda, even though they had given lip
service to the Equal Rights Amendment. Powerful corporate interests, donors to both parties, profited mightily from sex discrimination. Major business interests were notably absent from
our lists of ERA supporters, and while they may have hidden
behind Phyllis Schlafly's skirts for cover, many of them had
funded our opponents.

Things began to brighten a little as we went over the voting
statistics, because the numbers were crystal clear. In those targeted states that had failed to ratify, more than two-thirds of
the women representatives in the state legislatures, and nearly
100 percent of the African Americans, favored the amendment,
while less than 50 percent of white men were in our corner.
The single most obvious problem was the gender and racial im-
balance in the legislatures: Men constituted 94 percent of all
state senators, and 86 percent of all state representatives. If we
kept our momentum going, we might, indeed, vote some of
them *out* . . . and replace them with women dedicated to supporting equal rights.

If we ever wanted to have any chance of passing the Equal

Rights Amendment, we *had* to get those state legislatures in line.

Our mission was self-evident: We had to get more women and people of color into elected office. Period.

It was in many ways the perfect time for another major feminist push in Florida. Nineteen eighty-two was a redistricting year. With a marked statewide population shift to those urban areas that tended to be supportive of NOW and feminist issues, many new seats had been created; and conservative incumbents were especially vulnerable in their old ones.

At our urging, the ERA activists, angry, frustrated, and determined to show that women had some power, decided to stick around for another four months. Then we had to convince the more promising of them to run for office.

During the ERA campaign, some of the men we had supported for election because they said they were pro-ERA, were otherwise so uninspiring in their political views that we had had to keep them away from the NOW offices, so our volunteers wouldn't see what kind of politicians they were really working for. Too many of the men who claimed to represent us didn't seem to take women seriously at all. What we needed was to get our own people to run—and to win.

This represented a significant shift in NOW's strategy—what then-president Ellie Smeal called a "feminization of power." Instead of just trying to *influence* those in power, we would now *become* the people in power. We would get more feminist women elected. In the six weeks between the defeat of the ERA and the filing deadline for the 1982 elections in Florida, we conducted an urgent candidate search to convince strong feminist women to run for political office. As an immediate result, unprecedented numbers of women candidates ran for office in Florida that year: Twenty women filed for senate seats in the primary; fourteen of them went on to run in the general election; and nine of them won—eight of whom were pro-ERA. It was enough to *double the number of women in the Florida senate* (from four to nine out of forty). Revenge was sweet, too: of the twenty-two state senators who'd voted against passage of the ERA, ten lost their reelection bids. Eight of them lost to pro-ERA candidates. Two Florida senate seats went to African Americans (Arnett Girardeau of Jacksonville and Carrie Meek of Miami) for the first time since Reconstruction. (Carrie Meek again made history in 1992 when she and Corrine Brown became the first African American women elected to the Congress from my state.) The picture in Illinois, another key state that had failed to ratify, was similar: In the Illinois state senate the number of women doubled—from four to eight (seven of the eight were pro-ERA). And in North Carolina, Jesse Helms's Congressional Club candidates lost in all of the races they entered; NOW-supported candidates won several of those seats.

Our strategy worked. Not only did we get more women elected, but we also inspired new campaign workers and women voters by having candidates in whom we could believe with our whole hearts.

The gender gap (the difference between male and female voters' support for a candidate) had been decisive in many important statewide races, especially around the issue of the ERA. In Michigan, Governor James Blanchard had chosen Martha Griffiths (chief sponsor of the ERA in the U.S. Congress in 1972) as his running mate; the Blanchard/Griffiths ticket defeated Republican candidate Richard Headlee, who'd been outspoken in his opposition to the ERA. In New York, Lieutenant Governor Mario Cuomo (who had developed a vigorous women's rights platform) benefited from women's votes in the Democratic primary to defeat opponent Ed Koch, and the gender gap also helped him greatly in his gubernatorial race against Republican candidate Lew Lehrman, who outspent Cuomo by millions.

Legislative victories began to come more easily after the 1982 elections. Janet Canterbury had won election as the president of Florida NOW, and I became the state organization's legal counsel just before the statewide elections. Janet led us through the victories at the polls, then appointed a committee that drafted the Florida Educational Equity Act. It passed in 1984, prohibiting sex discrimination in schools in the state, which meant that women and girls in Florida still had the state law to rely on when the U.S. Supreme Court restricted coverage of the federal equal education laws. Although the Reagan/Bush eighties were shaping up to be a tough decade for feminists, it looked as if there would definitely be some bright spots along the way.

The real fruits of our labors continued to be evident years later. Seven years down the road our positioning of feminists in influential political positions ripened into a very satisfying victory for us. One of the candidates NOW had recruited and helped to elect in 1982, former nurse Jeanne Malchon, by 1989 headed the senate Health Committee, and blocked a potentially devastating piece of antiabortion legislation championed by the Florida governor, then Bob Martinez.

Over the course of the battle to defeat Martinez's proposal, I traveled with NOW's national caravan to an exhausting, seemingly endless series of rallies, strategy sessions, and news conferences throughout the state, all culminating in a massive abortion rights rally on the steps of the state capitol. The weeks—years, really—of organizing, lobbying, workshops, and demonstrations had enabled Florida's feminists to turn out a strong statewide showing. As I stood there looking out at the crowd of at least ten thousand, I couldn't help but feel a strangely ironic sense of déjà vu—accompanied by the unmistakable sensation of triumph. Seven years earlier I'd stood on the very same steps before a similar crowd. In 1982, despite all our attempts at putting on a brave collective face, we knew we would lose. But in 1989, with a friendlier state legislature, we knew we could win significant gains for the women of our state. And we did. Because of Jeanne Malchon, Martinez's proposals never even made it to the floor. "How sweet it is!" Ellie called out to the crowd; and ten thousand pairs of hands exploded in applause.

In retrospect, the decision to push ahead with the ERA campaign was a defining moment for NOW and for the feminist movement. Although time has diminished the fever of those days for many of us, the ERA was *the* hot issue of the early 1980s. The kind of wrenching emotions this issue evoked throughout the country would later characterize the Anita Hill/Clarence Thomas hearings in 1991, as well as the violent abortion rights struggle that continues in our country today. The political and personal intensity of the campaign caused emotions, long suppressed or contained, to burst into the open. They have never been resolved; they have never really left us.

FIVE

I n one way or another, all of my years in Miami were consumed with learning the ways of politics, power, and protest. Some of those lessons came at a terrible price, because in
those years, I also came face-to-face with political hatred and
violence.

Political violence, a daily reality in parts of the world, is a
horror that North Americans are largely sheltered from and
rarely asked to consider. My eyes had been opened to some extent in the years I'd been flying north and south through the
Americas, years of political instability and attendant violence
in much of the region; and by the time I was beginning to practice law, some of those Latin American tensions were spilling
over into my backyard.

I n Miami, no group of immigrants has left an imprint like the
Cubans.

Fidel Castro's New Year's Eve Revolution in 1958 was the
beginning of a new era for Florida. Thousands fled the island
nation as soon as possible; and hundreds of thousands left for
Florida over the next two decades. Many of these immigrants

had suffered the loss of their wealth and privilege in addition to the trauma of losing their home. They settled in the Miami area, raised families, and helped transform the city from a sleepy southern town into one of the fastest-growing and most vibrant metropolitan areas in the country. While some old-time Miamians resented the transformation, the Cuban influence was part of what I loved about the city. Others may have heard or intended xenophobia in a riddle that made the rounds in south Florida ("Why do Latin Americans like Miami so much? Because it's so close to the United States!"); I heard and felt affection and pride.

But the bitterness of the Cubans' losses caused an almost incurable infection in south Florida. A sort of government-in-exile was established and, with the help of the CIA and of right-wing groups across the United States, Cuban guerrillas trained in the Everglades. For years after the failed Bay of Pigs invasion, Cubans in south Florida still clung to the belief that they'd be going home following the violent overthrow of Castro's regime. It never happened, of course. But, hand in hand with their hatred of Castro and communism, some of the Cubans in Miami brought with them the use of violence—call it terrorism—as a political tactic.

In the mid-1970s, some in the Cuban community began calling for a dialogue with Castro in the hopes of improving life for those left behind in Cuba, especially their relatives, and of improving relations between the two countries. Right-wing Cuban groups responded with a terror campaign of bombing and maiming aimed at anyone who dared to express a less than rigid line against Cuba's communist government. All the problems I had seen plaguing the rest of the Americas were beginning to be mirrored right there in Miami.

A bomb a month exploded in Miami in September, October, and November 1974. These turned out to be dress rehearsals for a year-end finale in December, when five bombs exploded and a sixth was discovered and disarmed before detonation.

By the end of 1975, forty-five terrorist bombs had rocked

south Florida; twenty-four were disarmed between October and mid-December that year. Like too many others in Dade County, I told myself the violence was limited to the exile community; it had nothing to do with me. But some of the incidents were uncomfortably close to home. Bombs exploded in luggage lockers or were discovered and dismantled aboard jets at the airport. A large time bomb was found not far from my downtown office; another showed up on the doorstep of a University of Miami apartment building.

Within one four-week period in 1976, a bomb had exploded at the University of Miami prior to a speech by left-wing activist Angela Davis. Lawyer Ramon Donestev, who disagreed with the Cuban community's hard-line stance against Castro, was shot to death.

On April 30 of that year Emiliano Milian, a respected Cuban broadcaster on radio station WQBA, lay in the wreckage of his car, in a pool of his own blood in the station's parking lot. He had recently editorialized on the air against the wave of terrorism taking place in south Florida, urging his community to find another way to settle its political differences. Entering his car, he'd turned the key in the ignition and triggered an explosion. He lost both his legs. Stubbornly, he would survive. I felt nauseated, heartsick at hearing the news.

In 1977 alone, the FBI spent some $2.7 million combating terrorism in Miami.

Other regional conflicts were immigrating, too. In July 1979, Anastasio Somoza's government fell in Nicaragua, and the leftist Sandinistas gained control. For nearly a decade, Miami would be under the heavy shadow of events in Nicaragua as they played out locally and in the U.S. Congress, but immediately apparent to those of us living in south Florida was the sudden influx of another right-wing exile group whose hatred of communists often turned violent.

All the local jokes questioning Miami's claim to be part of the United States seemed a lot less funny during those years. I had just spent a great amount of energy getting through law school in the belief that the rule of law and the furtherance of our constitutionally guaranteed freedoms could make a better world. Did free speech, and political and civil rights really not apply in Miami? Could these rights simply be taken away because of the prevalence of a mob mentality? Without wanting to, I was learning about the use of violence as a political tool and the extent to which the presence of violence can test the limits of a free society.

Though I had quit flying in and out of the countries on a weekly basis when I finished law school, I wasn't away from Latin American affairs for long. As soon as I'd started working at Paul, Landy, with its substantial inter-American practice, I had joined the Inter-American Bar Association. The firm probably would have been happier if I had gravitated toward the association's corporate and commercial section, but I made a beeline for the human rights committee. The other members of the committee were mostly Central and South American lawyers looking for help in bringing international pressure to end abuses in their own countries. Their firsthand accounts of terrible political violence and their determination not to be intimidated helped shape my own response to the violence I would later face in this country. Together, we used our lawyerly skills to write letters and draft resolutions to bring publicity and build pressure, within the Organization of American States and the individual countries themselves, to end the violence.

I first met Judith Cisneros at an IABA conference in Cartagena, Colombia, in 1976. I'd become chair of the organization's women's rights section; Judith was a delegate from El Salvador. Since I'd flown to El Salvador many times and felt some familiarity with the country and its problems— particularly the disparity in wealth—I introduced myself to her after the morning session. Judith was a striking woman with thick black hair, a ready smile, sparkling eyes, and an enthusi-

asm for life that defied the grim situation of her country. She
and I hit it off immediately.

Judith worked as a legal adviser to the Salvadoran Commu-
nal Union, an organization of *campesinos*. She was also director
of the Salvadoran Demographic Association, which emphasized
family planning and women's rights. Although she was from a
well-to-do family and could have led a very comfortable life,
Judith had chosen otherwise. She spent her time traveling
around the Salvadoran countryside, holding what she called
"capacitation" classes.

During these sessions, Judith would teach the *campesinos*
how to deal with the modern world that was so rapidly invad-
ing and destroying their traditional ways. She taught people
how to use public transportation, how to open a bank account
and other practical skills. Many of the *campesinos* were illiter-
ate; some spoke only their local dialects. Judith taught them to
read and write in Spanish. She also described basic legal concepts, informing them of the rights individuals were supposed
to have under their country's constitution—and under international law.

"I also slip some discussion about women's lives into my
conversations with the men," she told me. "And when I meet
with the women, I talk about birth control and other women's
issues. I let the men come to their own conclusions—I just ask
them questions. Once, for instance, I was trying to get one of
the men to let his wife come to our classes. I asked him what
she did. He said, 'She doesn't work.' I said, 'Oh? Your wife
doesn't work? Then what does she do all day?'

"He started to describe a typical day. His wife got up two
hours before him, of course, to gather firewood and haul water.
She ground cornmeal and made tortillas by hand, then fried
them. She took care of the children and the animals all day,
and looked after the garden; she cleaned the house, mended the
clothes—none of this with anything more than a water bucket,
a hoe, and a not very sharp needle. At night she was the last
one asleep after cleaning up from supper. Well, when he fin-

ished this description, I said again, 'Oh, but your wife doesn't work, right?' Neither of us said anything more. But it was obvious that he had figured out some things on his own." Judith smiled.

"The next day, a woman came up to me and asked what sort of spell I had cast on her husband. I didn't know what she was talking about. But she introduced herself, and I recognized that she was the wife of the fellow I'd talked with the day before. 'He's a different man!' she told me. 'Before, he wouldn't even consider letting me talk to you. But last night, after he returned, he was so nice to me! He thanked me for making dinner. He said that I could come here today.' I thought she was joking about the spell. But she wasn't. She really thought I had bewitched her husband. And a few of the other village women came up to me later and asked me to do the same thing for them!"

Judith's laughter said a lot about her: It was full of the pleasure and satisfaction she got from her work. That was one reason why I loved being around her. I was inspired by her optimism in the face of such desperate conditions. From the first, I had the feeling that I'd met someone with whom I could do some very important work in the future. With other IABA members, Judith and I presented papers at conventions and drafted resolutions of support for local bar associations in Brazil, Chile, and Argentina. We published reports and wrote letters phrased in the language of diplomacy, urging this or that military regime to restore democratic rights. We believed that our actions, however small they might seem, would give hope and encouragement to the courageous people working in those countries. The cumulative effect of all of these efforts would ultimately turn the tide. But in the meantime, people suffered terribly.

I was similarly drawn to a Brazilian lawyer named Flavio Bierranbach, whom I also met through IABA. Brazil was then under the boot of one of the most brutal regimes in the hemisphere. The military junta had suspended the writ of habeas corpus in December 1968, and the human rights situation had deteriorated from there. (The junta had already abolished all political parties, extended their control over the legislative branch, and subjected the civilian population to the jurisdiction of the military courts.) By the time I met Flavio, thousands of Brazilians had been abducted, tortured, killed—many just because they were related to someone believed to be in the armed opposition; some because their names had appeared in a suspect's address book; others because they were university professors, journalists, artists, or intellectuals who had criticized the military. Despite the mortal risks he was running, Flavio was earnestly, openly committed to human rights. He had a deftness and humor about him; he loved music, fun, food; he was rotund and jolly and—at thirty-six—with light brown hair and a trim mustache, he was beginning to go bald. Like Judith, he was extremely well educated and spoke impeccable English. When I met him, he was a member of the São Paulo city council. He later served in the state legislature and went on to win a seat in the federal congress.

Flavio's sister Maria Luisa was also a lawyer. He told me how, in 1971, she'd been picked up by military police in the middle of the night and taken away for questioning. Why? Her business card had been found in the apartment of a suspected junta opponent. Flavio remembered waking to a hysterical phone call from his mother. He rushed over to the family home just in time to see Maria Luisa being pushed into an unmarked car and driven away.

He and his family knew they had to act fast; they contacted a relative in the military. After days of searching they were able to locate her. A week after she'd been dragged off, she was back home again. She'd been tortured, but—unlike so many other Brazilians—she'd survived.

Flavio's story stunned me. It touched me in a way that all the news accounts of the junta's gross human rights violations never had. Because, for the first time, I could see myself clearly in his sister's place.

* * *

During the Carter administration, U.S. policy had emphasized that the greatest danger in El Salvador came from the extreme right (which included important members of the government and armed forces). But the Reagan administration, elected in 1980, was preoccupied with balance-of-power politics and argued that communism posed the real threat to peace and stability in the region. This dramatic shift in U.S. policy meant a dramatic increase in aid and support to right-wing dictatorships and gave me good reason to worry about the welfare of my friends in Latin America. When I read press reports about the assassination of Archbishop Oscar Romero and about the four U.S. churchwomen who'd been murdered in El Salvador (both crimes were later established to be the handiwork of right-wing government death squads), I thought of Judith and of Maria Luisa Bierranbach.

As Reagan took office in January 1981, El Salvador, which had been teetering on the brink of civil war, exploded. The antifascist Frente Farabundo Martí para la Liberación Nacional (FMLN) launched an offensive against the government, and a bloody eleven-year war began.

Shortly after that I heard from Judith again. I was excited and relieved. It had been a while since I'd heard from her, and a part of me feared the worst. She was coming to Miami, she said; we made plans to meet at one of my favorite restaurants.

Anticipating our date, I wrestled with myself about what to say to her. The political situation made her work increasingly dangerous, and some part of me desperately wanted to urge her to quit. But as an activist, I knew how critical her work was. At lunch, instead of lecturing her about what danger she was in at home, I asked if the Salvadoran government had taken any action against her or her work.

They weren't pleased, she told me. They were against any efforts to educate people in the countryside, especially about concepts of democracy and human rights. A week earlier one of her coworkers, a priest, had been murdered by a death squad.

"Aren't you worried?" I blurted out.

A shadow passed over her face. "Of course, Patricia. I think about it every day. But if my life is going to mean anything, I can't stop doing work I know is important. As for the death squads, God willing, He will protect me."

We never spoke again. Within six months—on August 18, 1981—Judith was dead. She'd been murdered while leaving her home in a northern suburb of San Salvador: A carload of men blocked her way, pulled her from her car, and shot her point-blank in the face and chest. When her family reached her she was still alive; she died on the way to the hospital.

Such murders were becoming part of daily life in El Salvador. What happened to Judith was neither unpredictable nor uncommon. During the civil war, in fact, an estimated seventy-five thousand civilians—labor leaders, teachers, and rural organizers—were targeted and murdered. But, for me, Judith's murder put a face on these nameless numbers. This was the closest I had come to the violence that was happening all around me, and it had taken from me a dear friend and inspiring colleague. I asked myself the usual questions: Why had this happened? Would those responsible ever be brought to justice? *Why hadn't she been more careful?* But I knew the answer to the last one: Judith's work was her life and stopping that work was exactly what her killers wanted. I was also coming to understand, as Judith would have told me, that laying low doesn't guarantee safety. For her, there was no alternative to speaking out, to fighting back, to trying to change her country and the lives of its people for the better.

In my fury over Judith's death, I recognized that I had a responsibility to direct my outrage and energy for political activism toward my own government. Throughout the 1980s, the Reagan and Bush administrations would direct an estimated six billion dollars in economic and military aid to the right-wing government in El Salvador, in an effort to defeat the FMLN. It became a personal affront to me: My tax dollars were being spent to support the animals who'd murdered my friend. Writing lawyerly letters to dictators and drafting resolutions began to feel terribly inconsequential compared to the importance of stopping my own government from funding the slaughter.

But publicly disapproving of Ronald Reagan was not exactly a popular stance in Miami: Along with their hatred for Castro and communism, Cuban Americans by and large idolized the Gipper. After his election, right-wing Cubans were emboldened by his talk of the "evil empire" and of Cuban communists coming up through Mexico to invade Texas.

On May 21, 1983, fifty thousand Cuban exiles gathered to show support for Reagan during one of his visits to Miami. Like many such demonstrations, it did not exactly advocate tolerance of great differences of opinion. A man named George Kelly, driving by the demonstration, made the mistake of giving a thumbs-down when several Reagan supporters demanded that he honk his horn in appreciation of the president. Two men dragged him from his car and beat him up.

Many right-wing belief systems link feminism with communism, but the Cuban exile's hatred of communism was so fierce that it spilled over onto garden-variety progressives—and onto anyone opposed to fascism or right-wing dictatorships. While I myself had never been dragged from my car for refusing to wave to the president, the right-wing exile community in Miami did feel it had the right to "keep their eye on me" because of my immersion in feminist political activities, including opposition to Reagan's election and his anti-women policies. I received anonymous threatening phone calls. There were days when I walked around feeling watched—and distinctly unsafe. A Cuban businessman stopped a lawyer from my law firm one day and said, "You'd better tell Patricia to be more careful. Her name came up at our meeting last night."

I always suspected that this guy belonged to some anti-Castro paramilitary group. Clearly, he was capable of smaller acts thwarting democracy; I didn't appreciate the humor of it when he "jokingly" ripped the MONDALE/FERRARO sticker from

My first-grade picture always reminds me of my very first day of school. I insisted on going by myself and ended up in the wrong classroom initially, but that small mistake was worth it to me to feel so grown-up.

My parents married young, but waited six years before having their first baby, my sister Kathy, pictured here with my mother.

Unusual for his day, my father shared the housework when he and my mother were both in the workforce. Their big treat was a trolley ride to get an ice cream soda.

Our mother sewed the matching outfits Kathy and I wore in this photograph taken shortly before Kathy's death.

For more than a year my mother fought the child welfare department to bring my sisters, Susan *(left)* and Mary Lee *(right)*, into our family.

Dressed for the spring dance in 1961, my junior year in high school, I wore the white gloves that still denoted a true lady and were a required part of my stewardess uniform in 1968.

Shedding the white glove image for the summer in 1965, I posed with one of the "oulaws" at Six Gun Territory, where I danced at the Palace Saloon.

I had just been trained to evacuate a plane in 90 seconds and deliver babies at 30,000 feet. Still, the airline sold us for our smiles, so I put my best face forward in my Pan Am graduation picture.

Having grown up a half hour from Lake Michigan, I reveled in Miami's winters. Only the chance to work full-time for women's rights could have lured me north again.

Based on the Burma Shave signs I had seen growing up in the Midwest in the fifties, we began using rhyming slogans by the side of the road to promote the ERA.

As Equal Rights Amendment supporters boarded buses bound for Tallahassee that last year of the decade-long drive to put women in the Constitution, the exhaustion was plain on Kelly Flood's face.

As part of the final, record-breaking pro-ERA march on the state capitol the next day, the strength, determination, and pride we felt were equally evident.

I loved practicing law, and I know I made a difference working inside the legal system. *(Miami Herald)*

My white gloves made a comeback as Janet Canterbury, Bill Gamble, and I marched with our "Ladies Against Women" delegation in the Mango Strut, Coconut Grove's answer to the Orange Bowl Parade.

Now members cheered state representative Elaine Gordon and the defeat of Florida Governor Martinez' anti-abortion proposals in 1989 as a result of the strength we had gained in the elections after the ERA campaign. *(Tallahassee Democrat)*

Frustrated with their inability to outlaw abortion, extremists turned to violent confrontation at clinics like this one in Suitland, Maryland.

Carolyn Maloney, a successful candidate for Congress in 1992 *(bottom right)* joined NOW's protest against the Gag Rule (which kept women from getting information on abortion at federally funded family-planning clinics) during NOW's 1991 national conference in New York City. *(Sarah Feinsmith)*

Celebrating NOW's Silver Anniversary, former presidents, supporters, and founders of NOW included *(left to right)* Karen DeCrow, Muriel Fox, Aileen Hernandez, Judy Lightfoot, Molly Yard, Elizabeth Holzman, Ellie Smeal, me, and Gene Boyer.

In the tradition of the suffragists, I was arrested outside the Bush White House as NOW began a campaign of nonviolent civil disobedience in support of abortion rights during the 1992 elections. *(Reuters)*

Abortion rights hang by a slender thread in the Supreme Court, but in *NOW* v. *Scheidler* the court upheld our use of the anti-racketeering laws against violent anti-abortionists. *(Beth Corbin)*

Peg Yorkin, Molly, Ellie, and I met with Etienne-Emile Baulieu, creator of RU-486. Our efforts to make this non-surgical, safer means of abortion available to U.S. women were initially stymied by the Bush administration and anti-abortionists' threats and harassment.

I took the risk of bringing Israeli feminist Alice Shelvi and Hanan Ashrawi, then serving as spokesperson for the Palestine Liberation Organization, together on the same stage for a stimulating dialogue at NOW's Global Conference in 1992.

At the 1992 march on Washington, we celebrated Carol Moseley-Braun's victory over an incumbent who had voted to confirm Clarence Thomas. Moseley-Braun became the first African American woman ever elected to the U.S. Senate. *(Byron J. Cohen)*

With Rev. Jesse Jackson, Sen. Moseley-Braun, and others, I led the thirtieth-anniversary march NOW helped organize to mark the 1963 civil rights march and Dr. King's moving "I have a dream" speech.

Janet Canterbury *(bottom left)*, NOW officers Kim Gandy and Rosemary Dempsey, and I helped turn post-Anita Hill anger into constructive energy during our 1992 Elect Women for a Change campaign.

Celebrities like Martina Navratalova and Cybill Shepherd can help bring visibility to issues, as they did at the massive 1994 gay rights march.

Karen Johnson, to my left, joined our team of officers after a twenty-year career as an Air Force nurse. Karen's focus on women's health and freedom from violence and poverty was reflected in NOW's 1995 Rally for Women's Lives, announced at this news conference on Capitol Hill. *(Beth Corbin)*

Congresswomen Elizabeth Furse, Pat Schroeder, Eleanor Holmes-Norton and Connie Morella stood with Kim Gandy as NOW pressed successfully for passage of the Violence Against Women Act after the brutal murders of Nicole Brown Simpson and Ron Goldman. *(Beth Corbin)*

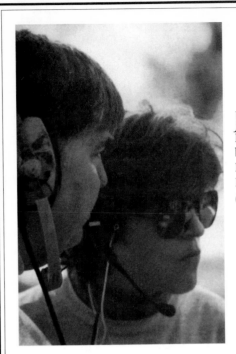

Janet Canterbury and Pat Silverthorn confer backstage at the 1995 Rally for Women's Lives.
(Barbara Timmer)

I have found that working to gain power to control my own life and to make positive change for myself and other women is an enormously satisfying way to live.
(Joanne Savio)

my bumper. But my feminist activities hadn't pushed the same political hot buttons that open opposition to Reagan's foreign policy would. To this émigré—and to many others like him—feminism may have been a demon, but communism was the Devil. Communists were the ones who had run his family out of Cuba. They'd taken everything he and his loved ones had possessed and believed in. His anticommunist hatred ran deep.

For its part, the Miami city government routinely (and disgracefully) acquiesced to the violence. After a 1983 protest against the U.S. embargo of Cuba resulted in a riot that left more than twenty-five people injured, Miami Commissioner Miriam Alonso called for the city to ban protest by *pro*-Castro groups—the ones who'd been on the receiving end of the assault.

Throughout 1983, political violence continued erupting in south Florida. That summer, a letter arrived on my desk from the Miami Free Speech Coalition. One of my law firm colleagues was listed as endorsing a campaign in defense of the constitutional rights to free speech and assembly in order to bring attention to the growing political violence in Miami.

We would like you to participate in a meeting in October, I read, and a sense of dread washed over me. It wasn't that I didn't agree with the need for a public political rights campaign in Miami. But I couldn't imagine having the energy—or the courage—to fight such a battle.

It was serious business. If I took on this fight, it would be a dangerous one. Judith's death was still foremost in my consciousness. So were my years of flying in and out of countries where political torture and assassination were par for the course. I already knew that political opponents in this city sometimes had their houses and their businesses blown up . . . and their legs blown off. Actively participating in the Miami Free Speech Coalition's struggle would put my personal as well as my professional life at risk.

I didn't respond to that particular Free Speech Coalition mailing.

Three years later, though, I would.

Not all of the violence in Miami was spillover from abroad; some of it was homegrown. Reagan's election exacerbated tensions between Miami's pro-Reagan Cubans and Nicaraguans and African Americans, who largely opposed him. In 1979, police had stopped Arthur McDuffie—an insurance agent, a veteran, a black man—after his motorcycle had run a red light. In the minutes that followed, McDuffie was beaten to death by a group of Dade County police officers. The police later claimed that he had resisted arrest. Nine officers were relieved of duty after McDuffie's death; five of them were tried on charges ranging from second-degree murder and manslaughter to aggravated battery and tampering with evidence in a cover-up. Their trial was moved to Tampa, where an all-white jury was selected. It was a long trial, plagued with irregularities and racial tensions; all five of the officers were white, two Latino. On May 17, 1980, the jury returned a verdict acquitting the officers on all charges. Liberty City and other largely black neighborhoods in Miami exploded. Dark smoke hung over the area for days.

I was in my law office when the trouble began, trying to force myself to concentrate on billable client work. I was staring out the window when I realized my assistant was at the door; she didn't wait for an invitation to burst in.

"Don't you realize everyone's packing up and heading home?"

We'd been ordered by the police to evacuate the downtown area; everyone was planning to hole up until the trouble blew over, waiting it out in their presumably safe suburban homes. As I made my way out of downtown, I followed news updates on the radio. By evening, the entire nation was watching Miami burn on national network news: Buildings blazed; cops shielded in riot gear from head to toe tore down barricades made of burning tires and fought in the streets with angry black youths. Eighteen people were killed, 440 injured. Florida's National Guard had to be called in to restore order. It seemed, to me, like newsreel footage from abroad.

For me personally, the only physical discomfort caused by the riots was having to drive around roadblocks. Psychologically, though, I had been shaken long before—ever since Arthur McDuffie's death. Sensitized to the reality of such state-sanctioned murder in countries like El Salvador and South Africa, I'd begun to realize that such injustice was a reality in my own country, too; but the actuality of riots in my own backyard disturbed me deeply. I understood the anger exploding throughout the city. On the other hand, I could foresee little progress resulting from the uncontrolled violence of the reaction.

Inevitably, I'd have more opportunities to consider the uses and abuses of violence at home.

In January 1983, a Miami police officer was called to a video arcade in a predominantly black section of Miami called Overtown. Within minutes of entering the arcade, he shot twenty-one-year-old Neville Johnson dead. Although the officer eventually was acquitted after convincing the jury that the shooting had been in self-defense, the incident triggered a wave of violence.

As news of the shooting spread, Overtown exploded like tinder in a lightning storm. Before Johnson's body could be recovered, people were rioting; by evening, buildings were burning again, rocks and bottles filled the air, and the tourist industry folks were very worried. Miami's second major riot in less than three years had blasted through the city's fragile facade of multiracial peace.

In January 1984, shortly before the officer's trial was scheduled to begin, I got a call at my law office from a woman named Jackie Floyd. I'd seen her at NOW functions off and on during recent months, along with a woman named Pat Silverthorn, but I knew little about either of them other than that they were members of the Socialist Workers' Party. Jackie was calling on NOW business.

"We'd like to get the chapter to pass a resolution about the trial," Jackie explained. "More than a dozen young black men have been killed by Miami police within recent months. Most of them nobody's ever heard about." Although she handled herself quite well, her anger was apparent, even over the phone.

"What do you see as NOW's possible involvement?"

"We're trying to get a variety of groups to monitor the trial. The police have been packing the courtroom whenever there's a hearing. NOW's endorsement would show them that civil rights groups of all kinds are watching what's happening in that courtroom. The project's being organized by a group called PULSE—People United to Lead the Struggle for Equality. It was formed by the mothers and other relatives of the victims to try to get some justice."

As Jackie described the mothers and sisters of PULSE to me, I couldn't help but see the obvious similarities between that organization and The Mothers of the Plaza in Argentina. For six years, every day, mothers and other female relatives of the *desaparecidos*—people taken away by the military regime, never to be seen again—had gathered to stand vigil in front of the national palace in Buenos Aires. Most of those women probably had never thought of themselves as political people; they certainly may not have wanted to get involved in a dangerous struggle. But repression by the state, blatant abuse of authority by the government, and the brutal loss of their own children and loved ones had drawn them in and forced them to protest. It sounded as if many of the women who belonged to PULSE had found themselves in a similar situation. Listening to Jackie tell some of their stories, it occurred to me that I had lived with the notion that abusive authorities and repressive governments were a fixture of life throughout South and Central America. But I did not want to believe that this was a regular feature of life in my own country's inner cities. Years later, when I saw the videotape of Rodney King curled into a fetal position on the ground while a group of white L.A. police officers viciously kicked and clubbed him, I thought again of PULSE: The questionable deaths or beatings, the continual failure to achieve justice through the court system—it all seemed terribly familiar.

"I'll bring Hattie Crews to the meeting," Jackie continued. "She lost her son, Anthony Nelson—she's one of the founders of PULSE. I'd like your support."

As Jackie and I discussed the Johnson shooting, I became convinced that NOW, as a civil rights organization, had to get involved. However, I knew that this opportunity to reach out to Miami's African American community would prove more complicated than it seemed. For one thing, Jackie was not your average NOW activist. She, Pat Silverthorn, and their friends were communists; and this, after all, was Miami.

Members of the Socialist Workers' Party had been in NOW since its founding, but they were not always welcomed with open arms. Both Jackie and Pat had zeroed in on me as a potential ally in their constant struggle to be allowed to participate. (I had spoken out against red-baiting—I saw it as a divide-and-conquer tactic, one that had served as an excuse for violence and repression in other countries.) But I didn't particularly welcome Jackie and Pat's attention at first. For one thing, their presence clearly freaked out some of the membership. (Actually, "freaked out" may be an understatement.) But our Dade County chapter had never had particularly negative dealings with them, and when I really looked impartially at most of the SWP members who were also members of NOW, I saw women who worked very hard and earnestly on those NOW issues they supported. When a demonstration on abortion rights came up, for instance, they'd do as much as or more than anyone else. On the other hand, when the chapter concentrated on getting out the vote for a Democratic candidate, they were likely to disappear. But I was taken by the discipline and commitment of those involved with the SWP. I was also surprised—and intrigued—that anyone would openly claim communist affiliations in Miami, of all places.

My own willingness to work with groups like the SWP bothered some of my colleagues in NOW. In fact, though many outside the women's rights movement assume that all feminists are cut from the same radical cloth, NOW, like most large women's rights organizations, has always included women who are determinedly mainstream and women who are proud leftists. I did not want us to weaken ourselves by excluding real activists from our movement out of fear because they called themselves communists.

I invited Jackie to bring PULSE members to the meeting. I also promised to work with her on the resolution she had drafted for us to consider.

The PULSE resolution Jackie read to me called on Dade County NOW to oppose any efforts to move the trial out of Miami or to exclude African Americans from the jury. All the resolution needed for maximum impact, I thought, was to have its sharp working-class rhetoric muted; Jackie implemented some of my suggestions to that effect. At the meeting, Hattie Crews, one of the PULSE mothers, whose tired face emphasized the difficulty of her life, helped Jackie present a personal view of life in Miami's poor black neighborhoods. I felt tension when several NOW members expressed having been troubled not only by police brutality, but by the violence of the 1980 and 1983 riots as well, a point I had wrestled with myself. Jackie, who had been a young mother living in Liberty City during both incidents and who had taken to the streets in 1980, explained her point of view patiently.

"To me, it was a week of *rebellion*—not rioting." The word *riot*, she went on to say, negated the fact that organized resistance had taken place. She had helped her neighbors keep police and National Guard troops out of the Liberty City area for several days and nights; they had organized patrols, and distributed food from looted stores, making sure everyone got what they needed. After 1980, Jackie had gotten a job working for the city in a program financed, in part, by funds distributed in response to the community uprising.

"By 1983," Jackie continued, "I'd decided that the violence hadn't produced an answer. Those rebellions were genuine responses, but they lacked any political leadership—so no real lasting political change came out of them." She believed, she said, that organizations like PULSE provided an alternative to unorganized violence and could help pull her community into more effective political action, and she thought NOW should get involved. Her carefully chosen words, and Hattie Crews's personal insight, moved the membership. Despite the general discomfort of many chapter members with PULSE's communist connections, the resolution passed.

Dade County NOW members occasionally found other common ground with the SWP. Members of both groups often turned out for protests organized by the Free South Africa Coalition, a broad group of community, campus, and city leaders working to promote official U.S. sanctions against apartheid in South Africa. NOW activists believed the fight against apartheid was a worthy cause; furthermore, it allowed activists of all kinds to strengthen our ties with local civil rights groups. The political goodwill created by our work together helped everyone.

I began to see that political coalitions, working with others where our agendas overlapped, were not only possible but imperative. As violence against all of us spread, I would draw on this experience.

P at Silverthorn and I didn't talk much at our first meeting. She impressed me as quiet, serious, and—at 5'2" tall, 110 pounds—diminutive. Later, after we'd become close, she would confide that she, too, had wondered how much more dangerous she'd made her life by openly professing communist convictions in that volatile, violent, commie-hating city. On more than one occasion, she confessed, she'd packed up her car in

fear and disgust, ready to head home to Denver, only to be per-
suaded to stay a while longer.

Pat came from a working-class Catholic family in Denver,
where her father had worked as an electrician. She spent her
childhood playing basketball, avoiding school, and getting into
various kinds of trouble until, just after her mother's death,
when Pat was seventeen, she attended her first meeting of the
Socialist Workers' Party. (She'd met them at an antinuclear
protest to which she'd been brought by the nuns from her
school.) Members of the SWP first taught her to read. Later,
having become a committed socialist herself, she worked as a
railroad switch operator in Denver, doing labor and political
organizing. She married another SWP member and, by the time
I met her in 1983, she had moved to Miami and was doing
factory work, still committed to the party, openly advocating
socialism to her fellow workers.

At eighteen, Pat had eagerly gone to her first NOW meeting
in Denver. Caught in a wave of anticommunist hysteria, the
chapter voted at that meeting to exclude all SWP members.
Angry and embarrassed, Pat concluded that NOW was an irrel-
evant, liberal organization, whose members were rude, to boot.
She was not convinced when her comrades in Miami suggested
she join the Dade County chapter. A committed political activist, however, Pat also realized that there were certain specific
issues around which the SWP and NOW could build a political
coalition of sorts. Keeping abortion clinics open was one such
issue. Convincing the powers-that-be to pay political heed to
the needs of poor women and women of color was another.

Working closely with Pat opened my eyes about the reality
of living as a political leftist in this country. I'd always dismissed left-wing paranoia as mere fantasy. After all, I reasoned,
our government had better things to do than harass political
activists. Back in the 1960s, although I'd never been involved
in the Vietnam protest movement, I remembered rolling my
eyes when activist friends started raving about their phones
being tapped. But my personal contact with Pat and the SWP

changed my mind; and a certain amount of my still-ingrained innocence was forever lost.

When the SWP ran Jackie Floyd for mayor of Miami in 1984, the party had to bring suit against the Florida Elections Commission, charging that forcing them to disclose their contributors was a violation of their constitutional rights. (This was based on a U.S. Supreme Court decision that prohibited the government from requiring disclosure of members and contributors when that disclosure put the organization's members at risk because of the unpopularity of their views.) I helped them get legal assistance. ("Patricia," Janet Canterbury sighed, "how did you let yourself get into *this* one?" Though by that time she was used to my tendency to take on every stray fight as if it were an abandoned cat or dog.)

The SWP also brought suit against the federal government for violation of their civil and constitutional rights. Watching this case unfold proved to be a somewhat radicalizing education in and of itself. The SWP discovered that the FBI had 9,801,114 pages of files on the activities of the SWP and the Young Socialist Alliance. The bureau had conducted an ongoing campaign to disrupt the lives of SWP members and destroy the party's relations with other groups. Attorney General Edwin Meese argued that surveillance and other activities were necessary "for the nation's vital interest of self-preservation." But U.S. District Court Judge Thomas Griese—no friend to the SWP's politics—nevertheless found that the party had not broken any laws and that "the FBI's disruption activities, surreptitious entries and use of informants" constituted "violation of the constitutional rights of the SWP, and lacked legislative or regulatory authority." He ruled in favor of the party for a large amount of damages.

Pat had been through a real political baptism by fire when she'd first arrived in Miami in 1983. Although I hadn't known her at the time, I might even have looked out my downtown office window (twenty-eighth floor, with an exquisite view of Biscayne Bay) one Saturday that May to see her and others fleeing a mob attack punctuated by rifle fire. Later, I'd remember the small article about it in the *Miami Herald* that had caught my eye: SHOTS FIRED AT EXILE RALLY. The article portrayed, almost good-naturedly, the arrest of a Cuban exile who had fired shots at fellow Cubans, thinking they were the "communists" he intended to intimidate.

Pat's personal account cast the incident in a more menacing light. The Latin and Central American Solidarity Association (LaCASA) had planned a protest of Reagan's policy in El Salvador. But, after listening to the constant threats and harassment of right-wing groups over the Latin airways in Miami, LaCASA canceled the protest. They decided to hold a press conference at the site instead, the point of which was simply to assert their right to exist—even in Miami.

That morning, when the group's representative tried to read a press statement, the dozen or so LaCASA activists there had to form a human chain around him for protection. Anticommunist thugs spilled out from behind trees and out of cars all along Biscayne Boulevard. The human chain was pushed and broken; the press statement was ripped from their spokesperson's hands. When the rifle sounded, they had already given up and were moving determinedly across the boulevard, trying to reach their cars.

Ironically, as the anticommunist Cuban exiles celebrated their "victory"—chanting "Viva Reagan!"—a late-arriving exile named Lazaro Sui fired a high-powered rifle over the heads of the crowd. Not realizing that LaCASA had gone already, he mistook his comrades for communists.

O ther violent events at which Pat and other activists were targets transpired over the spring and summer of 1983. A screening of a film held by LaCASA as a fund-raiser at St. John's Lutheran Church was threatened by a group who identified themselves as part of the right-wing paramilitary group Alpha 66. An angry mob gathered outside St. John's; again,

LaCASA was forced to cancel the event. Later that night, a fire-bomb was tossed into a shed adjoining the church, causing significant damage. At a subsequent NOW meeting, someone reported that the socialist bookstore in Miami had been fire-bombed, and several members of the SWP had received death threats.

Though I was not actually in the crosshairs of these assaults, the attacks concerned me more and more as my friendship with Pat deepened. Meanwhile, she and I had frequent debates about the merits of anticapitalist revolution. I didn't see the world in the same black-and-white terms that she and the SWP did. But Pat's courage and her willingness to stick it out as an open communist in Miami impressed me tremendously. When I first tried to envision this tiny woman trying to hold off a mob of angry right-wingers, I almost laughed. But, as I got to know her, I came to appreciate and respect the healthy defense skills she'd learned to abet her survival, both in Miami and in her life before. In the coming abortion clinic battles, these would prove invaluable to her and to me. And the next time a rally on Reagan's foreign policy was violently attacked in Miami, I would be by her side. I didn't necessarily agree with the SWP's political stands, but I certainly believed in protecting their constitutional rights—for all of our sakes.

By the spring of 1986, the increasingly savage battle between right-wing groups and progressive groups of all kinds reached a boiling point in Miami.

Giving millions of dollars in aid to right-wing guerrilla groups in Nicaragua ("Contra aid," as it was known at the time) had become a major congressional issue. I opposed U.S. involvement in the war in Nicaragua and objected to my tax dollars being used to arm and train right-wing forces there. I heard that the Miami Free Speech Coalition was planning a demonstration against Contra aid for March 23 at the Torch of Friendship in downtown Miami. The coalition had grown significantly, and the list of rally endorsers, this time, included more than LaCASA and a few known communist groups. People from Citizens for a Nuclear Freeze, a mild, middle-class organization based in the south Miami suburbs, were also listed. So was the Haitian Refugee Center. Several religious groups (Unitarian, Methodist, Lutherans, and Jewish) had signed on, too. ACLU members had agreed to speak and to provide legal observers; it was hoped that these observers would help ensure fair police and city protection, as well as provide a hedge against violence.

The growth of anticommunist violence in Miami had intimidated many people from taking activist roles in liberal politics throughout south Florida. In fact, people of all political stripes were afraid even to have conversations on the subject. Cuban lawyers and secretaries in my firm would not discuss Cuban American politics and the attendant violence even within the confines of the office. But it was clear to me and to others by now that keeping our heads in the sand only provided an illusion of safety and allowed the situation to get worse. My decision to speak at the rally necessitated some very conscious assessment of the personal risks involved, and a very real sense of dread at the idea of taking public stands that had cost others their legs or their lives. Nevertheless, I was absolutely convinced that a public campaign for political rights in Miami was the way to go. This time, when Pat and others from the Free Speech movement urged me to get involved, I did.

The coalition negotiated a permit with the Miami police. This would ensure our right to demonstrate legally; it would also put the police on notice that we expected protection if necessary. In the days leading up to March 23, the group organized a phone-drive call-in against Contra aid. As much of the press and media as possible were notified.

The usual threats had, of course, come to rally organizers. Right-wing radio stations issued their usual anticommunist call to arms. On March 21, 1986, the Contra aid bill was defeated in Congress. This political victory enraged our opposition even further.

So that morning, we fully expected a counterdemonstration. Pat and other organizers had earlier held training sessions at the Haitian Refugee Center for those willing to help with security. But it was stressed that security, after all, was really the job of the Miami police, who had been pushed (kicking and screaming, perhaps) into assuming their proper role as protectors of our basic rights. Beyond that, it was emphasized, activists working as security were supposed to help people remain calm, ease angry encounters, and, we hoped, keep things running smoothly.

The situation seemed fairly calm, I remember, when the first group of us arrived. The day was sunny. Bayfront Park, lined with gently swaying palm trees, was a marked contrast to the gravity of the day. A couple of hundred anticommunist protesters ambled around behind the orange-and-white-striped police barricades; a fairly large number of police were present, their cruisers blocking the street. I felt a surge of nervous adrenaline build in me as I listened to the war stories of two older protesters from the Women's International League for Peace and Freedom as they described what seemed like equally dangerous confrontations from their labor days in the 1930s. One of the women proudly pulled back her purple-blue hair to reveal a scar, received at the end of a Pinkerton guard's club. Organizing garment workers in New York City, she told me, had been as dangerous then as organizing opposition to Contra aid was now in Miami. I was not comforted.

By noon, we got started. It was a testimony to the progress the coalition had made over the years that as many as two hundred of us gathered there that day. This may seem like a small number; however, a few years earlier, getting so many demonstrators together for such an unpopular cause would have been unthinkable. We were determined to go through the speakers listed at a calm but brisk pace, then leave. We had no illusions about changing anybody's mind; no one among us expected to be liked or embraced by our fellow Miamians. This was no celebration of diversity. We would count it a victory just to survive—and to establish our right to demonstrate.

Within an hour, though, the hundreds of anticommunist demonstrators had become thousands. And they were straining the wooden police barricades. The city, showing its usual bias, had given the violent anti-Castro group Alpha 66 a permit to demonstrate right across the street from us. My first reaction was to scan the angry opposition mob for shotguns, pistols, slingshots, and M-80s. I couldn't see any firearms, but I did pick out quite a few rocks ready for the flinging.

I was more upset by *who* I saw standing there. In the midst of a group of well-dressed, important-looking people at one side of the mob was my old confidante, Roberta Fox. She wasn't the only politician in the crowd. Later Roberta justified standing with the other side by saying that a voice of reason was needed to moderate the passions on the right. In my anger, I thought it had more to do with the power of the Cuban vote in Miami: So many local politicians considered it political suicide *not* to show their support for the right wing, despite all the right-wing violence that had been going on in south Florida over the past decade. On the other hand, Representative Jack Gordon (who had been the chief sponsor of the ERA in the Florida Senate) stood with us at the rally.

A thin line of Miami police officers stood between the two sides. As few of them as they were, they would prove the only barrier between us and real injury.

As the time approached for me to speak, the mood became increasingly raucous and ugly. As I spoke, a frenzied crescendo of "COMUNISTAS!" and "DEMOCRACIA SI, COMUNISMO NO!" surrounded us. Occasionally, some rabid protester would throw himself over the police line, at which point a Miami cop would lead him back into the crowd. Well into the rally, two hundred of us huddled inside a circle of security. The air was thick with hatred, and with the threat of a mob out of control.

The throngs across the street began pushing against the thin

police line. When I close my eyes, I can still see this sea of angry
demonstrators, fists pounding the air, rushing those few blue
uniforms. The crowd's roar reached a dizzying crescendo at the
strongest point of each surge; I was terrified. It didn't look to
me as if there were enough police to hold strong.

I began to count backward, silently, in an attempt to calm
my stomach. Just as I reached "two," an egg came flying out
of the sky and cracked the sidewalk beside me, splattering my
left shoe with pieces of slimy shell.

Within a minute, a barrage of missiles—eggs, rocks, the odd
clawhammer—pelted us. Instinctively, I raised a NO CONTRA AID
protest poster over my head. Several others also began using
their limited softball skills to ward off flying objects and protect
our posterless neighbors. The two WILPF members dug in
firmly next to me, determined not to be moved.

As it seemed we were about to be overrun, a couple of yellow
Dade County school buses—their windows adorned with steel
mesh—arrived, and about thirty or forty riot-clad police
climbed out. The sight of police officers in riot gear—padded
vests, shields, serious clubs—had become a familiar sight on
Miami television in the 1980s, but I'd never been this close to
them before. And at that moment the intensity of the demonstration underwent a sea change. The final speakers finished
the program under a renewed volley of dangerous objects. By
that time the police agreed to get us out of there under their
protection.

The blue lights and wails of riot buses signified the demonstration's end. Seconds after we'd scrambled gladly into those
buses, hundreds of Contra supporters flooded the area our tiny
group had occupied. As the buses inched their way out of the
plaza, I looked back to see a bonfire made up of our placards. I
didn't watch for long. The sides of the bus were soon cracking
with rocks and eggs. I don't remember how long I actually kept
my face pressed firmly down against the plastic seat, hands
over both ears.

But by the time I finally looked up, things were quiet. We

were driving down another city street. Everything seemed amazingly serene, after what we'd all just been through. Pat was staring out the window, her face flushed.

"Some fun, huh?"

I could barely nod.

She pointed to my shoulder. "Well, at least you've got to-morrow's breakfast."

I glanced down to see that a well-aimed egg had turned my blouse into an ugly mess. It wasn't particularly funny, but both of us started to giggle nervously. Then we broke into giddy laughter.

The buses rode up to the Haitian Refugee Center, where, like veterans from a war, we swapped stories and struggled to come to grips with what had happened. When reporters began call-ing and showing up, we held an impromptu news conference, talked about the attack, but emphasized that we considered our action a success. We had stood our ground and made our point.

I dragged myself home to find James on the telephone, trying to find out whether I'd been hurt. He slammed the phone down, yelling.

"What the hell was going on out there?"

He'd seen the entire thing on the six o'clock news and was outraged. "What I don't understand," he kept saying that night, "is: where were the police?"

By the next day, that same question was ringing through the halls of the Miami City Council, the mayor's office, and the police department. Though our group had physically gathered only a couple hundred people to the demonstration, it seemed that the impact had been far-reaching; thousands of Miamians were as shocked as James had been, and they were expressing it loudly to any public figures they could reach.

Even Janet Canterbury, who always swore she couldn't re-member the difference between the Sandinistas and the Con-tras, was upset—not because she cared about Contra aid, but because she was furious at the idea that in the United States, it wasn't safe to say "what you damned well pleased" in public on a political topic.

In a welcome burst of committed journalism, the press also let loose with a barrage of criticism. One paper (the now-defunct *Miami News*) laid the blame at the feet of the Reagan administration, blasting in an editorial the anticommunist rhetoric it had been feeding the nation for the past six years:

> Are they on the side of the egg- and bottle-tossing dem-onstrators who would physically silence those who dis-agree with their views, or are they on the side of free and open debate, which is the essence of democracy? Some peo-ple must learn the meaning of free speech and free assem-bly. There is not a better time to teach them when, right under their noses, there's an object lesson in what has killed *democracia* elsewhere, and they and their conduct are it.

Of course, this had been the Miami Free Speech Coalition's point all along, though I wished we hadn't had to go through a riot to get it across. There is not a streak of martyrdom in me: I would have been just as happy to sit at a long table and negotiate an agreement with these people. But those who use violence and intimidation do not allow us that option. Some-times, putting yourself physically on the line is the only way to fly.

The political violence that I witnessed and associated with the Cuban community and with Latin American countries and politics was beginning to be felt in attacks on the women's rights movement in a way that we had not experienced since the struggle for the vote in the first two decades of the century. It surfaced over the issues of abortion and birth control.

The history of women's health is, to a large extent, a story of reproductive health and illness. Historically, even when it was a fervently desired event, pregnancy and childbirth put the mother's life and health very much at risk. Most women have had to bear more children than they could physically or economically afford to support and sustain. How many unavoidable pregnancies, how many live births—wanted *and* unwanted—did our grandmothers and great-grandmothers endure? Many women simply wore down, their bodies eventually collapsing from too many pregnancies and deliveries.

Birth control and abortion became widely available in the West only very recently (and only after extraordinary political struggle). Safe, reliable family planning methods have given twentieth-century women an unprecedented measure of freedom. The ability to control our own fertility gives women choice and timing, as well as improved overall health. And it's also given us the ability to enter spheres of endeavor other than motherhood. Birth control and abortion contradict the notion of woman-as-chattel or woman-as-childbearer—and nothing else. If we can control our reproduction, we can control our lives.

I am convinced it is this *freedom* that is at the heart of the abortion debate.

The right focused on the abortion issue to galvanize, organize, and expand their ranks. Archconservatives used *Roe* v. *Wade*, the 1973 Supreme Court decision recognizing the right to abortion, to politicize religious fundamentalists, rural evangelicals in the South, and urban Catholics in the North. Combined with the "states rights" (and racist) followers of George Wallace left over from his failed presidential bids—and with traditionally conservative business interests who had little or no stake in the abortion debate but who were traditional Republican supporters—this coalition eventually created a power base formidable enough to begin taking over the Republican Party and pulling it hard right.

* * *

The antiabortion movement grew increasingly aggressive and violent after Reagan took office in 1981. I saw the storm clouds approaching. I also felt the urgency working as Florida NOW's legal counsel; that was when I became privy to information on the shocking escalation of the antiabortion violence that was taking place in Florida and across the United States.

In August 1982, three members of the Army of God kidnapped Dr. Hector Zevallos and his wife, Rosalee Jean. Dr. Zevallos owned the Hope Clinic for Women in Granite City, Illinois. The kidnappers held them for eight days, threatening to kill them both if the doctor did not agree to stop performing abortions. They also demanded that President Reagan announce an end to legal abortion in the United States. The couple was released after Dr. Zevallos pledged to give up his practice. All of the kidnappers were later apprehended and convicted. In October 1983, one of them, Don Benny Anderson, was also convicted of two firebombings in Florida: one at the Bread and Roses Clinic in Clearwater, another at the St. Petersburg Women's Health Center.

In 1983 alone, 147 violent incidents were reported to the National Abortion Federation by member clinics. And in February 1984 the Hillcrest Clinic in Norfolk, Virginia, was firebombed. The initials AOG (Army of God) were scrawled on the sidewalk in front of the decimated building. Eight days later, the Prince Georges Reproductive Health Services in Prince Georges County, Maryland, was also firebombed. A man claiming to represent the Army of God called the local media to claim responsibility. By March 1984, forty-four violent incidents had already been reported that year to the National Abortion Federation.

In May 1984, the "direct action" antiabortion activists held their first national meeting in Fort Lauderdale. These were the people who advocated using force to stop abortion. Frustrated with the slow process of law and lobbying, they'd begun to employ terrorist tactics. On the eve of their meeting, NOW

President Judy Goldsmith and I held a news conference, drawing public attention to the seeds of violence being planted. Less than two weeks earlier, two Fort Lauderdale clinics had been sprayed with bullets from a .45 automatic. Holding up pictures of bombed clinics, we tried to spotlight the fact that this growing violence was being systematically directed against women and the health professionals who served them. The next day, I marched with hundreds of other pro-choice activists in Broward County to protest the national antiabortion group's militant strategies.

I was frightened by these so-called direct-action folks, as well as with their self-righteousness, "holier-than-thou" attitudes, and loud boasting. One of their leaders, Chicago's Joe Scheidler, had bragged sickeningly to an audience in Kansas just the year before that the rate of medical complications inside abortion clinics rose 4 to 5 percent when he was outside with his bullhorn. Scheidler publicly derided those antiabortionists who wanted to use the courts and legislatures to enforce their views, calling them "wimps for life." The ominous splitting off from the mainstream by direct-action antiabortion advocates became official with this gathering in Fort Lauderdale in 1984. Having seen terrorist-intimidation tactics in other contexts, I knew that things were about to become much more dangerous.

A month later, the Ladies Center in Pensacola, Florida, was bombed for the first time. So was another clinic in Pensacola, which never reopened. On Christmas Day the Ladies Center was bombed again. And so were the offices of Drs. William Permenter and Bo Begenholm, the other two abortion providers in town, both of whom stopped providing abortion services. I began to feel like Chicken Little: frustrated that I could not seem to convince anyone else that the sky really was falling.

Of course, the antiabortion terrorists were trying to shut down what was already a greatly threatened and increasingly inaccessible, if still constitutionally guaranteed medical procedure. By 1980 the Republican Party platform had become antiabortion; and a president who pledged to outlaw abortion altogether had been elected. A resolution was introduced in Congress (the Human Life Amendment) that would have banned abortion and some of the most effective forms of birth control and made that ban a part of the United States Constitution. Antiabortion members of both the House and the Senate began a drive to grant full U.S. citizenship to fertilized human eggs. When they couldn't muster the two-thirds vote necessary for a constitutional amendment, antiabortion members of Congress proposed the so-called Human Life Bill. Like the amendment, this bill would have allowed states to prosecute a rape victim who obtained an abortion, or a young mother who used an IUD for contraception, for murder. Any physician who prescribed the morning-after pill—and any pharmacist who filled the prescription—could be prosecuted as accomplices. This climate emboldened many private insurers to refuse health coverage for abortion and to increase premiums for fire, casualty, and liability coverage, driving many doctors, hospitals, and clinics to exclude this particular procedure from what they offered. Earlier, in a devastating blow, the Hyde Amendment, passed in 1976, had cut off Medicaid funding for poor women to obtain abortions.

The story of Rosie Jimenez's life—and death—was known to many of us. She'd lived in Fort Lauderdale, but, like many other farm workers in south Florida, she originally hailed from Texas. Rosie was determined to break out of the cycle of poverty that had trapped so many migrant workers. With one small child to care for, she went on welfare, and soon won a scholarship to college. Then she got pregnant. Unable to scrape together the money for a safe, legal abortion, she turned to an illegal abortionist. After an unsafe and unsanitary procedure, Rosie developed a raging infection. She died after days of fever and agony, the first known victim of the Hyde Amendment.

NOW and other progressive organizations lobbied hard and

successfully to defeat the Human Life Amendment and Bill and similar measures in Congress. Ironically, our political victory turned many frustrated antiabortion advocates toward terrorism. If they couldn't stop abortion through the force of law, they'd stop it through the force of violence and intimidation. After the 1980 elections, we knew that the rights to both birth control and abortion were at risk. Too many abortion rights supporters had become complacent after *Roe* v. *Wade.* Too few women had responded to the cutoff of Medicaid funding for abortions. Too many pro-choice voters had failed to take Reagan's threats seriously. Now it was clear that opponents of women's rights weren't going to stop at eliminating abortion for poor women alone; they were coming after *all* women, after *all* reproductive rights. And a growing number of right-wing groups had decided to shore up their opposition with physical violence.

As a way to stand up to the opposition and to support women who were trying to get abortions, and doctors and staff trying to provide them under these conditions, Dade County NOW organized a speak-out to coincide with the trial of the 1984 Pensacola Christmas bombers. We hit on the idea of a speak-out as a way to stop antiabortion opponents from setting the terms of the debate. They often spoke as if fetuses grew in petri dishes, not inside real, living women with real responsibilities, real hopes and dreams, real plans for a better future. When they *did* acknowledge women's existence, they portrayed us as being incapable of making moral decisions without some legislator, judge, doctor, or preacher telling us what to do. We knew that we needed to put women's lives into the picture immediately, to show people that women who had abortions were their daughters, sisters, wives, mothers . . . women like them. Telling our personal stories, we believed, would change the tenor of the debate; possibly, it would change minds, too. It's one thing to hear someone say that abortion is immoral, against the word of God, and should be illegal, in a vacuum. It's quite another to hear that same statement after listening to a woman talk about how an illegal abortion almost killed her—or *why* she made the decision to have an abortion in the first place.

To me, it seemed the ultimate irony. Our argument has always been that sexuality and reproduction are such personal, intimate parts of our lives that they should be protected against intrusion. Now, to support that argument, we were going public with some very private stories. The decision to speak out was emotionally wrenching for me and, I suspect, for every participant.

Intellectually, I was convinced that I should join the speakout. But it was an excruciating decision. Since my fight over equal benefits at Pan Am almost a decade earlier, I'd kept my feminist work at a safe distance from my personal life, working on behalf of what I thought of as broader issues affecting all women, as if "all women" comprised some category that had nothing to do with me! When I argued that abortion meant life and death for women, I was talking about Rosie Jimenez—not about myself. I knew that part of the reason I'd placed such a distance between myself and my work was my socialization; I'd been brought up with the idea that a good woman always put others first. It felt unseemly, somehow, to speak out on my own behalf. But I also realized that was only part of the story. I'd begun to understand that I shied away from going public with my own life because I felt ashamed. Realizing this, I had to start wrestling with the fact that I'd let other people define my morality.

I, too, had had an illegal abortion. And by speaking openly about it, by telling the world that I was not ashamed of it, I could finally begin to decide for myself what was right and wrong without any outside moral censure. In the context of my own life and my own spiritual beliefs, the fact remained that I had made the right decision to have that abortion, and it was the right decision, now, to speak of it.

Of course, just because something is right doesn't mean it's easy. To that day, I'd never even spoken with my own mother

about it—and I did not want to discuss my decision to participate in the speak-out with James. Even though I was sure it
was the right thing to do, I wasn't sure I had the strength to do
it if they objected; I wasn't yet sure I had the courage of my
convictions. So I didn't want to tell James or Mom, but I was
planning to get up in front of a microphone on the Dade
County courthouse steps and tell my story to several hundred
strangers (and, if the public relations people did their jobs, a few
television cameras). So, while I remember it today as a freeing
experience, I wasn't so sure at the time. I've faced larger numbers of reporters, notebooks, and tape recorders, but I've never
been as afraid to face the press as I was on that morning. It's
amazing how sheer panic can crystallize an event in one's
memory: I have a very clear image of how Miami looked that
day. By mid-morning it was hot, without a hint of breeze blowing through downtown's high-rise office buildings. The sky
was brilliant blue. Standing right in front of us on the courthouse steps was a Channel 10 camera operator wearing a
Miami Dolphins jersey. Sweat poured down his face; I felt my
own blouse sticking to my back, my heart pounding fast.

I don't remember much of what the first few speakers said; I
was too worried about what I'd say myself. Then suddenly it
was my turn. With my stomach knotted, knees rubbery,
mouth as dry as my palms were soaked, I found the face of a
friend in the crowd, focused on her, and told her my story.
"When I was barely twenty years old and a senior in college,"
I began, my voice shaking audibly, "I found myself pregnant. I
was shocked, since I'd been using birth control. And I was hor-
rified, because I was not yet in a position in my life to take care
of myself, much less a baby. I decided to have an abortion. I had
no intention of telling my parents. I didn't want to let them
down. To get an abortion in 1965 wasn't difficult—just dangerous and frightening. I had to go to the same people who dealt
illegal drugs and ran illegal gambling operations in the back-
room of the American Legion Hall in Knoxville, Tennessee. The
man who performed the abortions was an unlicensed foreign

doctor—or so I was told. He was also, by reputation, an alcoholic who needed the money to pay his gambling debts. This 'doctor' came to my apartment, gave me who-knows-what kind of drugs to ease the pain, and performed an abortion without incident. My only emotions afterward were overwhelming relief and deep gratitude. But I heard later that year that another woman who went to this same doctor wasn't so fortunate; he perforated her uterus. She had reason to be grateful, too, though. He could have left her to bleed to death; instead, he took the risk of dropping her off at the hospital emergency room on his way to the airport to leave the country. Illegal abortion was the leading cause of maternal death before *Roe* v. *Wade*. Making it illegal again will *not* stop women from having abortions. It will just mean that more of us will die or be maimed for life. Don't let that happen. Please."

The heavens didn't rumble in appreciation of my speech. Neither Ronald Reagan nor Joe Scheidler appeared suddenly to tell me they'd been wrong all along or to beg my forgiveness. Nor did the applause sound particularly loud. But I gave myself a standing ovation inside. At that moment, it was more than enough.

In fact, there was little public reaction of any kind to my personal story at the abortion speak-out. A couple of articles appeared in local papers. I received a few letters threatening me with eternal damnation—or with more immediate retribution, here on earth. The greatest impact had been on me. I had taken another step toward confronting the uncomfortable—and I'd lived.

Throughout those first few years of my growing involvement with NOW, James maintained a stance of basic nonparticipation in my political and professional activities. He wanted me to establish myself on my own, he said, to be strong and independent as a strategic way of enhancing my career. Neither law firm outings nor public protests and rallies were quite his style, in any case. We were drawn together partly because of, not in spite of, the marked differences in our personalities.

James and I had lived in the Miami area since the late sixties. We invested in land and groves in the Homestead area, twenty-six miles south of Miami. Over the years our personal regard and love for each other never diminished. This didn't happen by accident. To this day I credit James's persistence in not letting us slip away or fall apart. Both of us grew and matured immeasurably as a result of going through the process.

At the Second Annual Pro-Life Activist Conference held in Appleton, Wisconsin, in April 1985, explosives were the symbol; many attendees wore firecracker lapel pins, and the marquee at the hotel hosting the conference sported the phrase HAVE A BLAST. By the end of the conference, the participants had dubbed their coalition of direct-action antiabortion groups the "Pro-Life Action Network." They'd also proclaimed 1985 as "The Year of Pain and Fear" for "those who give and get" abortions.

Nineteen eighty-five *did* turn out to be a brutal year. Violence and harassment against abortion providers continued to escalate.

At NOW, we looked at the growing threats and incidents of violence. Then we looked at the White House . . . and saw that nothing was being done about it.

A full year before, NOW president Judy Goldsmith had sent telegrams to President Reagan, Attorney General William French Smith, and FBI Director William Webster, warning of "a campaign of terrorism and intimidation against American women exercising their constitutional right to obtain health care, including abortion if they so choose."

The hope was that, by highlighting the continued buildup of organized violent antiabortion activity in the United States, we could shame Reagan and his Justice Department into taking some action. But the administration's capacity for shame was greater than anyone could have imagined. After all, Reagan had invited Joe Scheidler to visit the White House. Apparently, the same president who loudly condemned international terrorism saw nothing wrong with entertaining the leader of one of this country's most fanatical organizations. As for Webster and the FBI: Webster stated that abortion clinic bombings did not constitute "terrorism" because they were not politically motivated and not committed by an organized group. This, despite the evidence to the contrary that had surfaced since the Fort Lauderdale conference. He added that the FBI would allocate resources only to investigate true terrorism (i.e., by terrorists who threatened to overthrow the government). Accordingly, attacks on abortion clinics were given low priority. No matter what the antiabortionists did, the silence from Washington was deafening. I thought about Judith. How frustrating to know what's coming and feel unable to stop it.

The Marches for Women's Lives were staged by NOW on both coasts—in Washington, D.C., on March 9 and in Los Angeles on March 16, 1986. We expected the march in the District to be huge, with hundreds of thousands of demonstrators attending.

We were also scared and prepared for trouble. The march organizers had received very specific and ferocious threats. I helped organize NOW security for the frontline marchers, and we took the task seriously. NOW president Eleanor Smeal was wearing a bulletproof vest. A trauma surgeon equipped with a trauma pack was "marching" with the VIPs in the second line. Though the feds had been unresponsive, the District had provided a SWAT team, whose sharpshooters lined the rooftops along the march route.

Meanwhile, we didn't want to be so secure that we didn't get our pictures on the news, so we had carefully coordinated frontline security procedures with the press. Periodically, on a count of "three," the security line (where I was) would duck down so the camera crews could get their shots of the celebrities and leaders on the front line. Supposedly, only those with press credentials could get near the front line. Suddenly, just as we came abreast of the White House, a group of antiabortion protesters led by Jerry Horn, an organizer of the Appleton conference and an advocate of violence, charged us. Masquerading as a journalist, one of his confederates slammed a TV camera into my head, knocking me down. Through the breach in the line, Horn charged right toward Planned Parenthood President Fay Wattleton. He screamed at Wattleton (who is African American), "Here's your little black sister, Fay! Here's your dead black sister!" and thrust what he claimed was an aborted fetus at her face.

Security people and uniformed police rushed Horn and moved the jeering knot of antiabortion protesters aside. The pace of the march barely slowed. Most of the thousands deep inside the snaking lines would never note the event at all.

Those of us who'd lived through it face-to-face would remember it, though. Despite the enormous pro-choice crowd they'd encountered, it was clear that these antiabortion extremists were willing to attack us directly and physically. Maybe it was their very real failure to win over majority opinion that gave them impetus for further violence as an outlet for their frustrations. Whatever the reason, they were unmistakably pushing for an increasingly deadly response.

Fourteen days later, on March 23, I was in Miami at the anti–Contra aid demonstration organized by the Miami Free Speech Coalition facing a mob out for blood and ducking a barrage of rocks and eggs.

Then on March 26, I was in my office when I got word that the Ladies Center Clinic in Pensacola had been invaded and two of NOW's people had been hurt. The voice on the other end of the phone trembled.

"Patricia, I think you'd better come up here as quickly as possible."

"What happened?"

"I—I'm not sure," Georgia Wilde stammered. "The clinic's been attacked, and I'm hurt."

As events would later show, Pensacola was the target of an extremely well-organized antiabortion campaign: The cluster of attacks there was not coincidental. Antiabortion leaders had held a one-day intensive training session in Pensacola to teach the locals some of the finer points of closing down a clinic. The instructors included the most violent antiabortion organizers in the country: Joe Scheidler (the so-called "Green Beret" of the antiabortion movement), author of the book *Closed: 99 Ways to Stop Abortion*; Joan Andrews, representing the Virginia group Defenders of Life, who'd been arrested more than 120 times for her antiabortion activity; John Ryan from St. Louis, director of the Pro-Life Direct Action League, who bragged of having been arrested 350 times but spending less than nine months in jail, and who proudly described himself as a "domestic terrorist"; and Earl Appleby from Washington, D.C., a self-proclaimed "ethical adviser" to North Carolina Senator Jesse Helms. In holding this training session, Scheidler, Andrews, Ryan, and Appleby were following up on plans made two years previously in Fort Lauderdale. To top it off they decided on a field exercise: The eager participants would put all their freshly learned tactics to the test by closing a local clinic. The logical target was the Ladies Center, now the only abortion provider between Tallahassee, Florida, and Mobile, Alabama, as a result of the 1984 bombings.

Georgia had gone up there to offer advice, assistance, and support to the staff and patients. Outside the Ladies Center, about forty abortion rights supporters were facing off against five times that many antiabortionists, who were playing "Happy Birthday," "Taps," and a funeral dirge over loudspeakers.

I took these right-wing picketers seriously. My experience

with anticommunist attacks in Miami had left me keenly attuned to the possibility of violence whenever and wherever the right wing made its stand. Unfortunately, too many others were forced to learn the hard way.

"I thought 'clinic closing' meant they would just surround us and try to keep women from getting in," Georgia said. "I really didn't think anything like this would happen."

Wanting to retrieve pictures taken at the march in D.C. from her parked car, Georgia had made the crucial mistake of opening a side door of the clinic. Four antiabortionists—former Klansman John Burt, his eighteen-year-old daughter Sarah, Karisa Epperly, and Joan Andrews—had burst in, violently knocking Georgia and clinic director Linda Taggert aside. Burt shoved Georgia up against a wall and, ramming his elbow into the base of her neck, threw his forearm against her throat, hard. The three women ran up one flight of stairs to the procedure rooms and started upending drawers and destroying equipment. Burt joined them; they didn't stop until a half hour later, when the police managed to drag them out. Only Sarah Burt walked; the other three—and two of their colleagues, who'd been arrested outside the clinic—had to be subdued by the police and dragged away, writhing furiously, while their comrades cheered them on.

More than anything, I think, Georgia called for reassurance, wanting to hear that she wasn't to blame for the violence, needing to hear that she was not alone. I told her to record exactly what had happened to her on tape, immediately; we'd need plenty of good evidence for court. Experience had taught me that witnesses' memories fade quickly, or are suppressed, if the memories are traumatic enough.

"Don't worry, Georgia," I told her. "You're not going to fight this one alone."

I made sure she'd been examined by a doctor to determine the extent of her physical injuries, not just for the court case, but for her own well-being. I promised her we'd make sure that she and the other women's rights supporters in Pensacola would have the support and assistance they'd need for the criminal trial and afterward. Florida NOW *and* the national office would become fully involved; she and her chapter would not be out there struggling on their own.

As I hung up, of course, I wondered how I was going to do all this. But I was determined to.

By that same evening, all four of the clinic invaders, charged with burglary, criminal mischief, and resisting arrest, were out on bail. Andrews and John Burt immediately returned to the Ladies Center, against the judge's orders; they were thrown back in jail and held without bail. After their trial in September 1986, Judge William Anderson gave the uncontrite Andrews a five-year prison sentence.

This was hardly the last anyone heard of her, though. Antiabortionists mounted a careful publicity campaign, trying to cultivate "Saint Joan's" image as a sort of martyr to their cause. Within months, the religious right had begun to compare her plight with that of civil rights activists in the 1950s. Said national antiabortion leader Tom Herlihy, "We will endeavor to address our fellow Christians as Martin Luther King attempted to address his fellow clergymen twenty years ago, using, whenever possible, his exact words." I was infuriated that he dared to invoke the name of Dr. King. Andrews tried to play her role in prison, but she had trouble with the nonviolence part; during an altercation with prison guards, she took out her glass eye and threw it at them.

But Jerry Brown, then governor of California, bought her act. He was one of many who wrote the Florida cabinet, requesting leniency for Joan Andrews. This particularly galled me; though not as much as the fact that the cabinet voted to grant Andrews clemency on October 14, 1988—more than two years before the end of her sentence.

For his part, John Burt claimed to have learned his lesson. Well, sort of. "I'd go out and blow up a clinic and have no qualms about it," he remarked, "except that I'm scared of being caught. I'm too old to go to prison for twenty years." And he added, somewhat prophetically, "People are going to get hurt and killed, if this trend continues—suppressing people with such hard sentences."

The nightmare didn't end there for Georgia Wilde, either. She continued to receive harassing phone calls and threatening letters. Her dog was poisoned to death. I tried to reassure her that the work she was doing was terribly important and she should be proud of herself for sticking with it. After a tough year, during which her husband died of cancer, Georgia decided she couldn't deal with the pressure any longer. She changed her name and moved to Atlanta. But it wasn't enough. During the 1988 Democratic National Convention there, antiabortion activists found her out. The threatening phone calls started all over again. It was the last straw; Georgia didn't have anything more to give. She left the field of reproductive health care entirely.

The violent trauma of the Pensacola clinic invasions and Scheidler's subsequent threats to a clinic in Delaware convinced us at NOW that if we wanted to put any legal pressure on the Pro-Life Action Network, we were going to have to do it ourselves. We'd been pressing as hard as we could for some help from our own federal government for years. But it was clear that neither the Justice Department, the FBI, nor the U.S. Attorney General's office could be counted on to protect us. We were frustrated and frightened. But there's a certain relief in giving up futile hope. There's also relief in taking responsibility for your own life and fate. Our new determination to go ahead and take the offensive with some action ourselves cheered us immeasurably.

Morris Dees, of the Southern Poverty Law Center, had extensive experience dealing with violent extremists in the deep South and had been married to an abortion provider. He'd also been involved, early on, in direct-mail fund-raising with NOW consultant Roger Craver. After the Pensacola incident he contacted Ellie Smeal, offering to discuss litigation strategies. I was brought in on the discussions as Florida NOW's legal counsel.

One of the associates in my law firm researched various legal strategies. We realized we had three basic choices: We could sue Scheidler and his cronies for violating federal antitrust laws, the antiracketeering statute known as RICO, or the civil rights law called the Klan Act.

Federal antitrust laws are primarily designed to protect an individual's freedom to enter and compete in the marketplace without obstruction. The goal of these laws is also to protect consumers from the effect of monopolies—and from the unfair pricing policies such monopolies tend to engage in.

The Klan Act (known to lawyers as Section 1985 [3] is the post–Civil War Civil Rights Act originally intended to provide a federal court remedy for newly freed slaves who were deprived of civil rights. In the years since Reconstruction, the Klan Act had been applied in many other situations where civil rights were denied for reasons other than race. However, the Klan Act had never been applied in any case of a woman's civil rights being violated. And I was skeptical about whether the court would ultimately allow us to use it against violent antiabortion groups.

This left the Racketeer Influenced and Corrupt Organizations Act. Originally designed to prosecute organized crime, RICO includes as racketeering activities arson, bombing, kidnapping, and extortion. Most importantly, RICO allows a case to be brought against those who are responsible for instigating those criminal activities, even if they have insulated themselves, as mob bosses generally do, with layers of organization that might protect them from being prosecuted under regular criminal conspiracy laws. I felt strongly that we could maintain a racketeering suit under state and federal extortion laws. These people were clearly using violence and threats of violence to try to force women and health care workers to give up their rights to receive and provide medical services. I was also fairly sure we would find ample evidence of their connections to the increased arson and bombing attacks on clinics.

Dees initially suggested that NOW, along with the Ladies Center and the Delaware clinic threatened by Scheidler, file a class-action suit under the federal antitrust laws; NOW would be representing its women members and other women who wanted to use reproductive health clinics, and the two clinics would be representing all the women's health care facilities in the United States. The suit would name Scheidler, John Ryan, Joan Andrews, the Pro-Life Action League, and the Pro-Life Direct Action League.

The SPLC had already demonstrated that federal antitrust laws could be used successfully against organized violent harassment: In 1982, they'd won a class-action suit on behalf of the Vietnamese Fishermen's Association of Galveston Bay, Texas. Vietnamese shrimpers in the area had been violently attacked; the SPLC proved that this violence was an organized intimidation tactic meant to protect the established white fishing industry from competition.

Using federal antitrust laws against Scheidler and his cronies also had real appeal for me and for NOW's national officers. It made practical and legal sense: Through organized violent action, the antiabortionists were increasing the price of abortions and other clinic services and denying abortion clinics the freedom to conduct business. Furthermore, if we won, we stood to force the defendants to pay three times the damages determined by a jury.

However, I knew that a federal racketeering complaint had those advantages and more. The racketeering laws would allow us to go after those antiabortion organizers who might never dirty their hands by lighting a match or pulling the trigger, but whose role in instigating the violence was undeniable. Personally, I leaned toward using racketeering as a legal strategy in addition to the antitrust laws. A big federal racketeering case would publicly show just who—and what—these terrorists were. The publicity we'd get from a high-visibility trial in which we compared antiabortionists to mobsters would do their movement a lot of harm. (Meanwhile, I was concerned that, by filing an antitrust suit, we might be playing into our opponents' hands by portraying abortion providers solely as businesspeople or, as Scheidler so often called them, "abortion profiteers.")

But pursuing the antitrust strategy had many benefits. And Dees was offering us free legal assistance. So we filed an anti-trust complaint in June 1986 in Delaware, where my associ-ate's research and personal experience clerking in northern Florida indicated that the precedent and judges were more fa-vorable. A short time later, we moved the case to federal district court in Chicago and dropped Joan Andrews, then still in jail in Pensacola, as a defendant in exchange for the other defendants' dropping all objections to jurisdiction and venue. Then began the discovery process: We took statements under oath from the defendants and were given access to their records, including correspondence and financial records. Over the next few years, NOW also filed complaints under the Klan Act in federal courts in New York, Virginia, the District of Columbia, and Maryland.

The legal process on the federal level is guaranteed to take time. Lots of time. By employing this particular strategy, we knew we were in for a very long ride.

But I had faith in the legal system. I was also thrilled to be using my training and experience as a lawyer to help lead a frontal assault on these criminals who were willing to use vio-lence to stomp on our civil rights and limit our access to health care.

Outsider by night (and weekends), insider by day. While I was giving more and more of myself and my time to my activist work, I remained highly committed to and ambitious for my legal career. I had left Paul, Landy & Beiley in 1978 for Arky, Freed, Stearns, Watson & Greer, a larger firm that was involved in the numerous corporate-takeover wars beginning to heat up all over Florida.

Arky, Freed had quite a few public companies as clients. I continued to practice corporate and commercial law, but moved from inter-American business transactions into a lot more banking and securities work. Miami banks and savings and loan institutions were cash-rich (partly because of the flight capital pouring in from Central America, partly because of the rampant Miami drug trade). Extraordinarily wealthy men were fighting one another to take over banks and corporations; out-of-state banking interests were trying to break into the state; and the atmosphere at my new firm was exciting.

Arky, Freed also offered as enlightened an attitude toward women as one could hope to find in corporate culture. Shortly after I arrived, an attorney named Allison Miller was named partner and others of us followed. And the women at the firm made sure in whatever way they could that the men didn't contribute to the sexism that still permeated the legal community. You didn't need a law degree; everyone could do something. Steve Arky's secretary Judy, for example, refused to book her boss at the Miami Club—one of the two exclusive dining clubs where lawyers met their business and banking clients—because the place refused to admit women. I'm not sure Steve ever knew why all his lunch meetings were at the Bankers Club; if he did, he never said anything about it.

I felt privileged to have work that allowed me to further my ideals. (Actually, after some of my earlier jobs, it was a privilege to have work that didn't utterly offend me.) It's also important to make practical, daily progress toward fulfillment of our goals. Working at Arky, Freed provided an atmosphere that encouraged me to express my feminism in daily professional dealings. I'd never compromise a client for the good of the women's rights movement. But, when I had a chance to infuse some feminism into my business practice, I'd do it.

My new firm gave me the chance to make a real difference. Most of our banking clients were subject to the same affirmative action requirements that had helped me in gaining equal compensation at Pan Am, since they too did business with the federal government. (Most national banks sell U.S. savings bonds and also serve as depositories of tax receipts for the IRS.) President Johnson had issued executive orders in 1965 and 1967 requiring all federal contractors doing at least $50,000 worth of business with the federal government to take affirmative action to end workplace discrimination. Still, many of our clients had not developed affirmative action plans and didn't seem to know they needed them.

Because I believe strongly in affirmative action, I always tried to use these federal requirements to create positive new programs that were designed to work to the benefit of my corporate clients and their employees as well.

A large pharmaceutical company, a major client of ours, was awarded a federal contract to provide drugs to the Veterans Administration and needed to establish an affirmative action plan immediately. I was assigned to draw one up.

My analysis of the client's workforce and personnel practices plainly showed that unskilled women hired by the company were immediately stuck in the packaging department, a veritable dead end. Comparably unskilled men, on the other hand, were assigned to semiskilled jobs that offered some training and at least some possibilities for promotion. I knew that the company CEO, a second-generation immigrant who had seen his own parents go through some very tough times in this country, would never have looked at himself as someone who condoned discrimination of any kind. But I had the facts; he'd have to face them.

"I'm sure you're not aware of what's going on, but you've got a problem here with your unskilled new hires." I augmented the point by telling him that if I were a plaintiff's lawyer I'd be able to take any one of the women out of the packaging department down to the EEOC then and there and hit his company with a discrimination suit—and I'd likely win.

Actually, had I walked into his office as an adversary repre-

senting one of the women and accused him of discrimination,
he probably would have told me to go to hell; then he'd have
dared me to take it before a judge. Because I was *his* lawyer,
though, and because he knew I was on his side, he heeded my
warning and told me to go ahead and implement the necessary
changes. It was, he said, common sense; and common sense
was always good business. I proceeded to come up with an affirmative action plan for the company that would work.

Through situations like this, too, I quickly discovered the
benefits of working for change on the inside. That particular
client listened to me because I approached him as another insider, as someone who shared his interests. This kind of approach is both honest and necessary; it makes change easier to
effect as well as accept. In any case, the work of insiders advocating social change is invaluable and has a profound impact.

No discrimination case, though, was as bizarre as the one
that arose when I was representing Guardian National Bank.

Now, if ever a client should have understood affirmative action, it was Guardian. The bank officers had come to Miami
from Cuba. They'd all been bankers in Havana before Castro
seized power, and they'd formed Guardian precisely because
they hadn't been able to get jobs in the lily-white Miami banking industry of the early 1960s. (The woman vice president of
Guardian had ended up selling cosmetics at Woolworth's when
she first arrived in this country.)

But they didn't actually have an affirmative action plan until
they received notice of a federal contract compliance review.
After researching their workforce and policies, I was sure we
wouldn't have any problems with the compliance review.

Unfortunately, during our first meeting, the affirmative action officer in Atlanta didn't agree.

"You don't have any blacks working at this company."

If I'd learned one thing, it's that you don't start a meeting by
telling some bureaucrat he's an idiot. So I calmly took out my
copy of the forms showing the employee breakdown and

started pointing out all the black employees at the bank. After I named half a dozen, the officer stopped me.

"No, no, no. Those aren't blacks. Those are SSAs."

"SSAs?"

"Spanish Surnamed Americans."

"They may be SSAs, but they're also black."

"No, no. They can't be both."

I'd come in here prepared for one of the easier meetings of my career, but this guy was beginning to try my patience.

"Well, what if we took Mr. Sastre down to the county court," I said, pointing to a name on the employee list, "and spent fifty dollars to change his name to Taylor—which is what *sastre* means in Spanish?"

"Well, then he could be black. But you haven't done that."

The meeting deteriorated from there. He threatened to bounce the matter up to Washington; I dared him to go ahead and do it.

Either Washington wasn't paying attention, or else maybe they liked my argument better than his. We never heard from anybody on the matter. In any event, it was an excellent demonstration to me that it's not as easy as I had first thought to find solutions to the problems of discrimination. No magic wand exists that can be waved once and for all to end injustice.

Developing a more sophisticated understanding from these kinds of learning experiences helped me tremendously as I became involved in NOW on the national level. So many businesswomen own companies today—women who hit the "glass ceiling" working for others and decided to build their own houses. When one of them comes to me complaining, for example, that some proposal for employer-provided health coverage is going to saddle her business with unbearable expenses, I can't dismiss her out of hand. I believe that progressive legislation like universal health care is essential and would be good for individuals and good for the country. But having seen government regulations in action from both sides of the fence, I know

that we must be wise and practical and fair if our policies are
to provide long-term solutions.

Some of my most satisfying work at Arky, Freed was done
on behalf of Eastern Airlines flight attendants. Knowing my
own background in the air and with NOW, when stewardess
Pat Fink was elected president of Local 553, she asked me to
serve as their legal counsel, handling grievances brought by the
union against the company on behalf of flight attendants who
had been wrongfully fired or disciplined. Now that I wasn't a
stewardess any longer, but a lawyer with some clout, it was a
special thrill for me to deal with airline industry management
to the benefit of my former peers.

Eastern seemed intent on union-busting, and the flight attendants' union was an easy target. When pilots or mechanics
went on strike they could cause devastating problems, but
flight attendants were still seen as replaceable parts. It became
obvious that the company was harassing flight attendants on
purpose, in a sense forcing the union to take more grievances
to arbitration. They instituted random drug testing; they
searched flight bags. At the smallest excuse, the company
would try to fire a flight attendant for "pilferage." The company's direct violation of work rules increased the number of
grievances and cost the union money as well as leadership time.

This was exactly the work I had envisioned for myself when
I left the airline for law school. I was helping large numbers of
women who were in the same position I'd been in, and I loved
it—but rather than satisfying my appetite for action, these
lawyerly victories only whetted it.

As far as I could tell, the firm was happy with my activist
work both inside and outside the office. More than once,
partners told me how much they liked my political involvement and the fact that I was giving back to the community

by taking on cases for individual women who needed help. (Of course, I did get dubbed the "pro bono queen.")

At the same time, they had to be questioning my ultimate commitment to the firm. All the pro bono work, satisfying as it was, didn't bring much cash into the Arky, Freed coffers. And I wasn't really willing to spend my free time in exclusive dining clubs cultivating relationships with bigshot clients, one of the ways to develop business for the firm and get named partner. As women get higher and higher in powerful corporate ranks, the pressure to conform increases proportionately. But I didn't want to lose track of why I'd wanted to become a lawyer in the first place, which was why I was working the equivalent of two full-time jobs: at Arky, Freed, and at NOW.

Partnership continued to elude me, and it embarrassed and frustrated me, although objectively I knew my impatience was largely unwarranted. Added to the fact that for more than a year I had worked night and day on the Equal Rights Amendment campaign, changing firms had probably added a couple of years onto that process for me. But I was nonetheless driven, ambitious, and still had something left to prove. Finally, in 1984, I made partner. But increasingly I had the feeling that I ought to be moving on. While I still got a competitive thrill from winning a case, I couldn't escape the fact that most of the time my work involved two wealthy guys fighting for each other's money. And aside from my professional pride, I had to ask myself, "Who cares if my rich guy wins?"

Of course, in retrospect I can see that I did make a difference with my clients in that law firm as an insider. Women play insider roles in all kinds of corporate and less glamorous work-aday settings, as well as in state legislatures and public offices; it's possible to pursue feminist goals no matter what you do between nine and five. And even for an individual woman, there may be many ways to play this out over the course of a single lifetime. But as time went on, as even the visceral pleasure of winning my cases diminished, feminist politics became the only thing that really interested me. Every woman has to find the role or roles that suit her. Ultimately, I wanted to make structural changes in our society, and I didn't think I could do that in my role as corporate lawyer. I'd never envisioned it as a lifetime career, anyway; I'd always thought of it as my bridge to something else.

In 1986 a seat in the Florida house opened up in my district. I began considering a run for public office.

The first person I contacted was Roberta Fox, who by then had taken Dick Anderson's seat as a state senator with NOW's help. Even though she had been on the wrong side of Biscayne Boulevard during the Miami Free Speech Coalition rally, Janet and I had stayed in her camp, and we were backing her for reelection. Roberta and NOW, Roberta and I, had enough goals in common that we mended fences and moved on. I knew I could rely on her for some no-nonsense advice. We didn't talk much about why I wanted to run for office or what good works I'd do if elected. Instead, she cut to the bottom line quickly.

"Who can you count on for support?"

The local flight attendant union, I told her; NOW and other women's groups; some of my business clients; maybe the trial lawyers, some other unions, and local Democratic Party groups—depending on who else was running in the primary. I thought it was a pretty impressive list. Roberta didn't.

"You're going to have to dig deep into whatever nest egg you have to make your campaign work."

The fact of the matter was that I'd bankrolled many of my own feminist activities. While I was making good money at the firm, and James had started selling paintings, our nest was not that full of eggs.

But it wasn't a lack of finances that dissuaded me from taking the campaign trail. Among other factors, it was a story about another state senator named Warren Henderson, who unwittingly provided me with a preview of the level of human maturity I could expect in Tallahassee.

Henderson was a member of the senate Natural Resources Committee. During a trip to St. Marks Wildlife Refuge near Orlando, Henderson, representing the committee, did his best to act like one of the animals. Actually, that's an insult to the animals. When other politicians pointed out one alligator with a dark, ugly face, Henderson, referring to an African American senator back in Tallahassee, remarked, "But Girardeau's not here!" During the rest of the excursion, he also threw the word *nigger* around liberally.

Women were hardly spared that day, either. When someone suggested that the group find a bathroom so that women members might relieve themselves, Henderson, who'd been relieving himself behind bushes and trees throughout the day, remarked: "When women have equal equipment, they can have equal opportunity!" Then he bodily picked up *Orlando Sentinel* reporter Donna Blanton and twirled her around on his hip.

The good senator had what he considered an acceptable excuse for these actions: he was drunk. He and some of his buddies had been tossing back beers all day; when he got out into the sun, he reeled. ("Alcohol," he lamented later, "has been my best friend and my worst enemy in life.") He simply passed off the day as nothing more than a rough one at the office. "Gosh. I guess I'm just sorry. I always try to conduct myself reasonably in public. But we've all had good days and bad. This was one of my bad days."

Despite Henderson's protestations, "bad days" didn't seem particularly uncommon—for him or for many of the other elected legislators. A sort of frat party/stag club atmosphere pervades Tallahassee. Janet Canterbury once told me about a senator at the capitol building who'd shoved his way into an elevator packed with NOW delegates, gleefully hollering, "Hello, ladies! Who's gonna get lucky tonight?!"

"It's almost as if, since they have to be good little boys at home with their wives and kids and constituents, when they get to Tallahassee they figure it's party time," she speculated.

The thought of constantly working in these conditions didn't appeal to me after all. I salute those women who do, but I knew I could not return to those same kinds of attitudes I'd left behind at Pan Am. I couldn't imagine how I'd stand it if I had to spend all day, every day, trying to change the customs of this particular culture.

Not surprisingly, James was against the idea of my running for office from the start. He craves privacy; he always has. As my political activities increased and became more and more public, he grew increasingly protective about his own personal life. The last part he wanted to play was the role of candidate's husband. He was also concerned that the brutality of political life would hurt me. Roberta Fox and her husband, Mike Gold, were friends of ours; we'd seen what it could be like.

But the deciding factor for me was that, even if I did win the election, I would be starting over as a forty-one-year-old first-year legislator; in a system based on seniority I'd have to spend years fighting my way through the political morass of state politics, working my way up through yet another well established pecking order, just to get the power I already had as a leader in NOW, as Janet Canterbury's closest ally, and as a member of a prestigious law firm. I wanted to have a bigger impact, and I wanted it sooner rather than later.

That was the end of my electoral aspirations.

Afterward, I tried to sort out why I had decided what I did and what that meant. I knew that Roberta Fox and Elaine Gordon had both been very effective working in the Florida legislature. But I realized I'd become much more grandiose in my ambition. I believed that I really could accomplish something within NOW—on the national level, in Washington.

In 1987 the paid officer position of treasurer at NOW's national action center in Washington, D.C., became vacant.

In retrospect, I don't think I'd even have considered the position if I hadn't first made partner at Arky, Freed. I couldn't have stomached the thought of people whispering, behind my back, that I'd left the law because I just couldn't cut it. (In recent years, Rush Limbaugh has played upon this idea that career feminists are part of a "those-who-can't-do-protest" front; even back then, I wanted to know, and I wanted everyone else to know that it wasn't the case for me.) Ironically, the fact that I'd reached this goal cleared the way for me to leave commercial law—for good.

I was excited at the prospect of going to NOW's Washington headquarters as an officer to work with and learn from the president, Ellie Smeal. At the same time, the thought of uprooting myself petrified me. I ran to fill the vacancy, but upon learning that I'd won the board election, instead of celebrating I went into a state of shock: my stomach ached, my hands sweat. I felt as if I was back at FSU again, preparing to convince my classmates to join in my complaint about a sexist textbook or on the courthouse steps taking part in the abortion speak-out. My sense of turmoil at embarking upon something new, untried, and very real was the same.

The law career had been my safety net for many years by then. When things got too crazy at NOW, I could always bury myself in a case and forget other problems. Despite my commitment to feminism, I'd considered myself a corporate lawyer for the past twelve years; that was my identity. Now, though, I was going to become a professional feminist activist—with nothing to fall back on.

I was also afraid of the very real prospect that NOW would eat away at every remaining inch of my personal life. I'd seen other activists give everything to the organization, until there really wasn't anything else left in their lives. I knew I did not want that to happen to me. I wanted to keep the perspective that my life outside NOW had always given me. I wanted to go to the movies sometimes, read books, take a vacation.

I'd also have to leave Miami for Washington, D.C.—it was a full-time job and there was no choice in the matter. This meant that James and I, for the first time since becoming seriously involved with each other nearly twenty years before, would have to live apart. We'd need to maintain two separate house-holds. And, after two decades in south Florida (it had been our home since 1968) I felt comfortable there. I liked being a com-paratively big fish in a relatively small pond! I'd be leaving a community where I'd planted deep roots of every conceivable kind; where I'd developed an extensive support system over the years that was political, financial, and personal. In the world of Florida politics, I was a mover and a shaker. In D.C., especially at first, I would be a friendless little politico in a city that had more politicos than parking meters. I'd be all but a novice—one of many.

But it was my relationship with James that presented the most significant part of the whole emotional dilemma. He had established himself as an important citizen in Homestead, not only as proprietor of our avocado and mango groves, but as a spokesman for the farming community both in Tallahassee and Washington. There was no question he'd stay based in Florida; I'd have to go on my own.

The two of us tried valiantly to sort out the ramifications of living in separate cities. But the emotional impact of drastic life changes can never be wholly sorted out in advance.

The practicalities seemed obvious enough: I would need to find an apartment in D.C.; one or the other of us would have to travel almost every weekend so we could see each other; my salary would be cut in half; I'd no longer be contributing sub-stantially to our shared assets; and watching every dollar would again become a way of life for me, alone, in a distant city. We *knew* all these things. But knowing, understanding, does not always make the accompanying feelings easier. Even as James and I struggled through this turbulent period, still, a profound love and respect existed between us and bound us together.

Along with the practical questions of maintaining a two-city, two-household relationship, there were the big, emotionally terrifying questions. James and I were both substantial, inde-pendent adults, each committed to personal growth in our own

right. We had no doubt in our minds that we could survive
without the other—eventually, perhaps, even thrive—if we had
to. If we wanted to. But we didn't want to. Would *we* survive
this move; and, if so, what new directions would our relationship take, what form would it grow into, in the uncertain future?

Janet Canterbury and Pat Silverthorn were my mainstays.
Janet listened as I agonized. She encouraged the move from a
political point of view; personally, she had a lot of ambivalence
about it. Pat also told me that she believed that devoting myself
full-time to the feminist movement was absolutely the right
thing for me to do, even though it meant we wouldn't be seeing
each other on a day-to-day basis. But I had no idea what I'd do
without them.

To all these and other equally weighty questions, I had no
obvious answers yet.

You say you want real autonomy, I told myself, real freedom. Well, there's a price to be paid; and here's the piper, coming around to collect. Will you take responsibility, pay the price
that goes along with the growth? And if not now, when?

At times I tried to minimize the impact of the move. I would
rationalize it all: I had traveled a lot as a flight attendant, I told
myself; and I'd been gone nearly every weekend during the past
few years on NOW business.

But this would be different, and I knew it.

A deep ache lodged itself in my heart. This will be one of the
hardest things you ever do, I thought. It was true.

I packed some things. Like a true Southerner, I didn't own a
winter coat.

SIX

Washington, D.C., capital of the most powerful nation on earth, is a city where the politics of power lie heavy in the air, as palpable as the springtime scent of cherry blossoms. Other cities in the world are magnetic centers of activity, too—where business is conducted, edifices constructed, wars plotted, nations created and destroyed, where the streets cram with traffic and people hurry purposefully—but, in Washington, so many of the deals struck or lost involve the raw material of human life. The quality of human life—of your life, and mine—hangs there in the balance with each government decision that is weighed, or influenced, or made. The city, with its monuments, parks, and buildings, is designed after the model of Paris and Versailles: There are carefully placed centers and hubs, wide boulevards lined with police barricades or trees. From the Hill, it's easy to believe that every road must lead there. No city on earth is quite like it.

Turning points are never easy. And this move from Miami to D.C. was no exception. Emotional difficulties aside, a lot of big practical details needed to be attended to all at once. First things first: I had to rent a modest place to live. My good friend Barbara Timmer helped me find an apartment in the Adams

Morgan section of town, a racially and ethnically mixed neighborhood that's both residential and commercial. It could not have been more unlike my quiet, rural neighborhood in Homestead. Luckily, Barbara lived in the same building. (Janet and I had helped Barbara get elected as executive vice president of NOW in the early eighties, and she remains part of the organization's national network. A seasoned political strategist, she worked for Geraldine Ferraro's vice presidential campaign and has worked for Congress as well as in the private sector.) Having her close by helped immeasurably. When I got too gloomy or homesick, Barbara would walk me down the two blocks from our rent-controlled building to D.C.'s Eighteenth Street, a street that immerses you in the international atmosphere for which the city is famous. Within a six-block radius of my new home, I could eat my way around the world in French, Jamaican, Salvadoran, Ethiopian, Senegalese, Indian, or Italian restaurants (to name just a few).

Part of the reason I'd made the move at this time in my life was to work with Ellie Smeal, NOW's dynamic, forceful, and inspiring leader. I knew that if I wanted to pursue a career in political activism, Ellie's tutelage would prove invaluable. So despite the difficulty and inevitable loss entailed by the move, being in D.C. also filled me with excitement, enthusiasm, and hope. But the people I'd left behind were impossible to replace. James and I had given each other continual support and companionship for two decades. Over the past several years Pat Silverthorn and I had become increasingly close. And I'd grown to rely on Janet Canterbury's intelligent advice, sense of humor, and loyal friendship.

I had to accustom myself to working in surroundings that were far from luxurious, too. Without realizing it, I'd been spoiled in Miami; over the years I'd gotten used to all the perks of working at a posh downtown Miami law firm. NOW's national action center in D.C. was a different story. The workers there were still using manual typewriters. And there were no assistants or secretaries to take dictation or run off copies for me.

One of the first things that came across my desk was a complaint filed by a woman suing NOW, President Reagan, Federal Express, and a lot of other defendants, alleging that we'd all conspired to break her nose. Obviously bogus, but we had to file a response. While looking for someone to type up and file a reply in court, I was struck for the first time by how dramatically my circumstances had changed and by how limiting that change from for-profit to not-for-profit work could be. The carpet stains and the peeling paint on the walls in my new place of work were constant reminders: In many ways, the party was over. But in other important ways, the fun had just begun.

As treasurer my responsibilities involved managing the finances of the national organization: paying bills, reviewing invoices and requests for reimbursement, managing cash flow—or lack of it. Former NOW president Judy Goldsmith had spent a lot more than she'd taken in; throughout the three years of her term she overspent by an average of nearly forty thousand dollars a month, and the organization's negative net worth ran over a million dollars. When Ellie Smeal came back as president in 1985, NOW was in financial shambles. Once she took office Ellie instituted stringent austerity measures. NOW might well have gone under financially if she hadn't. Her successful race had divided the organization deeply, though, and the bitter polarization and conflict continued for many years, leaving lots of internal fighting in its wake. By the time I joined her in Washington, we were still conducting business on a cash-only basis with many of our vendors.

My new duties also included public speaking and executive committee responsibilities—lots of work, in fact, that had little to do with NOW's finances. Of course, I'd brought with me all the interests and legal expertise I'd developed over the years; so I stayed involved in litigating against antiabortion terrorists, just as I had in Florida. When President Reagan nominated Robert Bork for the Supreme Court, I took a lead role in analyzing his legal writings and translating them into lay language for NOW's activists, and I helped draft the organization's congressional testimony against him. I also continued to work on global feminist issues, meeting with women from other countries and helping to develop formalized international programs and strategies. I buried the confusion and isolation I felt by staying busier than I'd ever been.

The first eight months were the hardest. I spoke to James, Janet, and Pat on the phone every day, seeking comfort and advice. Having left one world behind, trying to gain a good foothold in this new one, I often felt as if I'd fallen into some strange crevice between worlds, between realities; and, in this strange limbo land, I was the only one around for miles and miles.

At times I nearly went crazy from loneliness, and from that most deceptive enemy of all: self-pity. But all emotions are fleeting in the end. And the turning points in my own life have taught me that every difficult experience has its crescendos, its peaks of maximum difficulty after which things tend to get a little better. As athletes and soldiers alike say, sometimes the only way out is through.

At an absolute peak of loneliness and despair I found two wild cats starving in front of my apartment building and, identifying with them like crazy, caught them and took them in. It wasn't easy. Barbara Timmer got her hand bitten all the way through to the bone trying to help. They proceeded to break everything that wasn't nailed down. One night, coming in late, I stepped over the threshold, kicked off my shoes, and stepped immediately on some large shards of glass from a vase they'd shattered. It cut right into my flesh, and I bled copiously. The cats prowled around hissing. I sat there on the floor thinking, "I am going to bleed to death here in this rundown apartment, alone except for a couple of wild animals who will probably eat my corpse!" In shock, I tied my sock around the worst-cut foot to try and stanch the flow of blood. Then I lay on my back and, holding both feet in the air, managed to drag a phone toward me and dial for help with one shaking finger.

Time healed the soles of my feet and soothed some of my loneliness; and I began to get the hang of my new job. With that came a real sense of enthusiasm and excitement. And belonging! I began to understand the style of working in D.C. It was a place where people played political hardball. I'd had some experience with that in Miami, over the years; my work for NOW, participating in actions against right-wing violence, and as a corporate lawyer had proved good training ground. My work as a flight attendant also proved valuable. After all, I'd spent seven years walking up and down airplane aisles, taking people's garbage and thanking them for it, which was exactly what women had experienced with politicians in Washington for too long! I vowed that we'd no longer take their garbage; we'd take their jobs. And it's also true that my experience as a lawyer in hostile corporate takeovers was good training for dealing with some of the more rugged internal politics of NOW. But the stakes in Washington always seemed higher, somehow; I couldn't forget that our wins and losses here had a direct, profound impact on the lives of many people.

It took a couple of years to feel truly comfortable with my new work and surroundings, and to develop a real support network of friends and political allies.

Those cats, by the way, became quite fat and gentle. They're now an integral part of my family.

There's a price to be paid for moving into any new position of power. For women entering nontraditional spheres of activity, the cost can be high, but so can the gains—although these may not be as apparent at first.

Months or years of loneliness may seem interminable when you're smack in the middle of them. They certainly felt that way to me. But, in retrospect, I see that during those first couple of years in Washington I developed new skills professionally and personally, made new contacts, developed important new friendships, and got a glimpse of the way this country operates at its very core. The loneliness and occasional feelings of powerlessness that I did feel, learning the ropes in Washington and at NOW's headquarters, were painful, but they were also signals to me of real maturation and growth. As my own competence in these new surroundings grew, I became a stronger human being—and a much better activist. I became more politically savvy. I became more honest with myself, better able to evaluate my own strengths and weaknesses, to use the strengths to achieve my goals, and to work on eliminating the weaknesses.

This had profound positive ramifications for my personal life, too. Unavoidably, my personal relationships changed. My growing sense of who I was and what I wanted resulted in a deepening of my relationships with my family and friends. Ironically, despite the geographic distance, I was able to feel closer to those I love and to relate to them more honestly as I became more confident and happier.

But make no mistake: learning Washington's ways was no mere exercise in self-actualization. I had come to play in the majors, and both the tools and the rules were new. I'd been a star minor leaguer in Florida. But D.C. was "The Show," for sure. Traditionally in our country, women play softball; men play hardball—and hardball is widely recognized as the "real" baseball. But the differences between these games are superficial, and the gender division between them artificial: There is no reason on earth why women cannot learn to play hardball well; we simply have to practice some different techniques. In doing so, we often find that our years of playing softball have given us some excellent training indeed.

And something else: Our years of living, working, negotiating, and loving as women may give us a distinct advantage. Because we so often become the caretakers and guardians of others, women understand that political hardball is no mere game; we understand how intimately, how profoundly the decisions of those in power affect the very real lives of our families, our children, ourselves, and all of our loved ones and neighbors. "Hardball" is shorthand for something important and real, an international pastime with enormous impact. As caretakers, women understand this. What better training is there for making difficult, important decisions that affect the real day-to-day lives of large numbers of people?

In Washington I began to understand just how well all of my minor-league softball playing had equipped me for the ultimate game of real-life political hardball. And it was in Washington that I learned to play major-league hardball—for keeps.

Of course, nothing ever goes quite the way we plan. Six weeks after I'd moved from Miami to D.C. to take over as NOW's national treasurer, Ellie Smeal surprised everyone with the announcement that she would not be running for a second term. She'd decided, instead, to take advantage of a great opportunity: to join Peg Yorkin in starting a new organization, which they planned to call the Fund for the Feminist Majority. To put it mildly, this sent people in the national NOW office into a tailspin. Ellie is a living legend among NOW activists, and she had guided us through some incredibly tough times. We'd all come to rely on her, and the thought of moving along the tightrope of feminist politics without her in charge put some women—including me—into a panic.

Janet Canterbury was in Washington that week, and Ellie called both of us into her office to break the news personally. She told me one reason she felt secure leaving NOW's presidency was that she thought I was ready to take over the job. I was too shocked to be flattered. I'd only been in the district six weeks; I hardly knew how to fit my key into the new apartment door—never mind having a firm grip on the politics of NOW and of Washington in general. I was also disappointed—and furious. I'd made the decision to come to D.C. in the first place because I wanted to work with Ellie. She is a savvy political organizer whom I liked and respected, and I'd looked forward to learning the ropes of national politics under her guidance.

"Ellie," I told her, "I'm really very angry about this! I disrupted my whole life, came to Washington to work with you, and you have the nerve to tell me you're leaving?"

"It's because you're here that I can leave," she responded.

I had always thought I would run for president eventually, but I did not yet feel ready. I still had so much to learn. There was another reason as well. I knew that if I ran for president, I'd have to deal with a disruptive loss of privacy—and with questions about my private life that I didn't want to answer in public. I had made some unconventional choices in how I was living my life, and I hadn't figured out yet how I'd frame my own honest responses—and I knew they'd have to be honest—to all the questions that would inevitably arise.

For any woman seeking power in the public arena, these questions would be unavoidable, doubly so for a feminist. Ellie, for instance, was married and lived with her husband and two children; nonetheless, she'd been subjected to a continual barrage of accusations and attacks on her sexuality. (She'd even threatened a defamation suit against one major media outlet after they'd reported that she was a lesbian. Surprised, I asked her if she considered being called a lesbian defamatory. She did not, she told me; the story was defamatory because it portrayed her as a liar—for allegedly being a lesbian but representing herself publicly as heterosexual.) Molly Yard, not only married and a mother, but a white-haired grandmother to boot, was alternately charged with being a dried-up old prune or an active lesbian.

Sexual innuendo of every conceivable stripe ("she's frigid"; "she's a lesbian"; "she slept her way to the top") is used to try to keep women out of power. If that's what our opponents made of Ellie and Molly, what would they do to me? For I had two people in my life, and one of them was a woman.

I talked it over with Ellie. As long as I was comfortable with my life choices, she said, she didn't think my concerns should stand in the way of me running or serving as president of NOW.

But if I was comfortable with my choices, I certainly wasn't comfortable—or interested in—discussing them publicly for a variety of reasons both personal and political. As I'd enthusiastically sought and gained roles of increasing political prominence in NOW—first in Florida, now nationally—the part of my life that I could call "private" had decreased proportionately. On those rare occasions when I was able to step back and gain a little perspective on things, I realized how tremendously the loss of my own privacy affected the people whom I loved most. After all, they had not chosen to have their privacy diminished or invaded; it was something they risked and suffered because they loved me. The loss of time also took its toll on my relationships as I struggled to meet the demands of learning and doing my new job. I felt responsible; I felt guilty; I felt torn apart. And I knew that, if I became president of NOW, every last shred of my private life would cease to be private altogether. I didn't look forward to that, especially since I knew just how dramatically it might happen. I also worried that the inevitable publicity might hurt NOW as well.

I alternately felt sorry for myself, angry at Ellie, and then guilty at blaming her for wanting to do something else for the women's rights movement.

All things considered, it seemed like the wrong time in my life to risk making yet another major change.

NOW officers and staff members gathered in Ellie's office late that afternoon, all hoping to change her mind. Ellie tried to make it clear to us that she really was leaving, and she made no secret that she wanted me to run for president. The atmosphere in the room was funereal.

Molly Yard took it upon herself to become Mother Hen.

"Hey!" she boomed, banging her fist on the table. "What is wrong with you people? This is a great opportunity for Ellie and a great opportunity for the movement. We should be congratulating her! We should be recommitting ourselves to do anything to help NOW after she's gone!"

"You're right, Molly! Are *you* willing to be president?"

Molly glared at me—for it had been my voice. "I don't know," she said, a little more subdued.

The whole room was silent then as we pondered the question of Ellie's successor. Then Molly jumped in again. "I do know that, whoever it is, NOW's going to stay strong! Because we're not going to accept anything less!"

Within a few days, I was spared the pain of making any immediate decisions about my future. NOW action vice president Sheri O'Dell visited me.

"I just wanted to let you know that Molly says she's willing to run for president, Patricia."

I told her that was fine with me. In truth, I was relieved. Molly serving a term as president would give me three years to prepare myself to run. Molly Yard and I came from the same NOW caucus and shared the same politics within the feminist movement. We both believed strongly in having NOW remain an independent political force; we both were unshakably committed to getting more women into policy-making positions; we both wanted to maintain and develop a powerful activist program that worked in the streets as well as the suites. Whatever conflicts she and I had were conflicts of personality and style. True, I respected rather than liked her, but we agreed that we could and would work together for the good of the organization. It was widely taken for granted in NOW circles that if I didn't try for the presidency I would run for executive vice president. I did wind up on the ticket—alongside Molly—in that position. With Ellie's help, we convinced Kim Gandy, with whom I'd served on the national board, to give up her law practice in New Orleans and run with Molly, Sheri, and me as national secretary. (It would turn out to be among the smartest moves we ever made. Kim now serves as executive vice president, and is a key member of my team of officers.)

I'm pretty sure I wasn't the only one who felt relief at having Molly head the ticket. The spotlight would be on someone else for a couple of years. Within NOW, people knew that my candidacy would have opened the organization up to a barrage of attacks at a particularly vulnerable time; and, while the other officers would have supported me against all of the lesbian-baiting that would have taken place, they preferred not to have to worry about it. So did I.

Molly's style of leadership was very different from Ellie's. Ellie had always focused on the big picture, and she was very intent on making lasting political change; anything that might fragment her ability to concentrate NOW's resources on the key issues on our agenda she'd just as soon have thrown right out into some incinerator—NOW's vast volumes of incoming mail, for instance! As president, she'd always forcefully insisted that the organization follow through with the priorities our members had established and focus on action rather than administration. (It's true, of course, that the president has a great deal of authority both by the bylaws and by the force of her personality—and Ellie has a powerful personality. But it is our chapter delegates, voting at the national conference, who set the priorities, and our national board, setting the budget, who determines how those priorities are implemented.) Both Molly and Ellie were hands-on kinds of leaders, but in totally different ways. Molly often stayed in her office late into the night, responding *by hand* to the vast numbers of letters we received.

My experience working with both of them would prove invaluable to me as I refined my own goals for the organization. Like Ellie, I thought it was important to keep our staff time and other resources focused on political and grassroots organizing. However, like Molly I also knew that many of the women writing to us—whether members or not—were desperate for our help: I myself had come into the movement because NOW offered help to me, an individual woman, when I faced discrimination. I decided I would, as president, develop ways to improve our communications, not only with those seeking help, but also with members writing in suggestions and chapter and state activists writing with their questions and comments. I would only trash incoming mail from obvious opponents and obvious loonies. On the other hand, I would only respond personally to select correspondence: The rest could be handled by one of the other radical innovations I planned—word processing and mail merge.

One of the organizational projects I enjoyed most during my time as executive vice president was initiating NOW's first National Young Feminist Conference. I knew how important young activists were and are; as they're so fond of telling us, they aren't just leaders for tomorrow, they're leaders today! I was convinced that we needed more systematic, widespread leadership development and skills training in NOW. This would make us a lot more effective at things like membership recruitment, action planning and goal setting, fund-raising, and media outreach. It would also reduce the amount of internal conflict we had within the organization. Confident, creative people also tend to be willing to learn new skills, embrace new coworkers, and try new strategies, rather than react defensively when their ideas are questioned. What we do in Washington can have little or no impact if it's not accompanied by serious organizing at the community level.

My years as NOW's executive vice president were years of tremendous political turmoil in the United States. The struggle for abortion rights was high on our agenda. In May 1988, Operation Rescue burst on the scene with four days of massive attacks on women's health clinics in the New York City area. Then in July during the Democratic National Convention, Operation Rescue began a four-month siege of abortion clinics in Atlanta. More than twelve hundred participants were arrested, at least thirty of them on felony charges—eight for assaulting a police officer, six for terrorist acts, and sixteen for false imprisonment. In early October, Operation Rescue ended the attacks in Georgia as it geared up for its first National Day of Rescue on October 29, 1988.

The emergence of Operation Rescue also pushed Randall Terry to the forefront of the violent antiabortion forces. Unlike Joe Scheidler who with his hulking figure looks the part of a villain, Terry was telegenic and charismatic enough to cover up the ugly side of his movement's activities. In Binghamton, New York, Terry was well known to the clinic staff: during a protest he organized there a pregnant clinic worker was punched in the stomach. She was taken to the hospital and miscarried several weeks later.

Publicly Operation Rescue spokespeople always claimed theirs was a peaceful movement. But training tapes distributed by Terry argued it was necessary to "physically intervene with violence . . . with force," because "that is the logical response to murder. And abortion is murder." Operation Rescue began laying the groundwork for the wave of terrorism that would lead to the antiabortion murders in the 1990s.

We continued to pursue the litigation strategy I had helped to develop in Florida, but in light of the escalating attacks we needed a short-term as well as a long-term plan of action. Local NOW activists had been defending women from attacks at clinics since at least 1985, and when Ellie Smeal brought a proposal to NOW's national board to expand this into a national program, the board voted for NOW to organize the effort. Even as I was serving temporarily as lead counsel for the antitrust complaint NOW had filed against the antiabortion extremists, as executive vice president I created NOW's proactive clinic defense program, which we called Project Stand Up for Women.

Our clinic defense strategy served several purposes. It was primarily designed to keep clinics open, and to provide a positive pro-choice presence for patients and staff alike. If the antiabortionists were going to keep on trying to close clinics down, we wanted politicians and the press to know that we were equally committed to keeping them open—and that we had enough abortion rights activists on hand to do just that. The Project also took advantage of the vast numbers of our supporters eager to stand up to the bullies at the clinics. In addition, our clinic defense strategy provided us with the opportunity to gather information for our lawsuit. We always had legal observers at each site. Their job was to gather evidence on the antiabortionists who took leadership roles. Our observers could later serve as witnesses at trial. We had photographers on site at every clinic defense; they got stills and videos of antiabortion organizers. (As a bonus, we also found that the presence of photographers served a security purpose. Clinic defenders who were being hurt began calling for the cameras instead of the police, who seldom responded as quickly as our activist photographers.)

We wanted to turn every attempted clinic blockade into an opportunity for Operation Rescue to further incriminate itself. I was also confident that, with all the information we were gathering, we'd have plenty of evidence eventually to prove racketeering charges against Joe Scheidler, Randall Terry, and their cronies. (In the fall of 1988, we finally amended our complaint to include counts under RICO and to add Randall Terry and Operation Rescue as defendants.)

In fighting for our rights against violent opposition, a free press and media can provide invaluable visibility. Unlike our long-term litigation strategy (which has only been given sporadic coverage by the mainstream press), our confrontations with the antiabortionists at the clinics often turned into media events. This was fine with us; we wanted as much public exposure of organized antiabortion terrorism as possible.

Early on, NOW's clinic defense strategy ran into a lot of fearful resistance on the part of some clinic directors—the very people it was designed to defend. Some of them seemed to believe that if they ignored the right wing's violence, it would not touch them. But the preservation of rights, like the preservation of freedom itself, requires constant vigilance—and the best strategy in the face of a campaign of violence and intimidation is to confront and expose it.

At a Planned Parenthood meeting in New York City in 1989, I found myself having to defend NOW's direct defense strategy to a group of clinic administrators who didn't want to risk getting any media attention or antagonizing antiabortion opponents. They believed—or wanted to believe—that if they just maintained a low profile the antiabortionists would leave them alone. Some of them also argued that having clinic defenders there during antiabortion attacks would create even more chaos outside their clinics and make the experience even more traumatic for their patients and staff. I could tell that some of them had been speaking with local police (who often complained that NOW's presence during an attempted clinic blockade made it more difficult for them to do their jobs).

I responded by pointing out that most police departments had hardly proven themselves worth counting on when it came to removing Operation Rescue protesters from clinic grounds. Even when the police did respond, it took them hours to clear protesters away from clinic doorways. In any case, NOW had never stopped the police from doing their job. Plenty of times, though, we had been the ones who had kept clinic doors open when the police were either unwilling or unable to do so.

My case was helped by a clinic director from a Planned Parenthood affiliate in the Midwest. "We've been attacked with and without you folks," she said, "and I'd rather have you there every time—if for nothing more than the morale of my staff." Her people felt isolated from the pro-choice community, she told us; more than anything, they wanted to know that their efforts weren't unnoticed or unappreciated.

Over the years, most of the resistance of abortion providers to NOW's clinic defense strategy evaporated. In many cases we were able to make sure that staff and doctors could get into their clinics and that women could get the services they need. And based on what we learned about Operation Rescue, our refined blueprint for action became even more effective.

The most important thing was to get to a targeted clinic first. That meant arriving early enough, and in sufficient numbers, to form a human corridor that ran from the street or parking lot up to the clinic door. Once Operation Rescue arrived, our task was to stand firm for the rest of the day. (This required a tremendous amount of sheer stamina, physical and psychological strength, commitment, restraint.) We also acted as escorts and provided moral support for staff and patients.

Operation Rescue was an organization with a strict hierarchy of command. The movement's pawns were under orders not to do anything unless instructed by their leaders, which was why, at clinic blockades, you usually saw their bigwigs running around with bullhorns. If we could cut off these lines of communication, their attack would usually falter. Our people were endlessly creative in finding ways to shut down these leaders (much like guards on a basketball court!). We'd surround those men—they were always men—chanting, singing, mooing, whatever it took to drown out the bullhorns. This looked pretty silly. But it worked.

We worked hard to avoid escalating any kinds of conflict.

One of NOW's most important strategies was to prevent the mass arrest of Operation Rescue demonstrators during blockades if access to the clinic could be kept open. Trespassing was merely a misdemeanor under the law—the equivalent of an unpaid parking ticket. And Operation Rescue wanted its people arrested; mass arrests helped them cultivate their desired public image of being willing "martyrs" for the "unborn."

Each clinic defense required extensive planning. There was simply too much at stake to leave things to chance. We found that in most targeted communities, NOW could generate crowds at least two to three times the size of Operation Rescue's. We knew the support for our work was widespread; poll after poll reiterates the fact that a majority of people support a woman's right to abortion. Part of NOW's job was to go into local communities and mobilize grassroots support: to help the housewife in Fort Wayne, Indiana, or the nurse in Buffalo, New York, make a difference.

Along with Project Stand Up for Women staff and activists, I conducted an intensive program that organized and trained tens of thousands of activists all over the country in nonviolent clinic defense techniques. We wanted individual communities to be prepared for local disturbances, and we wanted to be capable of a nationwide response to Operation Rescue's second "National Day of Rescue." (The first National Day of Rescue, in October 1988, saw Operation Rescue attack clinics in some forty cities in the United States, and in Toronto, Canada, prompting some twenty-five hundred arrests.) On the second National Day of Rescue, in April 1989, NOW officers traveled to various locations around the country to provide support for local abortion rights activists. Molly led a rally near Detroit, Michigan. Kim Gandy joined our supporters in New York City. I participated in a clinic defense in College Park, Maryland. And other national leaders took part in other events throughout the country.

By any measure, our efforts that day were a success. In Boston approximately three hundred antiabortion demonstrators were met by more than six hundred Project Stand Up for Women participants. In Los Angeles our supporters outnumbered Operation Rescue demonstrators three to one and kept a planned clinic blockade from even getting started. In Woodbridge, New Jersey, one hundred brave women and men made sure that all the patients entering and leaving an abortion clinic were fully protected from the thirty Operation Rescue demonstrators who tried to block their path.

In dealing with police departments, I always tried to understand their point of view. They hated clinic attacks as much as we did. The numbers that they needed to do their job meant that not only were off-duty cops required back on duty, but they were also forced to use police with no special training in crowd control—a potential disaster since these situations inevitably involved ugly confrontations with citizens. A defense diverted and consumed the force's energy for at least an entire day. The flood of arrests that followed could clog up a police department, especially in a small city or town, for weeks. To avoid these problems the police sometimes suggested to clinic staff that they close temporarily, anyway. They claimed not to have sufficient police power to protect them. They negotiated with everyone—even with the lawbreakers themselves, trying to reach an agreement, for instance, that Operation Rescue would be allowed to keep a clinic closed longer in exchange for an agreement that their troops would walk, instead of having to be carried, to police vans and would give their real names instead of Baby Jane or John Doe.

One of the many injustices inherent in the approach of most police departments was that they treated clinic confrontations merely as part of a war between two opposing factions, without stopping to think that one side (ours) was committed to maintaining law and constitutional guarantees, whereas the other side (Operation Rescue's) was committed to breaking the law and curtailing women's rights. The police focus was on keeping the peace, not protecting a woman's right to abortion. There were, however, plenty of law enforcement officers who saw these clinic attacks as the criminal actions they were and who were prepared to help us. Whenever possible, we tried to get local police in targeted towns to contact these officers in other cities where Operation Rescue had already hit. Police in Atlanta, for instance, were always willing to brief other jurisdictions about the group and its tactics.

NOW's primary role remains to influence society's institutions, not to provide services ourselves. Clearly, we were neither trained nor equipped to act as police. Part of our political strategy, therefore, included organizing pressure on those responsible for local law enforcement to make sure the police did their job. We also pushed for local and state laws that would create mandatory buffer zones around women's health facilities. These buffer zones would be similar to the quiet zones around hospitals. And we began to push Congress for a federal clinic access bill.

Our strategies proved successful. They gave us confidence going into volatile situations. But they could not take the anguish out of such events. Clinic defenses were emotionally and physically wrenching for everyone involved. My most visceral experiences as an activist have come while I was on clinic defense duty: an intense rush of adrenaline, mixed with a healthy dose of fear, that temporarily alters the nervous system.

Lost in the drama, of course—and, too often, neglected or ignored in our national discourse on abortion—were the women for whom these clinics provide services. Some of them stayed home to avoid the conflict, trauma, risk of public humiliation, personal injury, and death. Many, most of them poor women, with these clinics their only access to health services of any kind, were kept from receiving the help they so desperately needed. (At the clinic in Maryland I helped defend on OR's second National Day of Rescue, forty women had appointments scheduled—and canceled—that day. Ten women were coming for abortions. The other thirty were coming for a variety of gynecological procedures. One woman who hadn't gotten the word about the cancellations showed up but was prevented from entering the clinic: She had come to renew her birth control pill prescription.) Others, attempting to keep their appointments, found their very lives at stake. At clinic defenses I saw doctors and patients trapped inside cars in the sweltering heat, surrounded by violent antiabortion demonstrators. I saw women hemorrhaging on the streets outside clinics, unable to enter and receive medical treatment because of an Operation Rescue blockade.

Eventually, we did begin to see payoffs from the political and litigation strategy we'd been pursuing against Randall Terry, Joe Scheidler, and Operation Rescue.

Local prosecutors and judges began to take notice. Following

Operation Rescue's 1988 attacks in Atlanta, Randall Terry was convicted on felony charges of inciting police assault and criminal trespass. Though his bail had been paid by Moral Majority leader Jerry Falwell, Terry announced after his conviction that he would no longer pay any fines. He claimed that it would be "immoral" to do so. I felt sure it meant that, just as we'd hoped, contributions to Terry were down and he was trying to reassure donors who didn't want to see their money going to pay contempt of court or criminal fines, much less damages to clinics or NOW. After serving five months for refusing to pay his fine, Terry was released from prison in Atlanta. The fines against him had been paid anonymously; apparently Terry found that a more "moral" course of action. He went directly from jail to the Press Club in Washington to announce the closing of Operation Rescue's national headquarters in Binghamton, New York; NOW's lawsuits, he said, had driven them to the brink of bankruptcy. (Terry and OR never voluntarily paid any of the judgments or contempt of court fines resulting from our lawsuits against them.) In December 1989, federal authorities had seized two Operation Rescue bank accounts (including one for their payroll) in satisfaction of a federal court judgment. In the fall of 1990, federal marshals seized what Terry insisted was Operation Rescue's last account—getting only $1,200. (Meanwhile, we knew that OR received money filtered through other organizations, and that they opened bank accounts just long enough to cash the checks. Eventually, they turned to check-cashing operations: We knew because we were sending them small contributions to try to locate their assets.)

It became increasingly clear to us how effective our litigation strategy was. We had our own "spies" within the Operation Rescue organization. Reports began filtering in to us: The financial pressure caused by our litigation was causing a lot of disruption in the ranks; various leaders were busy blaming each other; Terry had come out of prison to try to regain his control over the organization.

At his news conference, Terry had also been forced to admit

that fewer and fewer people were willing to take part in block-ades. Spending a night in jail with their friends might have some appeal to an antiabortionist with fantasies of easy "mar-tyrdom." But when we went after their bank accounts, cars, and other material assets, the adventure quickly lost its roman-tic appeal. OR participant Adele Nathanson paid $25,000 in set-tlement of a $50,000 judgment against her for violating a court order we'd won banning clinic assaults in New York City, and we made sure that word was spread among the OR ranks.

The numbers confirmed the decrease in blockades and block-aders. Clinics belonging to the National Abortion Federation had reported 182 clinic blockades with 11,732 resulting arrests in 1988, and 201 clinic blockades with 12,358 arrests in 1989. By 1990, those numbers had dropped to 34 clinic blockades and 1,363 arrests.

In April 1990 Randall Terry announced that he was stepping aside from the day-to-day operations of Operation Rescue in order to focus his attention against "Godless, pro-abort judges who serve as lapdogs and lackeys to the National Organization of [sic] Women." He couldn't have played into our strategy more perfectly, I thought. If the U.S. attorney general started getting calls from federal judges who were being personally targeted, the federal government might finally be forced to take some action. Also, judges insist on their orders being taken seri-ously, and by this time several of them had been faced with Operation Rescue's continual contempt. And, as much as they may strive for impartiality, judges read the papers, too.

I felt as if we were making progress.

During my time as executive vice president I came to un-derstand more clearly the unique perspective I could bring to the presidency: the perspective of someone who had functioned—and functioned well—in the world outside the women's rights movement. The negotiating skills I'd learned as a business lawyer and my experience of "women's work" as a stewardess would prove useful to the organization. My work as a flight attendant, as well as my work in corporate law, gave me the ability to empathize with a wide variety of women's experiences. I also believed that these experiences enabled me to communicate with many different kinds of people, from many different backgrounds. Especially in light of the ongoing attacks we faced during the Reagan years—attacks that are only more intense now—I urgently wanted us to expand the movement, to include all the women's rights supporters who'd begun moving into positions of power, all of the people nationwide who had come to agree with our agenda, even if they didn't describe themselves as feminists. By the time I did run for NOW's presidency, I also knew that I was ready to take on that task.

As the 1990 elections drew closer, there was considerable worry about Molly's health. She'd already suffered a series of transient ischemic attacks (what laypeople refer to as mini strokes). Being president of NOW is incredibly stressful; many of us were concerned that she wasn't up to another three-year term. Sadly, Molly began to fall asleep at meetings—sometimes even in public. In the past, I'd heard her speak admiringly about an English politician who dropped dead right in the middle of a speech—just as he was gesturing dramatically to make a point. She seemed to like the idea, but none of us wanted her to die in office.

Many people in the organization were pushing for me to run for president. I too thought the time was right. George Bush's reelection effort in 1992 was going to be critical; we had a lot of feminist women ready to run for Congress. The truth also was that Molly had failed to reduce NOW's enormous debt substantially. Painful but necessary decisions had to be made; I felt that I could make them. After three years as a senior officer— three years wrestling with the hardball politics of Washington, three years of almost constant traveling, three years of expanding my knowledge about women's issues well beyond the boundaries of south Florida—I'd lost all of my earlier ambivalence about being ready to lead the organization. I was comfortable enough at the national level to feel that I knew just how the organization could change for the better, and I was eager to have a shot at putting my plans into action. As president, I would include prominently on my agenda things like aggressively implementing more grassroots strategizing and organizing to enhance our political clout, more outreach to and through the media, targeting traditional women's magazines and talk shows, and expanding the base of our membership. I wanted to do more organizational outreach to other parts of the women's movement, especially poor women and women of color who are organizing in their communities. And I wanted to strengthen our alliances with other social justice movements: the civil rights movement, the lesbian and gay rights movement, labor as well as welfare and disability rights groups. I felt there was room for us all to learn from one another, to better appreciate the different roles we all played—and to see these roles as complementary. This would help us coordinate our work more effectively.

And—after three years of really thinking through strategy, talking it over with various public relations and fund-raising people in the feminist movement, discussing it with my family and searching my own soul for some hard-to-get-at answers—I felt I was ready to deal with the inevitable controversy that would arise over my personal life.

There'd be plenty, I knew.

But Molly still wasn't ready to step down from the NOW presidency. She had some projects to wrap up; she wanted to be president for one more term. After a series of difficult, open meetings with NOW activists around the country, we reached a compromise. We'd run together again—with the understanding that in December 1991, halfway through her term, she'd retire and I would assume the presidency. Unlike many traditional decisions made in Washington, this one wasn't

reached in a smoke-filled back room. Lots of people were involved in the discussion, and all the NOW delegates to the election conference knew about the plan before they voted. Kim
Gandy agreed to continue as national secretary. We recruited a
high-energy, experienced organizer from New Jersey, Rosemary Dempsey, to join our team as action vice president, and
agreed that when Molly retired, Ginny Montes, a savvy electoral strategist who'd been born in Honduras, would join our
team. We were reelected with little opposition.

Unfortunately, things didn't go as planned. In April 1991,
ten months after reelection, Molly suffered a massive stroke
that incapacitated her for months. We tried to convince ourselves that she could manage a quick and complete recovery.
Molly was an incredible fighter; we expected her to be back at
the helm in time for the national conference in New York City
in July. And, right up until a week before the conference, Molly
herself expected to make it. But her doctor forbade her to go.

"What if I go anyway?" she asked, defiantly.

"You could have another stroke, and if you're lucky you'll
die. If you're not lucky you'll survive, and you'll spend the rest
of your life completely dependent on other people."

That was enough to convince the fiercely independent Molly.
As executive vice president, I was thrown immediately into her
place, taking over all of her duties, including that of making
the keynote speech in New York on one week's notice.

The conference created a major media splash during an otherwise slow Fourth of July weekend. We'd scheduled an action
to protest the Gag Rule (a Reagan/Bush policy that prohibited
women who use federally funded family planning centers from
receiving information on abortion). Then, just days before the
conference, President Bush nominated right-wing conservative
Clarence Thomas to replace Justice Thurgood Marshall on the
Supreme Court, and we expanded our action to include opposition to the nomination. About five thousand New Yorkers
joined us for the march up Sixth Avenue and rally at Central

Park. I was thrust into the spotlight as NOW's spokeswoman; the *New York Times* included a profile of me in its coverage.

After the conference, I decided not to do any more personal interviews until I officially became president that December. I wanted to encourage Molly in every way possible to work hard on her own rehabilitation and to return to work whenever she was able. I feared that a lot of stories about me acting as president of NOW would make her feel unneeded or prematurely pushed aside. So when *The Advocate*, a national gay magazine, called that summer asking for a personal profile, I explained why I would not do the interview until that fall—and then only on the condition that they not use it until after I took office in mid-December. They were very understanding, and, in exchange for holding off on running the story until year's end, I agreed to give their reporter an exclusive.

NOW's national board had scheduled a meeting for the first week of December. I assumed that would give me plenty of time to discuss *The Advocate* interview with all the board members; it would also give us plenty of time to alert our state coordinators and chapter leaders. I wanted to give our activists every opportunity to prepare themselves for the firestorm of controversy and political backlash that would ensue.

Alas. *The Advocate* wound up releasing advance copies of the interview to the media over Thanksgiving—a week before our board meeting. This blew my plans for alerting the NOW community in advance. Playing the angle for all it was worth, the magazine ran the interview as a cover story, with a teaser: "America's Most Powerful Woman Comes Out." As I joked later, in a National Press Club speech, I thought that was a bit of an overstatement. The part about my coming out, that is. In one sense, I had never really been "in" any closet. It's just that, before I became national president of NOW, my personal life wasn't news.

In another sense, though, I had not "come out" at all. I had carefully crafted what I would be willing to say publicly about my life. What I told *The Advocate*—and seemingly dozens of other suddenly curious newspapers and magazines—was this: I have a husband, and he is very important in my life. I also have a companion, and she is very important in my life, too.

Most of the interviews that followed were spent trying to explain why I would not claim the label "lesbian" or "bisexual" or any other label to describe my sexuality.

I knew that no matter what I said about my personal life, I could not avoid being the target of unwanted commentary, so personally and politically, it was important for me to find the right balance. I wanted to be open, to avoid being hypocritical. But I wanted to be seen as a whole person. I also needed to draw the line at what I considered appropriate to discuss publicly. I'll defend to the end another person's right to decide otherwise, but I decided that for me the line stopped at talking about my love life.

The more of a public figure I have become, the more I have felt a need to maintain some zone of privacy in my life. The presidency of NOW is a workaholic's dream; the work is urgently important and there's always more of it to do. Even as an ambitious attorney in a competitive field, working overtime on the ERA countdown campaign, I'd been able to share more time with family and friends than I could as president of NOW. In other words, whether I took it public or not, I already had precious little that was "private." I also felt keenly responsible for protecting my loved ones from harm.

These were the private reasons. The political reasons boiled down to this: I am absolutely determined to resist our culture's obsession with evaluating women on the basis of our sexuality. Some women might resist this reductivism by claiming the right to define their sexuality in public on their own terms. I have resisted by saying (in more polite terms), "It's none of your business." By refusing to participate in that game, I feel I can underscore just how strong society's need is to characterize and judge women in sexual terms—and that it's unacceptable to me.

In the past, society rested on a thorough presumption of heterosexuality and more emphasis was placed on whether women were chaste, fertile, and could produce a son to inherit the family's wealth (thus ensuring the legitimation of the male bloodlines). The question "gay or straight?" didn't come up. Today the presumption of heterosexuality is less universal because in recent decades, lesbians, gays, bisexuals, transgendered, and transsexuals have staked a positive claim to the labels. But women are still measured by our physical attractiveness and our compliance with the expectation of sexual availability to men.

What became clear to me during the first few months of my NOW presidency was that many people don't seem to know how to act around a woman if they have no neatly packaged way to define her sexually.

When it comes to questions of sex, my own life has been something of a roller coaster, with all of the thrill as well as the fear of that exciting ride. I bear the legacy of having grown up in the Indiana heartland in the 1950s, hardly an atmosphere that promoted clarity or openness about sexual issues. While I'd eagerly tried to participate in the sexual revolution of the 1960s, I'd never quite been able to rid myself of a profound ambivalence, especially in light of the double standard for women and men.

When I first became a women's rights activist, I still carried with me the legacy of being raised on the idea that sex was absolutely not something to discuss in public. So, although I wasn't aware of making any conscious decision to do so, I concentrated my efforts on issues like economic and legal equality for women—nice, clean issues untainted by sex. As a lawyer I stayed the path: I helped form the Florida Feminist Credit Union, which gave women access to loans; I took employment discrimination cases; I advocated the Equal Rights Amendment. Subconsciously, perhaps (and in any case, naively), I actually believed that these were somehow safe issues that would not jeopardize my standing as a respectable downtown lawyer.

I also cared passionately about improving women's lives, and it seemed to me then that we had the greatest chance for progress on economic issues. By the time I became active in the Equal Rights Amendment campaign, most people understood that economic opportunity for women was only fair. Even the most conservative politicians would preface an attack on feminism or the ERA by saying something like "I believe in equal pay for equal work, but . . ." By the mid-seventies, few were willing to say—out loud, at any rate—that women didn't deserve equal pay, equal educational opportunities, equal access to credit.

The sexual issues, however, were a different story. And they still are today. I never saw economic issues as a shrine before which all our other concerns ought to be sacrificed. But abortion and lesbian and gay rights were emotionally provocative issues that could be cast in moral terms, allowing opponents to demonize anyone who advocated them. I worried that raising these more controversial concerns would hurt the movement. At best, the so-called "radical" sexual issues could distract the general public from other matters that impacted on a much broader cross section of women. At worst, of course, this might stymie the entire movement, and thus make economic equality harder to realize. So I was receptive to the argument that we could make progress on equal employment, education, and credit—not to mention child care and recognition of homemaking as work—if we'd only stop trying to shove things like abortion rights or lesbian rights down people's throats. The temptation to try to consolidate our gains on these more widely acceptable issues, which a majority of people seemed to agree with, was great.

I'd seen firsthand the frightening strength of antigay fervor fifteen years before in Miami. In 1976, Dade County Commissioner Ruth Shack had found herself in the center of a political minefield when she sponsored one of the nation's first human rights ordinances banning discrimination based on sexual orientation in housing, public accommodations, and employment. On January 18, 1977, by a vote of five to three, the commission passed the ordinance. Almost immediately a vicious campaign to repeal it was launched. Its titular head was the scripture-spouting singer Anita Bryant, well known at the time as spokeswoman for Florida orange juice. (Just like her political cousin Rush Limbaugh, many years later. Is there something in that juice?)

Bryant and friends named their anti–gay rights group "Save Our Children." They stoked a hysterical fear in the community, equating homosexuality with pedophilia and claiming that stopping discrimination against gays and lesbians would lead to the widespread molestation of small children by homosexual teachers and police officers. Within six months, Dade County voters repealed the ordinance by a vote of 208,504 to 92,212. Even Commissioner Shack seemed chastened by the loss. Her reelection campaign in 1978 was brutal. Inspired by her courage and leadership, I volunteered to help—it was one of my first ventures into the battlefield of electoral politics. Most of my time was spent sitting in a windowless room phoning long lists of voters. But phonebanking suited me just fine. Insecure as I was about being linked with "the gay rights candidate," I was glad for the invisibility.

The phonebank script I was told to stick to made clear that Shack's campaign advisers felt it was necessary for her to distance herself from the very ordinance she'd introduced. At the top of the page were instructions on how to respond if the person on the other end asked about the antidiscrimination law.

"This election is not about gay rights," we were told to say, "the voters have already spoken on that issue." Then we were supposed to steer the conversation to a safer topic. Looking over the script, I silently surveyed my fellow phonebankers. Of the fifteen or so in that room, ten were probably gay men. Others, like myself, were there because of, not in spite of, Shack's leadership on gay rights and other feminist issues. Who were we trying to kid?

To me, that campaign epitomized the political dilemma facing feminists. Shack won reelection, which seemed to confirm her strategy of downplaying the gay rights issue, and as a result, she was able to continue bringing her much-needed perspective as a feminist and gay rights advocate to the commission. On the other hand, by downplaying her own commitment to gay rights, she seemed to be validating the political closet.

Over the years I have learned that sexual issues cannot be isolated from the rest of our politics, any more than sexuality can be separated from the rest of our lives. Our opposition acknowledges the indivisibility of these hot-button issues, too; and they wouldn't let us ignore them even if we wanted to.

During the ERA campaign, while we were emphasizing the discrepancy in men's and women's wages, Phyllis Schlafly, lead anti-ERA campaigner and prominent skirt for male pols and business interests to hide behind, was arguing that the ERA meant abortion on demand, homosexual marriages, and unisex toilets. In the late 1970s, her monthly newsletter warned about the potential evils of the ERA with headlines like WOMAN CABBY RAPED, CO-ED WARDS TIED TO RAPES AT PSYCHIATRIC UNIT, and THE AN-DROGYNY TREND. Trying to scare her readers into thinking that passage of the ERA would have apocalyptic effects on our society, she hammered away at the issue of lesbian and gay rights, continually warning her readers about the "dangers" of homosexual marriage. Of course, she linked the women's rights movement to lesbianism, releasing special "studies" like "NOW, Lesbians, and ERA."

This campaign had an effect. The arguments about the ERA were diverted from the question of whether ERA supporters had valid economic and legal arguments; instead, they shifted to whether we represented the "average" woman or were radical lesbians seeking to destroy the family.

The impact of this became obvious to me during an early experience with the divisiveness of homophobia. I remember it well: I had never seen Leanne Seibert so angry. As I walked into our Dade County offices that final year of the Equal Rights Amendment Countdown Campaign, a fuming Leanne confronted me, waving a newspaper around and muttering something about slander.

"Look at this stupid piece of trash, Patricia!"

It was a copy of a newspaper from Hialeah. Leanne had circled an anti-ERA editorial and, in blazing red ink, she'd underlined a sentence claiming that the board of Dade County NOW was "100 percent lesbian."

"They'll be sorry they printed that lie! We'll sue them!"

"And say what, Leanne?" I quipped. "That only *half* the board is queer?"

I was trying to defuse a volatile situation. But I also wanted Leanne to think about what she was saying. She's a strong, committed feminist; I have never once viewed her as homophobic. But as soon as some right-wing rag called her a lesbian, she started screaming defamation. She reacted the way most of us are conditioned to react whenever someone questions our heterosexuality.

On the other hand, who was *I* to give Leanne lessons? I wasn't anywhere near as blasé about that article as I'd pretended to be. My immediate instinct for humor hid my own discomfort. To me, lesbian rights and abortion were murky swamps that I, too, was trying to navigate on a personal as well as a political level.

NOW itself had struggled initially with those issues, too. In 1967, a year after the organization's founding, NOW members at the second national conference adopted legalization of abortion as a priority. But NOW lost a number of members who felt strongly that the organization should stick to economic issues. In those early years, many NOW members also tried to keep lesbian activists out of NOW chapters. Betty Friedan made national headlines when she warned against the so-called "Lavender Menace." But in 1971, delegates at NOW's National Conference voted strongly that lesbian and gay rights should be considered a feminist issue, and again we lost some members over that.

By 1975, NOW had included lesbian and gay rights as a national priority. At the International Women's Year Conference in Houston in 1977—the broadest-based, most democratically elected meeting of women in our country's history—Betty Friedan herself helped lead a successful campaign to include a lesbian rights plank in the U.S. Plan of Action.

It's significant, though, that despite this history of gradual acceptance on the part of the women's rights movement the controversy over lesbian rights has never really ended altogether. Many good women's rights supporters continue to cling to the illusion that we could win other priorities on the agenda if only we'd abandon this one.

Looking back on the history of the modern feminist movement, I'm confident that the industries that profit from discrimination against women and the politicians who are indebted to those industries would not have suddenly embraced the ERA even if every lesbian had been purged from the ranks of the movement and shoved back into the closet nationwide. Somehow, too, I doubt that the U.S. Chamber of Commerce or the National Manufacturers Association would have encouraged George Bush to sign the Family and Medical Leave Act if we'd only been willing to turn our backs on young women's and poor women's right to abortion. But in my early years of activism, none of this was quite so clear to me.

My own father personalized the dilemma. When I went to visit my folks, he would pick me up at the airport wearing an ERA YES button. And he could work up a lot of righteous indignation over the fact that, as a woman lawyer, I might not have the same career opportunities as a man. But during the 1977 Dade County fight over the human rights ordinance, he'd argued vehemently that lesbians and gays should not be allowed to become teachers, or child care workers, or anything else that brought them into contact with children. My own uncertainty in defending my position at the time made me that much more adamant and angry in response. But after the defeat of the ordinance at the polls, we let the subject drop.

My mother stepped into the picture characteristically by sending me a newspaper clipping. I was surprised to open it to a short article she'd also shared with my father. Under the headline CHILDREN OF GAY PARENTS NORMAL, the article cited a study showing that children of homosexuals were no more likely than those of heterosexuals to turn out gay themselves.

I was pleased with her for sending it, and I was probably overeager to show it to Janet Canterbury, who was still a relatively new friend. I wasn't prepared for her angry response. In fact, she exploded.

"That's an insult, Patricia! What do they mean, 'normal'? Where do they get off, implying that we're some kind of abnormal freaks?"

My face fell; I'd brought her the article as proof of my family's feminist enlightenment. On the other hand, I could understand her anger at being characterized as "abnormal." But my capacity for lawyerly talk kicked in: "As a scientist, you know good and well that the term refers to the frequency of occurrence. Even taking the highest estimates, you must admit that being gay falls outside the statistical norm." That was my best defense.

I couldn't help but be a little chagrined, though, at how much I had to learn.

(Later, Janet would say that my discomfort with sexual issues was probably more regional than familial. She's always claimed that women from the Midwest can hardly stand having bodily functions, much less talking about them; whereas women from the South revel in such talk among themselves, especially about their "female troubles." I have to admit that she had Midwesterners of my generation pretty well pegged.)

Getting to know Janet and NOW's other lesbian activists greatly eased any early discomfort I had working on lesbian and gay rights and deepened my love for all women, in the end. When I think about the life of our action vice president, Rosemary Dempsey, for example, I can't imagine *not* addressing lesbian rights as part of the feminist agenda.

In June 1980 Rosemary had to fight to keep custody of her son and daughter. This was a precedent-setting case (*Belmont* v. *Belmont*), one of the first to establish—no, to acknowledge—that two lesbians could provide a good home and family for their children.

Many years later Rosemary had to go to court again: this time to win the right to care for her own mother, who had Alzheimer's. Other family members argued (unsuccessfully, thank goodness) that Rosemary's mother would be better off spending her final days in an institution, rather than with a loving lesbian family.

At the time of Rosemary's child custody case, even some members of NOW's national board had argued that we should not get involved for fear of hurting the organization. But the majority voted to support her. Eventually, more and more of us became convinced that working on lesbian and gay rights issues would actually strengthen the movement. Political movements must be built on idealism and principle. And fighting for civil rights for all of us is, quite simply, the right thing to do. After my election to NOW's national board as Southeast regional director in 1980, I had also become convinced that another, very pragmatic reason exists for feminists to make lesbian and gay civil rights a priority: fear of being identified as a lesbian is used to scare women away from the women's rights movement.

When I was regional director during the final year of the ERA Countdown Campaign, I began an informal experiment during new member sessions in my chapter. I'd ask participants how many of them had mentioned to a family member, friend, or coworker that they were coming to a NOW meeting that night. Quite a few hands would go up. Then I'd ask, "How many of you got a response like 'That bunch of dykes!'? Or something more subtle like 'I thought you were married!'?'' Invariably, most of those same hands were raised again, accompanied by nervous laughter—and sighs of relief. They weren't alone.

I continue to conduct this informal experiment today—with exactly the same results—when I give speeches on college campuses across the country. And for every person who comes to a chapter meeting or speech despite antigay comments from family and peers, I wonder how many have been scared away. Homophobia is effectively used to keep women in line regardless of our sexual orientation.

As I saw firsthand how homophobic fear was manipulated to weaken and divide the feminist movement, I became more and more committed to taking a public stand on the issue. As regional director, I actively encouraged NOW chapters in the Southeast to organize lesbian rights projects. When Janet Canterbury was elected president of Florida NOW in 1982, I asked her to appoint me chair of the new state Lesbian Rights Task Force. I'd come a long way!

The fact is that, while my heart and brain said that standing up was the right thing, my stomach still had a way to go. I continued to worry about the reaction among clients and partners at Arky, Freed: Would they be freaked out because one of their lawyers took a public stand on this particular issue? Would I be testing the limits of their tolerance for the rest of my feminist work? Eventually, I convinced myself that the risk of consequences did not outweigh my responsibility to work on a civil rights issue I'd come to see as fundamental. And if that put my standing in the business or legal community at risk, so be it. I knew I was a good lawyer. And Arky, Freed was a progressive law firm; otherwise, I'd never have worked there. If my public stance bothered some of my more straitlaced colleagues, maybe I could use the opportunity to talk with them and help change their perceptions.

Over the next few years, I became so visible on the topic of lesbian and gay rights that, when the post office handled anything addressed to "Lesbian Rights Task Force, One Biscayne

Tower'' they knew which firm in the thirty-eight-story building to deliver it to, and my firm's mailroom knew to send it to
my office. And when none of the consequences I'd feared came
to pass, I gradually moved from being afraid to becoming more
and more outspoken and willing to tolerate the social tension
of raising issues that made me and others uncomfortable.

In the fall of 1985 I was invited to be keynote speaker at
what I called the take-a-judge-to-dinner banquet organized by
my old friends at the Florida Association for Women Lawyers.
The room was filled to capacity that night with professionals
all dressed up and on their best behavior. I began my speech re-
creating some of the more amusing cultural clashes that had
taken place at that year's NOW conference in New Orleans,
which had received widespread media coverage because of Ellie
Smeal's upset victory in a bitterly contested election for president. (I must confess that I thought Andrea Dworkin et al.
moving through the French Quarter on a Saturday night during the NOW conference gluing paper plates on top of explicit
ads for strip shows made quite a show themselves—one I'm
sure the tourists on Bourbon Street still talk about to this day.)
I moved on, in my speech, to suggest that members of the audience plan fall vacations in Vermont and enjoy the foliage while
canvassing door-to-door to support a state ERA on the ballot
there. Then I took a deep breath and began to talk about lesbian
and gay rights.

A hush fell over the audience. Later one of my friends who
had been seated at a table in the back of the room reported
overhearing a woman whispering to her neighbor, ''But I
thought she was married!''

''Well,'' the other woman hissed back, indignantly, ''she's *not*
wearing a ring!''

This comment confirmed beyond even my capacity for denial
that by speaking out on lesbian and gay rights, I was inviting
questions about my sexuality. There was no way around it. But
avoiding gay rights does not guarantee immunity from such
questions. Straight, lesbian, bisexual, or ''no-comment,'' any

woman who tries to take a place in the public sphere has to contend with opponents who will find any number of ways to use sexual or gender issues against her. This had become painfully clear to me at the 1984 Democratic National Convention in San Francisco.

NOW had waged a big campaign to get a woman on the ticket in 1984, and I'd been an energetic participant and organizer. When Walter Mondale came to the NOW conference in Miami Beach that year, I had helped organize the enormous floor demonstration which greeted him with chants, "Run with a woman! Win with a woman!" That July, I happily traveled to the Democratic National Convention as a Mondale delegate.

That convention should have been one of the peak moments of my career as a feminist activist. Geraldine Ferraro had just been named as Walter Mondale's vice presidential running mate—the first woman ever to run on the presidential ticket of any major party in our history. But that same convention also included one of my darkest days as a feminist—one that still makes me cringe when I remember it, more than a decade later.

The night Ferraro accepted her party's nomination, I was absolutely elated. Many of the male delegates had yielded their seats to female alternates. For the first time ever, a National Convention floor was filled with the proud faces of women. Even those of us who consider ourselves hard-nosed, hardball-playing political veterans were a little misty-eyed that night. (At the same time, before the new vice presidential candidate gave her acceptance speech, we were careful to whisper to her under our breath, "Don't *you* cry!")

But my exhilaration that night was matched by my sinking feelings the following day.

It began when I jumped into the taxi that was waiting to take me from my hotel to San Francisco's Moscone Convention Center. I didn't know what the day would hold, but all good things seemed possible. We had a woman running for vice president! The taxi driver delivered the first blow.

"What'll happen if Mondale gets elected?" he asked, turning

to face me with a goofy grin. "What?" I asked faintly. I had the feeling I wasn't going to appreciate his reply. I didn't. "We'll have *three* boobs in the White House!" he guffawed, and peeled out onto the road. When I didn't laugh, he glared at me in the mirror. "Ahhh. You feminists have got no sense of humor anyway."

I guess I wanted to prove him wrong about that. Feminists *do* have a sense of humor. If we didn't, we wouldn't be able to survive. So I spent the rest of the ride regaling him with every antimale joke I'd ever heard. "What do you call gross stupidity?" I asked him, happily delivering the punch line: "One hundred forty-four men!"

He didn't laugh at that—or at any of my other jokes, either. Maybe cabbies just don't have a sense of humor.

But if responding in kind made me feel better for the duration of the ride, my brothers at the Democratic Convention did their best to kill what remained of my good mood. The first thing I noticed upon returning to the scene of the previous night's triumph was the new batch of campaign buttons being sported on far too many lapels:

FRITZ AND TITS.

Ferraro had been a vice presidential candidate for less than twenty-four hours, but she was already being reduced to her body parts. I was indignant, not to mention disgusted. For all her apparent heterosexuality, Geraldine was as susceptible to the slings and arrows of sexual politics as any other woman striving for a fair share of power.

W omen leaders and politicians have had their sexuality challenged from the earliest stirrings of the feminist movement in this country. Although they could not bring themselves to use the word *lesbian* or *sapphist*, newspapers in 1848 did describe participants at the first women's rights conference in Seneca Falls, New York, as "mannish," and pointedly noted, too, that Susan B. Anthony was a "spinster." The goal, then as now, was to make women retreat from activism—and from each other.

During NOW's 1990 national conference in Los Angeles, at a lunch meeting we had arranged with top women politicians who had come to the conference to help raise money for the NOW PAC, I had a chance to hear some stories from the front lines of this war. At a private room at the L.A. Hilton, Ellie Smeal, Molly Yard, Janet Canterbury, Kim Gandy, and I were treated to lunch with a veritable Dream Team of political talent. Sitting at the table were Democratic candidates Dianne Feinstein, Barbara Roberts, and Josie Heath. Feinstein and Roberts were running for governor of California and Oregon. Heath had set her sights on the U.S. Senate seat from Colorado. Barbara Hafer, who was campaigning for reelection as auditor general of Pennsylvania, kept Janet from being the only Republican at the table. Our hope was that this lunch would be a chance for us to get to know these women a little better. There was no set agenda. After Roberts brought up how upset she'd been at some recent lesbian-baiting in her campaign, the conversation quickly became a forum on sexual politics.

We listened as, one by one, each politician related the same kinds of war stories. Whether married, divorced, single, with or without children, Republican or Democrat, each of these candidates had suffered similar attacks. And not all their attackers were frothing-at-the-mouth homophobes or obvious right-wingers. Pete Wilson, Feinstein's opponent in the race for California governor, was hardly Jesse Helms; yet his supporters had begun a whisper campaign against Feinstein, accusing her of being a lesbian.

Aside from being labeled "lesbians," the women in that room had other things in common. They were all confident, competent, ambitious, assertive, and advocated women's rights. These qualities are, to my way of thinking, what their opponents really mean to attack when they call them—or you, or me—"lesbians." No matter what our backgrounds—no matter what our true sexuality—all women leaders have to deal with this.

NOW has learned to incorporate this reality in the advice we give to women political candidates and activists alike. "Before you start, you'd better map out a strategy for how you're going to respond when you start getting called a lesbian," we counsel. "It's not a question of whether you're gay or straight, and it's not a question of *whether* it's going to happen; it's just a question of *when*."

This became glaringly clear once again when Janet Reno became the Clinton administration nominee for attorney general.

Here's how Reno, a model of self-deprecation and the highest-ranking law enforcement official in the United States, introduced herself to the nation at the National Press Club on July 1, 1993: "I'm not anything different from what you see. I am a fifty-four-year-old, awkward old maid who is not a great speaker. I can be impatient. I do have a temper. My mother accused me of mumbling. I am not a good housekeeper. I don't put much priority on housekeeping. . . . My fifth-grade teacher said I was bossy. My family thinks I'm opinionated and sometimes arrogant. And they would be happy to supply you with other warts that I have, too."

After Zoë Baird and Kimba Wood had both been forced to withdraw their names from consideration for the post—the press had really gone to town with "Nannygate"—I began joking that the only woman who could get the job would be a childless woman with a dirty house. Apparently the White House took the idea seriously. As did Reno, who described herself that way.

No sooner had everyone breathed a sigh of relief that Reno would not have a problem over household help than tongues started wagging again and rumors abounded . . . about the new nominee's sexuality.

"Oh, a woman in her fifties? Never married? Hmmm . . ."

As a single, middle-aged woman with no children, Reno may as well have had a sign COULD BE A LESBIAN painted in bright red letters on her forehead. The minute her name surfaced for the position of attorney general, the buzz around Washington wasn't about whether she was tough or qualified enough to handle the job; her professional history made it clear that she was. What inquiring minds wanted to know was whether Reno was heterosexual.

I may have inadvertently fed that speculation when I mentioned to a couple of journalists that I'd played softball against Reno in a women lawyers' league back in the late 1970s in Miami. The point I'd been trying to make was that Reno, whom I admire greatly, was tough and assertive and had a single-minded sense of purpose; you didn't want to be in her way when she ran bases. But these reporters acted like playing softball was a sure sign of lesbianism. (Back in my Indiana junior high school in the late 1950s, kids used to say the same thing about wearing yellow on Thursdays.)

This wasn't the first time Reno's sexuality had been used as a political football. In 1988, a born-again antipornography crusader, John B. Thompson, tried to unseat Reno as state attorney in Dade County by claiming she was a closeted lesbian. During one campaign event, he handed her a piece of paper on which was printed a multiple-choice question, and announced to the crowd that he'd give her four days to answer. The sheet read: *I, Janet Reno, am a* ☐ *homosexual,* ☐ *bisexual,* ☐ *heterosexual.* At that point, Reno put a hand on Thompson's shoulder pityingly. "I'm only interested in virile men," she told him. "That's why I'm not attracted to *you.*" This moment of inspiration prompted Thompson to file battery charges against Reno. The charges were thrown out of court. Thompson also lost the election campaign.

He later tried to avenge himself by badgering the Clinton administration with tasteless (and baseless) rumors about Reno's sexual behavior. Ironically, the only group that seemed to take him seriously was the gay rights group Queer Nation, which specializes in "outing" public officials. They called a press conference to state that the new attorney general was "more likely than not" a lesbian.

Reno apparently felt compelled to deny not just that she was a lesbian, but that she had any sexuality at all. By that time a veteran of sexual politics—and of playing political hardball— she was adept at using the "awkward old maid" routine as an effective low-key defense. When asked point-blank about her sexuality at a Miami Airport press conference, she gave her standard reply: "The fact is I'm just an awkward old maid with a very great affection for men."

Implying that she was straight-but-celibate was not an option for another powerful insider, Roberta Achtenburg. When President Clinton and Housing and Urban Development Secretary Henry Cisneros nominated her for the position of assistant secretary for Fair Housing at HUD (which would make her the highest-ranking open gay ever to serve in an administrative position), conservatives immediately attacked her as a lesbian. North Carolina Senator Jesse Helms, relishing his self-designated role as arbiter of our morality, called Achtenburg a "damn lesbian." Furthermore (he told anyone willing to listen) she wasn't just "a garden variety lesbian." She was "a militant activist mean lesbian, working her whole career to advance the homosexual agenda."

"What's the difference between a lesbian and a 'damn lesbian'?" I began asking audiences whenever I gave a speech. "A 'damn lesbian' is politically active."

It wouldn't have seemed so funny if these slings and arrows had somehow managed to keep Achtenburg from serving in the government. But the Senate confirmed her by a strong vote of 58–31; even Senator Sam "Don't Ask, Don't Tell" Nunn voted in her favor.

Lewd bosses and crude coworkers try to use sex to keep women "in their place," just as much as cynical politicians do. Men who feel threatened by having to compete with women on an equal basis often try to shove the relationship back into a sexual context, in which, since the Garden of Eden, men have been dominant—and women have taken the blame. They sometimes use sexual harassment and lesbian-baiting as a one-two punch.

While serving in the Persian Gulf War, Captain Victoria A. Hudson, a NOW activist from Florida, was repeatedly harassed by her section leader, a battalion operations officer with the rank of major. He refused to give Captain Hudson time off duty unless she wrote him an erotic letter. When she objected, he spread the rumor among the ranks that she was a lesbian.

Women seeking to break into nontraditional fields—whether as politicians or soldiers, neurosurgeons or welders—often face sexual harassment. But they also face the accusation that such harassment would not befall them if they were only a bit more "virtuous."

Any adult behavior on the part of a woman opens her to potential allegations of sexual misconduct. Any woman, no matter what her sexuality, can find herself under attack just because she is perceived as being sexual. When I was in law school, we were taught that the perfect rape victim, from the prosecutor's viewpoint, was a woman who was old enough to tell her story but too young to have ever smoked a cigarette, had a drink, or gone on a date. Anyone else would prove fair game for the popular, effective, and easy "blame-the-victim" defense. I remember reading, in the 1970s, that the increase in rape on military bases was one of the problems caused by women in the military! It sounded like a problem caused by *men* in the military to me. But try to offer a feminist analysis of that absurd charge, and it's likely to be dismissed or attacked by antifeminists as evidence of "man-hating" or of some other deep-rooted sexual psychosis.

Women leaders of any kind are also plagued by those who insist that their activism is merely a manifestation of sexual frustration. Oklahoma NOW president LoReacy Moses found this out when she took on the University of Oklahoma athletic department.

The school's athletic director had begun making weekly

radio broadcasts from Hooters, a restaurant chain whose logo
is an owl with eyes designed to look like a woman's breasts; the
waitresses are required to wear tight T-shirts and miniskirts as
their uniform. LoReacy and other NOW activists in Norman,
Oklahoma, protested that this broadcast from Hooters encouraged sexual harassment in the athletic department and created
an atmosphere in which women were not taken seriously—
either as athletes or as employees. Driving her teenaged sons to
school one morning, she turned on the radio in time to hear a
local deejay deliver his analysis of the Hooters controversy: All
LoReacy Moses needed to clear her mind, he said, was "a good
screw."

This is a classic mode of attack against women who speak
out; it demeans our political stance by claiming that we seek
power in order to soothe frustration over some alleged inability
to "catch a man"; and, at the same time, it implies the threat
of sexual assault as "deserved" punishment for daring to step
out of line.

So the dangers of advocating for controversial positions, of
speaking out on your own or someone else's behalf, are real.
I long ago grew strong enough to take a confident stand on
these issues in public, but in the aftermath of *The Advocate*'s
story, I had to examine how I was embodying that belief in
my own life. Other people may take a different road and speak
proudly to the world about their sexual identity (or identities)
and the choices they've made. I am no less proud of who I am,
but even with all I've learned, the Midwesterner in me would
still rather be left alone to muddle through my relationships
and sexual choices in private. I have tried to be honest about
my life, while insisting that women, including me, are much
more than the sum of our sexual activities. I believe that together we are making progress toward a world that is a more
open and, yes, safer place.

In the days of our grandmothers and great-grandmothers,

women were constrained from having any sexuality at all. Corsets, chastity belts, and in some cultures genital mutilations, religious strictures, social conventions, and laws, served to control and restrict this area of women's lives. Sexual pleasure—although it most certainly occurred—was not supposed to be among the things a proper woman wanted. You could say that the first "closet" encompassed the entire realm of women's sexual expression!

Entwined with all of this have been the very real risks for women who have permitted themselves sexual expression. Nevertheless, even in the teeth of enormous social sanctions and personal costs, women as a whole and individually have made great progress in honoring of our own sexual choices, in freeing ourselves to express our sexual natures honestly. I myself have made unconventional choices in my personal life—and I have known other women who have made their own, very individual, life decisions. Whether it's the choice to be out as a lesbian or bisexual, or to say "no comment"; to be single and celibate or to have multiple partners; to devise alternative families or to affirm our right to marry and have children in conventional nuclear family structures, I see the decision to make our own choices as empowering and necessary, even when we feel we might be making mistakes, wrong turns, or be heading into uncharted territory altogether. Though some of our nearest and dearest may be displeased and try to enforce their way of looking at the world, and though we may fear—rightly or wrongly—society's retribution, the important thing to understand is that we *do* have choices. The essence of feminism for me is the freedom to live our lives as we please, and to reinvent the world as we do so. The risks are there. But so is the possibility for progress.

In many ways, the entire history of social progress is the history of movements and individuals presenting ideas that at first seem so radical as to threaten the very stability of that society and that then go on to become accepted as essential to a just society. This was true of the transition from monarchy to

our form of representative government; it was true of the abo-
lition of slavery. That's how we got voting rights for women,
racial integration, the introduction of the eight-hour workday,
and an end to child labor. In the late 1960s, when NOW first
advocated public child care and early childhood development
programs, like Headstart, child care was seen as a commie plot.
Now all but the most conservative politicians understand that
with so many families dependent on the income of women to
survive, child care programs are a national necessity. The same
historical process will mean the universal acceptance of other
feminist goals eventually, including the right to make our own
sexual choices and a guarantee of full civil rights no matter
what those choices are.

If I seem overly optimistic that sexuality, sex, or gender can
be eradicated as political weapons, there are a couple of reasons.
First, optimism is the life's blood of political activists. If I didn't
think we could change society, I'd still be managing corporate
takeovers in downtown Miami.

I know that attitudes and opinions can change. If we keep
advocating our positions honestly, consistently, persuasively,
we ultimately have a great effect. Take my father: In 1977,
during the campaign against the Dade County human rights
ordinance, he and I were at loggerheads about lesbian and gay
civil rights. In those days he seemed as intractable on this issue
as anyone I've ever come across. But in 1983, he and I were
pushing a shopping cart together through the Publix supermarket in Punta Gorda, Florida (where he and my mother had
retired several years earlier). I told him how nervous I'd been
when they'd made the move. He seemed surprised.

"I knew I'd been singing the praises of Florida for years, Dad.
Every time I wrote or talked to you during the winter, I'd make
sure to mention that it was eighty degrees down here before I
asked about the latest snowstorm in Indiana. But when you
said you were going to move, I wasn't so sure. You'd lived in
Valparaiso for so long. All your friends were there. I was afraid
you'd be homesick and hate it here, and it would be all my

fault. But I shouldn't have underestimated you like that. You're getting more out of Florida than I am! When you and Mom got certified for scuba diving, I really started to feel better about getting older myself.''

''I don't like the getting-old part,'' he admitted. ''But I *am* glad to find that, as I get older, I'm still willing to learn new things. And I don't just mean the diving. Remember those fights we had about Anita Bryant and the gay rights ordinance? How could I ever have argued against it! *Of course* we need civil rights for everyone! No one should be discriminated against. I don't even know what I was thinking.''

Has any daughter ever gotten a better present from a parent?

SEVEN

When I became president of NOW in December 1991, one of my first steps was an energetic campaign to reach out to women beyond NOW's membership. One vehicle would be the mainstream media, especially those magazines and television and radio shows that attracted large numbers of women readers, viewers, and listeners. It had been easy for feminist leaders to discount some of these mass-market outlets in the past: Twenty years earlier, for instance, every major women's magazine in the country was headed by a man, and there was little room in their pages for what we had to say. Now, nearly all of those magazines are headed by women—many of whom call themselves feminists—and I wanted to get to know them and their readers. I made appointments with the editors-in-chief or editorial boards of every women's magazine that would see me.

In early 1992, I was in the New York offices of *Glamour* magazine. Even though I'd been assured by Kim Gandy that *Glamour* actually paid a lot of attention to women's issues, I'll admit that I was on my guard. The cover of the first issue I saw in the office was hyping a story on "The Kissiest Lips." I became acutely aware that my own lips were conspicuously unpainted.

As I hung my coat in a small alcove near the receptionist's desk, though, I saw something that made me feel right at home. Hanging on the bulletin board in the coatroom was a sign-up sheet for *Glamour*'s bus to the March for Women's Lives—the massive abortion rights and reproductive freedom march that NOW was organizing. I immediately smiled to myself: I looked forward to seeing the kissy lips of the *Glamour* delegation in Washington in the spring. So much for the stereotypical image of women's rights supporters.

I did the daytime talk show circuit: *Donahue, Sally Jessy Raphael, Rolonda*. I wrote commentary for *Elle* on the priorities of the women's movement and for *Ebony* on the impact Dr. Martin Luther King, Jr., had on my life.

The large national advertisers of cosmetics and cleaning products that support the women's magazines have exerted a great deal of control over what does and doesn't go into those publications over the years: they seem to think that serious issues don't put readers in a buying mood. But those readers must want more from a magazine than pleasantries, because they have demanded and, with the advent of women editors, have gotten more straight talk on women's issues. When I met with the editor of *Ladies' Home Journal*, the first thing she said about her readership was that they were "mainstream, mainstream, mainstream!" But she went on to say, "And they're angry about the same things NOW's members are angry about—whether it's sexual harassment, date rape, or lack of research on breast cancer—regardless of whether or not they call themselves feminists!"

Being president of NOW means that I have to be constantly wary of preaching to the converted. It's important to reach out to a wider audience as often as possible. It's easy to keep giving the same speech, over and over, and fun to talk to supporters who are already on the bandwagon. But that doesn't do much to broaden the appeal or the effectiveness of the women's rights movement, and it doesn't do enough to change women's lives.

* * *

The power of "mainstream" women and men made itself felt like a hurricane following Anita Hill's grilling before the U.S. Senate Judiciary Committee. When I became president, two months had passed since her dramatic testimony; new members were pouring into NOW at five times the normal rate.

Until Hill came forward during the Clarence Thomas hearings, sexual harassment hadn't really been in the forefront of our country's consciousness. Like the issue of violence against women, it was often seen as a personal problem of individual women rather than a societal problem many women must face specifically because they are women. As in cases of rape or domestic violence, the burden of shame—and proof—was on the woman, not on the man or men who had harassed her. But Anita Hill changed all that dramatically.

Hill, a law professor at the University of Oklahoma, had worked under Supreme Court nominee Clarence Thomas when he was head of the Equal Employment Opportunity Commission. During his confirmation hearings, she came forward to charge that Thomas had sexually harassed her, that he had pursued her beyond the point that was appropriate, and that although she had firmly turned him down, he regularly made exceptionally crude sexual comments and suggestions. The Senate Judiciary Committee did not make her charges public and closed the confirmation hearings without calling her as a witness. When the story was leaked to the press, all hell broke loose.

NOW didn't immediately jump to Hill's side. We were already strongly opposed to confirmation of Clarence Thomas to the Supreme Court, but that was a separate issue: We had made no bones about our distaste for his nomination. Thomas, even while serving as head of the EEOC, had declared his opposition to affirmative action and had identified as "clichés" women's legitimate complaints of job discrimination. He had praised an article that equated abortion with the Holocaust, then claimed with a straight face, under oath, during the hearings that he had never discussed *Roe* v. *Wade*, even in private conversation, and had no opinion on the subject. He had demeaned his own sister for what he said was her dependency on welfare when she was already back in the workforce and had been on welfare for only a short period of time while she cared for an elderly and ailing aunt. So we certainly didn't want Clarence Thomas on the Court, but we couldn't and didn't automatically back Anita Hill until we knew the whole story. Only after watching the testimony of Thomas and Hill and all the other witnesses did we say we believed her.

But first we had to fight to get the hearings! When the story broke, the Senate Judiciary Committee initially refused to re-open the hearings to take testimony and publicly address Hill's charges. The senators' patronizing attitude that the public had no right or need to know touched a nerve for women and men across the country, but women were particularly outraged by the committee's arrogance in thinking it could continue to deal with sexual harassment by sweeping it under the rug. We helped organize that deep anger into pressure on the senators, and within just days the hearings were reopened.

Watching the all-male Senate panel skewer Anita Hill, I was disgusted and angry. But the political strategist in me was dancing with joy. These guys were digging their own graves, and women all over the country were watching while they kept right on shoveling. Those senators didn't even have the imagination to improve on that well-known, tired old tactic of blaming the victim. Their reliance on portraying Hill as the stereotypical "woman spurned"—or as a mentally unstable (read: "hysterical female") employee—in order to account for her allegations of sexual harassment was a page from some dreadfully outworn book. Millions of women nationwide, remembering their own experience with harassment, asked themselves: *How dare they?*

The magic of Hill's stand was that, by being courageous enough to tell her story in front of the world, she gave other women the courage to tell their own stories, too—to anyone who would listen. Nationwide there was a sudden, cathartic release of guilt and shame, built up over the years, by women who'd kept their experiences of sexual harassment secret. Wonderfully, the release of all this pent-up energy threatened to blow out the phone lines at NOW.

Normally a big news event concerning women's rights will keep our phone lines busy for a couple of days—with reporters looking for a quote and NOW members and others calling in to let us know their concerns. But Hill-Thomas brought on more than two weeks of massive phone activity—so much so that we had to install a backup switchboard and bring in teams of volunteers to help field the calls.

The vast majority of calls were from women who felt the need to tell us their stories; they knew we'd listen. They wanted all those senators to listen, too. But mostly, they wanted to know what they could do. They wanted to take action. (Some right-wingers called us, opining that Hill was a political "prostitute," but we simply told them they had the wrong number and suggested they dial the *American Spectator*.) The membership rolls of local NOW chapters swelled, too, with women who were eager to become politically active. According to the calls, and to conversations I've had in the years since with women all around the country, the Hill hearing was the first time that many women had made the connection between what goes on in Washington and what goes on in their lives, and the first time they had seen such dramatic evidence of what it means that women have been excluded from the Senate and other positions of power.

We also received a lot of calls from men who felt they'd contributed to the problem of sexual harassment by ignoring it. I remember one that I took myself. It was from an elderly man who told me how, thirty years earlier, his wife had complained to him about being sexually harassed at her job. "I just kind of shrugged it off," he said, choking back tears. "I didn't take her seriously. I told her she was being oversensitive. Now she's gone. And I never got a chance to apologize."

Actually, it was a man who, in retrospect, summed up the

kind of national reaction sparked by the behavior of the Judiciary Committee. He burst into the NOW Action Center in D.C.
one afternoon. In his blue suit and red tie, he didn't look
different from the thousands of other people who occupy
Washington's law and lobbying offices, although he did have
memorably bright, curly red hair and a wild sort of look in his
eyes.

"I should have been here before! I should have done something to help!" he cried, to no one in particular. Then he threw
two fifty-dollar bills on our receptionist's desk and promptly
left.

I wanted to harness this national anger and desire to "help"
and turn it into something constructive. I remembered all the
years of being a flight attendant, suppressing my own hurt and
rage at being treated with disrespect—all the years of allowing
myself to be alternately patronized and harassed because I just
didn't have the tools yet to fight back. I didn't want other
women to go through that; not if NOW could help it. What
began with Hill, Thomas, and a few cynical or thickheaded senators quickly became a grassroots movement of the best kind.

As usual, politicians were slow to catch on. But once they
did, they started elbowing each other to hop on the bandwagon. And this, in turn, opened a window of incredible legislative opportunity.

"*Of course* I'm against sexual harassment in all forms . . . but
Anita Hill was lying." This became a popular excuse for senators who voted to confirm Thomas that winter. So, when the
Civil Rights Act of 1992 came up, they—and President Bush—
were trapped. The bill provided, for the first time, a right to
trial by jury in cases of sexual harassment and other job discrimination; it also permitted the awarding of damages, instead
of just back wages. (I'll never forget one of the women who
came to Washington to support the Civil Rights Act: Literally
running from her boss, she tripped and fell down some stairs.
She was injured badly enough to be out of work for days, but
under the existing law, she couldn't even get compensatory

damages to cover her medical expenses, let alone punitive damages.) Congress had passed the bill before, in 1990, but President Bush had vetoed it, calling it a "quota" bill. This time when the bill came to his desk for signature, the power of the outrage over the Senate's treatment of Anita Hill had magically transformed it into a legitimate civil rights bill, and Bush felt compelled to sign it. It was a major victory for women.

The national momentum from the Hill hearings continued into the Year of the Woman elections of 1992. Alan Dixon of Illinois, one of the Democrats who voted for Thomas, may have been shocked when he woke one spring morning to find that Carol Moseley-Braun had pulled his Senate seat out from under him, but it was no surprise to the NOW activists who'd campaigned for her. The power of ordinary women doesn't often show itself so blatantly—or so overwhelmingly. But when it does, it's awesome.

NOW kicked off the 1992 campaign season with another March for Women's Lives, this one a massive abortion and reproductive rights march on Washington, D.C.

Not everyone in the movement was charged up about the need for a march—at least, not at first.

But there are solid reasons for doing mass actions. We use them to organize and to inspire. A mass action builds our strength and our momentum—and shows that strength to politicians and to ourselves. Successful mass actions also have positive "hangover effects": the tremendous individual and group efforts needed to organize a big march expands our lists of contributors and supporters and provides an opportunity to develop skills and activism at the grassroots. These new community organizers can continue to expand that network and use it to turn out the vote or bring constituent pressure for an issue. One day of marching can mean hundreds of hours of phone calling and shopping mall petitioning by inspired volunteers.

Marching has a galvanizing effect on individual activists,

whether they come from big cities or from rural parts of the country that may not have large feminist support networks. Dr. Susan Wicklund, an ob-gyn from Minnesota who I asked to speak at the 1992 march, had attended the 1989 march on her own. Walking way in the back at the earlier event, she found herself wondering what she was doing to help, besides coming to Washington and waving a sign. "I was here at the march in 1989 with my mother and my daughter. I was in private practice, and I said, 'This is ridiculous; why am I not doing something? Within two months I was working in the clinic. I now work in three states providing abortions to rural women, many of whom travel ten to twelve hours to get their abortion." As a result of Susan's decision to become an abortion provider, she and her family had endured threats and harassment at the hands of a vicious antiabortion group calling themselves The Lambs of God. They camped out in her driveway, they invaded her house, they invaded her daughter's school, they put logs across her driveway so that she couldn't leave in the morning. She received graphic, gruesome death threats. Eventually, she had to have armed guards with her in her own home.

Considering that the presidential election was only six months away, it wasn't surprising that politicians were eager to make their way onto our guest list at the march. With an anticipated audience of 750,000—not to mention the massive television and press coverage—the March for Women's Lives was a politician's dream.

Clinton's people called, asking for their candidate to be given a chance to address the crowd, but we declined. The point of the day was to have all the politicians *listen*, for once, to all the women who were fighting for our rights and for our lives. Clinton's people were actually very gracious; we worked out a deal whereby Clinton and his delegation would be able to march behind his own banner near the front. Even then, it was obvious that the man could run a very savvy campaign; he knew when not to push too hard.

The same could not be said for Jerry Brown and his people. First, a group of Brown supporters jumped in front of the march with a banner touting Brown's 800 number. I grabbed a bullhorn and yelled, in my most commanding flight attendant voice, for them to back up. I then called for the facilitators to move the official front line and the welfare rights delegation in front of the Brown crew. Later, once the day's speeches had begun, Brown insisted on having a few minutes at the microphone. I managed to ignore him until he somehow convinced Ellie Smeal to lobby me. The rock group Toad the Wet Sprocket was playing onstage at the time, and it was difficult to hear anyone.

"Patricia, Jerry really wants to talk!"

"Forget it!" I shouted back. "I already told him, no presidential candidates!"

"He's driving everyone crazy back there! What am I supposed to tell him?"

"Tell him I remember Joan Andrews!" And I felt both pleased and powerful for being in a position to remind him and tell him no. I hadn't forgotten that when Joan Andrews was playing martyr after being arrested for her Pensacola abortion clinic attack in 1986, Brown had been one of the politicians clamoring for her release.

Later on that week Brown came to see me at NOW's national offices, and we talked it through. I don't like to hold a grudge, and I was glad to put it behind me, but it sure did feel good to say that after all those years.

The March for Women's Lives also provided me with an opportunity to strengthen NOW's ties with other movements.

Twenty-four hours before the start of the march, the National Welfare Rights Union, the National Anti-Hunger Coali-

tion, and the National Union for the Homeless held a Summit
for Survival at Howard University. This had been brought
about by the work of an extraordinary man named Faith
Evans, who had worked for the United Church of Christ in their
social justice section and served as president of the Religious
Coalition for Abortion Rights. NOW had hired Faith as an
organizer for the march. Rising above a violent and poverty-
stricken childhood, he had spent a lifetime dedicated to economic justice and reproductive rights, and he was determined
that NOW connect with the welfare rights women. The summit
was originally scheduled for Houston, but Faith convinced the
groups to move it to D.C. so they could take part in the march,
convinced the United Church of Christ to fund the move, convinced me and other NOW leaders to attend, then sat back and
waited for us all to figure out how to talk to each other.

I wasn't surprised to find a very angry group of attendees at
the summit. I'd have been angry, too, if I was getting unfairly
blamed for the economic woes of an entire nation while my
family went hungry and homeless. It seems as if an entire generation of shallow 1990s politicians has taken up California
Governor Pete Wilson's grotesque remark that the devastating
welfare cuts he was trying to push through in his state would
just mean that welfare mothers would be able to buy one less
six-pack a week.

"I'm glad the president of NOW could take the time to be
with us here today," said Maureen Taylor, president of the
Michigan Welfare Rights Union. "Though I wonder where
NOW was last January, when I was freezing in a tent city for
the homeless in Detroit and couldn't get anybody on the
phone!"

Maureen's opening volley set off a flood. For the next forty-
five minutes (or at least it felt that long) I sat and listened to the
ways NOW had failed them. We hadn't helped when Michigan's governor decided to push thousands of poor women off
the state's welfare rolls; babies had died of exposure and mal-
nutrition while NOW sat idly by.

My first impulse was to get defensive; to present the list of poor women's issues that we had tirelessly promoted over the years, to explain how busy we were with so many projects that benefited all women, including them. But being defensive closes down communication, and we were there to communicate. Besides, when someone says you've acted in a classist or a racist manner and that they're angry at you, the answer is not "You have no right," the answer is "I'm sorry." So I waited until things calmed down a little, took a deep breath, and stood.

"All I can say is that I'm sorry for the times we haven't been there for you in the past. I'm sorry we let you down. But the reason we're here is that we want to go forward and work with you—starting with tomorrow's march."

The following day the front line of the march and the rally speakers included representatives from the Summit.

In the years since that first meeting, NOW has worked closely with the women on welfare, and especially Marion Kramer, president of the National Welfare Rights Union and the Up and Out of Poverty Now! coalition. This alliance has helped me realize how utterly susceptible to poverty women really are. "Most women can't ever imagine being on welfare," she says. "But I can't tell you how many poor women used to have lots of money, a car, and a fine house. Then one day, all they had was three kids and nowhere to go. For many women, poverty is just a paycheck or an illness or a divorce away, and many women fall into poverty because they're fleeing an abusive relationship."

Through Marion and Faith, I also met a woman with two kids who worked a double shift to support them after her divorce from a batterer. When she had a heart attack, with no health insurance, they were evicted and ended up homeless. As we worked on these issues, I also learned how many NOW members had had to rely on the federal safety net to stop their economic free-fall. Women like Karen Johnson, a national vice president of NOW. Karen's three sisters and her brother were still quite young when their father abandoned the family and they were forced onto welfare. The help they received enabled Karen's mother to raise her children to become productive adults. Karen won a scholarship and, like all of her siblings, got a college education. After twenty years as an award-winning Air Force nurse, Karen brought her experience on global issues and her strong management skills to our team of national officers, along with her commitment to economic justice.

I also used the March for Women's Lives to begin building stronger ties to Reverend Jesse Jackson's Rainbow Coalition.

Reverend Jackson has consistently backed women's rights and I admired his work in bringing women, civil rights, labor, religious, and other groups together. So I sought him out personally shortly after I became NOW president. At our very first meeting when I asked for his support for the march, he helped me to understand why abortion and reproductive rights had to be seen and presented within a broader context to address the concerns of the African American community. That day, Reverend Jackson reminded me that the right to give birth and the right to determine a child's fate are not taken for granted in his community. "Only two generations ago," he said, "we had our babies sold out from under us. The idea that abortion, birth control, or sterilization could be used to 'control the black population' is a very real fear among African Americans, and we must be concerned with the right to choose to have and raise our families as well." I explained that the march had been called for reproductive freedom as well as for abortion rights and that ending poverty was on our agenda as well, because we did understand those connections. And most African American civil rights leaders, including Reverend Jackson, understand the dangers of allowing the government to coerce us one way or another in our reproductive lives. In the end, not only did Reverend Jackson agree to participate, he also cut public service announcements for broadcast in D.C. I did similar personal outreach to C. Delores Tucker from the National Political Congress of Black Women, Dolores Huerta from the United Farm Workers, and other women leaders, and we carried out a massive mail and phone campaign to the entire women's rights community. The march turned out to be the largest and one of the most diverse the movement had ever had.

Throughout the 1992 election campaign, it became quite clear just how vehemently abortion opponents feared the coming of a pro-choice president. Picketing at clinics shot up dramatically during that time—from 292 incidents in 1991 to 2,898 in 1992. Blockades doubled from 41 to 83. And it began to look as if the co-opting of the Republican Party by religious right-wingers would continue unchallenged.

What happened at the Republican National Convention in Houston that year highlighted the depths to which the party of Lincoln was prepared to sink as the two Pats—Robertson and Buchanan—took center stage.

The low point of the convention's rhetoric came during Pat Buchanan's keynote speech, when he was heard to call for a "cultural and religious war" in this country. The language of many of the other speeches delivered at the convention was also offensive, and it seemed dangerously and deliberately inflammatory.

The mood was ugly. Young Republican thugs broke up a news conference held by Democratic National Committee chairman Ron Brown by hollering and pounding on the windows. Another group followed National Public Radio political correspondent Nina Tottenberg around, shouting at her to reveal who she had had affairs with because they mistook her for the woman reporter who had asked George Bush at a news conference about his long-rumored affair. I guess all women reporters look alike. While this kind of hatred was being verbally splattered about the Astrodome, the surrounding streets of Houston were also filled with strife. On the third day of the convention, a demonstration for gay and lesbian rights was broken up by police on horseback swinging billy clubs and cracking heads.

I was busy at the time with my own battles across town, as our three-way strategy in the struggle for abortion rights—politics, litigation, and clinic defense—all came together. To take advantage of the presence of the media and the conventioneers, Operation Rescue and the Lambs of God had planned to shut down Houston abortion clinics; Planned Parenthood, a local physician, and other plaintiffs, having done their homework in advance, had already gotten a Houston judge to issue a temporary restraining order barring trespassing on clinic grounds. At 5:00 A.M. I was at the clinic, dressed for combat; by 10:30, as part of the litigation team, I'd race to the courthouse, using the bathroom to change into my lawyer clothes. (At one point I'd literally had to crawl through the legs of clinic defenders, journalists, and camera operators to serve a court order on Keith Tucci, then head of Operation Rescue.) As soon as court was adjourned, I'd be in front of a microphone, trying to get our message about the violent and illegal tactics used by OR and Lambs of God out to any politician who might be listening—and to the voters.

As testimony at the hearing clearly showed, Tucci's organization, local abortionists led by a man named Flip Benham, and others habitually went out into the community to harass people in their homes as well as at the clinics. One abortion provider had had his home surrounded by antiabortion hecklers with bullhorns during his family's Sabbath meal. Someone threw a brick through his dining room window. His daughter suffered so many threats and such harassment by antiabortionists that the doctor had enrolled her in a private school out of concern for her safety, a measure she bitterly resented.

Cross-examining the doctor in court, Benham asked, "Doctor, isn't your real objection to us that we're trying to create a *Christian* atmosphere around your home?"

The doctor was Jewish. Enough said.

Four of the Operation Rescue bosses were tossed into jail for violating the injunction, leaving their ranks in chaos.

That week in Houston was also the first time I'd encountered the theological phenomenon called "imprecatory prayer." This was the first time I'd heard of people praying for bad things to happen to those of us who didn't agree with them. One doctor connected with a targeted clinic had a heart attack; the praying activists were very pleased and congratulated themselves on the success of their imprecatory prayers. All over Houston, I heard our opponents say, "We're praying for you, Patricia!" A few months later, with Hurricane Andrew whistling in my ears as it passed over my house in Homestead, Florida, I wondered if they'd take credit for that, too.

As disgusted as I was by the so-called "Christian" atmosphere pervading Houston that week, I was also certain that from my point of view the Republicans couldn't have chosen a better time to shoot themselves in the foot. The glow of triumph from Desert Storm had worn off; the economy was sinking slowly. Although they didn't know it at the time, the religious right-wingers buried the Republican Party's chances for winning that fall. They—and the GOP leadership—had badly misjudged the mood of the voters. People were interested in hearing about solutions to the grave, practical problems that had created fissures in the quality of their lives: issues like the economy, health care, and education, not about government imposing a right-wing religious agenda on all of us.

It's my belief that the Republican National Convention tipped the scales against George Bush. In the same period that our televisions brought us images of young neo-Nazis in Germany burning buildings in attacks on Turkish Moslem immigrants, we got a glimpse on national TV of how truly frightening our own religious right can be—and voted against it, in droves.

As excited as I was at the prospect of harnessing all of the post-Anita Hill feminist energy for the 1992 elections, it's also a fact that I found the 1992 presidential race a far from joyful experience.

Clinton did say some appealing things, not least of which was his campaign promise to have, as president, "a cabinet that looks like America." Since according to the most recent census, women constitute 51 percent of the population, that sounded good to me. But with his conservative views on welfare and other issues affecting women, he was hardly our ideal candidate. Our strategy was to continue focusing on recruiting and supporting feminist women candidates. By doing so, we would turn out many more women's rights voters. Naturally, the voters we galvanized were also anti-Bush voters—and Clinton benefited, along with our candidates. (Women ended up providing Bill Clinton with 56 percent of his votes.) But our slogan in 1992 was "Elect Women for a Change"—not "Elect Clinton for a Change."

This was a strategy we had already field-tested in Louisiana in 1991. From any feminist, progressive, or garden-variety liberal point of view, Louisiana was political swamp water. With a total of three women state legislators (2.8 percent of the entire legislature), Louisiana had passed the nation's most restrictive antiabortion law in 1990. The law had been tacked onto a flag-burning bill. The quality of the debate in the legislature over the bill had been almost unbelievable: While arguing against an exception in the law, which would have allowed abortion in the case of incest-related pregnancies, state representative Carl Gunter reminded his colleagues that "the way we get thoroughbred horses and thoroughbred dogs is through inbreeding."

NOW established "WomanElect 2000" in Louisiana. Kim Gandy (who became NOW's executive vice president when I assumed the presidency), who was from Louisiana and had practiced law in New Orleans, went down to run it, because you can't send just any Southerner to Louisiana. (Kim had just returned from her honeymoon and had to leave her new husband for long periods during their first year of marriage.) The statewide campaign focused on organizing local activists, teaching grassroots campaign techniques, and helping to identify and recruit feminist women candidates in their own communities. We also provided political consulting, technical advice, and volunteers. The response was unprecedented and amazing: Within the first few months we'd recruited more than twenty strong feminist candidates to run for state house and senate seats, and more were in the pipeline.

Meanwhile, we also had to make a decision about the Louisiana governor's race. The Democratic candidate was Edwin Edwards. A former governor who'd been indicted twice (but not convicted) for accepting payoffs, Edwards once bragged that the only way to get him out of office would be to catch him in bed "with a dead girl or a live boy."

Ordinarily, I wouldn't have stopped on the street to shake his hand. But that year Edwards had managed to find himself running against the one candidate in the world who could make him look good in comparison: Republican nominee David Duke, an ex–Ku Klux Klansman who had shed the sheet but not the beliefs of the Klan.

Some NOW activists pressured us to boycott Louisiana and its crazy election altogether. I admit, it was tempting. We'd turn on the TV to see Duke giving his stock campaign speech about "reverse discrimination"; then switch the channel to find Edwards joking that both he and his opponent were "wizards under the sheets." Using our best leadership skills, we couldn't have drummed up support for Edwards even if we'd had the stomach for it ourselves. But the dilemma we faced was perfectly encapsulated by a bumper sticker that made it onto many cars in Louisiana during that time: VOTE FOR THE CROOK. IT'S IMPORTANT.

We resolved it by working on "WomanElect 2000." If we kept our focus on getting women candidates to run—and getting women to vote—we could dump pols like Carl "That's how we get thoroughbreds" Gunter, and we'd probably stop Duke as well. If we could pull out the vote *for* women's rights, we were confident that would also be a vote *against* David Duke.

When the final tally was in, it turned out that we were right: the votes of women and African Americans had saved Louisiana from electing a Klan governor.

After the election, Louisiana looked a lot better. The number of women in the state legislature had more than tripled. Anti-abortion candidates lost both the lieutenant governor's and the attorney general's offices, and five antiabortion incumbents, including Carl Gunter (who, at the national NOW headquarters, we'd nicknamed "Mr. Sensitivity"), lost their seats to pro-choice candidates.

Throughout the nation, women's rights candidates won in droves in 1992: On a national and state level, 702 candidates that NOW PAC had endorsed were swept into office. Afterward, though, many activists settled back into a celebratory kind of daze. And many progressive organizations were so excited about having access to the White House, for the first time in twelve years, that they made the fatal mistake of relaxing their vigilance.

A lot of abortion rights supporters also breathed a premature sigh of relief. Clinton was heading for the White House after a dozen years of the antiabortion policies of Reagan and Bush. The elections saw nearly a doubling of women in the U.S. Congress (from roughly 5 to 10 percent). We were elated. We had tripled the number of women in the Senate, which sounds so much better than saying we had gone from two to six women out of a hundred senators! Approximately one-fourth of the women in this newly elected Congress were women of color. And, like Clinton, all of the new women had campaigned as abortion-rights supporters.

Dianne Feinstein of California was sworn in a few days before the other new senators, since she was filling the unexpired term of Pete Wilson, who had stepped down to make a successful run for governor of California. The day she was sworn in, the gallery was overflowing with supporters, campaign workers, family, and friends. All of us had fought long and hard for this day. I sat next to Kate Michelman of the National Abortion and Reproductive Rights Action League.

Now, the Senate is a pretty stuffy place. Formality rules there. When Native American Senator Ben Nighthorse Campbell of Colorado, who moved up from the House in 1992, started showing up at work wearing bandannas and bolos with string ties, there was actually serious discussion as to whether his attire met the Senate's dress code requirements. (They decided that it did. And no one mentioned his ponytail, which I assure you was the first one seen on the Senate floor since the days of powdered wigs.) Most senators take themselves *very* seriously. But after Feinstein took her oath of office, the gallery erupted, not with polite applause, but with wild hoots and fists pumping and waving in the air—a celebration more worthy of a triumphant home-team crowd at a football game. As other senators lined up and solemnly shook Feinstein's hand, Senator-elect Carol Moseley-Braun—the Senate's first elected African American woman—ran up and threw her arms around Feinstein, and the gallery erupted again. Maybe it was my imagination, but it looked to me as if Senator Robert Byrd, the powerful senator from West Virginia, had suddenly developed a nervous tic. The Senate would never be the same.

But for those of us with our political ears to the ground, there were a few ominous warning signs cropping up around us already. Amidst all the hoopla Kate Michelman leaned over to me and asked, "Is your mail working?" She was referring to the mass-mailing letters our organizations send out asking people to join or make a financial contribution.

"Our members are still responding," I replied. "But our prospecting for new members is so bad we've simply stopped." Kate nodded grimly and confirmed that NARAL was experiencing the same thing. We shared a moment of worry that stood in sharp contrast to the celebration exploding around us. We were right to be concerned: By the end of 1993, NOW's membership had dropped by 25 percent. The election victories had lulled many of our supporters into a dangerous complacency.

Although we had cause for concern, I also felt a certain vindication when I saw the impact of having such an increase in the number of women in Congress. We had worked hard to elect the women, believing that they would bring a valuable, new perspective to government. And they have. In addition to a fuchsia scarf or a bright yellow blouse in among all the gray and blue suits, the new members brought their experiences as women to the floor of the Senate and House, and they spoke from their hearts.

During debate preceding passage of the Family and Medical Leave Act, I remember Feinstein telling her colleagues how she had been fired from her first job when she got pregnant. The senators must have been as moved as I was when Patty Murray spoke of her friend Melinda who had just died of ovarian cancer; they voted a record amount of money for research on women's health. I will never forget Carol Moseley-Braun's passion in describing the impact of racism on her life, as she successfully urged her colleagues to reverse the special protection they had extended to the Daughters of the Confederacy's insignia. And, I was so proud that the strong leadership of Barbara Mikulski and Barbara Boxer helped NOW build the pressure that led to Bob Packwood's resignation from the Senate more than three years after the story of his sexual harassment and abuse broke. Even in the current Congress, Nancy Kassebaum is pushing for reforms so workers could change jobs without losing their health insurance.

And yet, when the Senate voted for the Republican welfare bill that would have plunged millions of women and children deeper into poverty—Carol Moseley-Braun stood alone among the women senators in opposing it. NOW had worked hard to stop Congress from ripping large holes in the federal safety net that had been in place for more than sixty years in this country. We had successfully pulled together coalitions and drawn in other women's rights groups to stand up for poor women and their children. We had made sure that the voices of poor women themselves were heard in the debate, so the lawmakers would understand how many women fell into poverty because they were fleeing a violent relationship, how many of us were only one paycheck or one job away from poverty ourselves. I had been arrested in the Capitol rotunda for a nonviolent protest the day the House passed its version of the bill. The vote against a federal guarantee of a minimal, subsistence level of support was a devastating loss to all women. And in light of the women senators' votes, it was a loss that forced us to reassess our strategy of electing more women in order to advance our issues.

The women's votes had not gone unnoticed by reporters either. But despite the media's invitations to do so, I resisted the strong temptation to lash out at the women and to renounce the strategy. I am convinced that to effect real, lasting social change, we need women and women's rights supporters both outside and inside the system. And while we must hold women on the inside accountable, the same as we do any public official, we must also value and recognize the difference in the roles insiders and outsiders play.

The truth is until we have more women and women's rights supporters in Congress, the cabinet, and the courts, in boardrooms and newsrooms, in the pulpits and inside university administrations, the impact of outside groups like NOW will never be as strong as it could be. When state legislators failed to ratify the ERA in 1982, we learned an important lesson: All the grassroots work in the world won't result in progress if there aren't enough women in elected office. And the same applies to other institutions as well.

Why? Well, for one thing, women have a different experience in life. We are still the caregivers of the very young and the very old. Women are more likely than men to live in poverty and to face violence in our own homes. We are the ones who get pregnant. As a result, women have a different perspective and different priorities in policy making. I know this is a gross generalization, but the record is clear: Women in office take leadership on different issues and vote differently than men. We are more likely to support public education, health, and child care measures. Women have a better record on antidiscrimination and antiviolence bills. We are in favor of abortion rights and reproductive freedom in greater numbers than men.

Even conservative women are sometimes allies on our issues. When Congress had to decide whether to override President Bush's veto of the Family and Medical Leave Act, Republican Ileana Ros-Lehtinen voted against her own party's president. Ileana, a Miamian and the first Cuban American woman in Congress, is among the most conservative members of the House, but the story circulated in Washington that she told the White House lobbyist, "Don't tell me we don't need family and medical leave. I've got young children at home."

To take another example of the different priorities women bring to power, in the 102d Congress, the one that served before the 1992 elections, 74 percent of the women, but only 47 percent of the men, were taking leadership as cosponsors of the Violence Against Women Act. Now, I appreciate the men who served as sponsors, and I know Senator Joseph Biden and Representative Chuck Schumer were driving forces behind VAWA. And it doesn't mean I don't wish the other 26 percent of the women had been on board. But if the gender split in Congress had been even close to what it is in the general population, that twenty-seven-point gender gap would have meant that the bill would have passed easily. With only 5 percent women in Congress, there just weren't enough of us there. After the 1992 elections, the 103d Congress, with 10 percent women, finally passed the bill.

I want women to have a fair share of power, because I want to make progress on women's issues. Of course, that means that in a given race, I may favor the man over the woman, if he is stronger on women's rights issues, and NOW's political action committee has endorsed men over women in those circum-

stances. But if I had to choose in the dark, with no other information, I would choose fifty-fifty women and men and take
my chances from there. As we get more women in positions of
power, we have to concentrate on how to work more effectively together with them.

In the women's rights movement we have not yet begun to
use an inside/outside strategy to the fullest. One of the great
assets of the movement, built up over the past thirty years, is
the extraordinary number of women and women's rights supporters in policy-making positions inside the institutions—
private as well as public—that shape our society. But too often
we find ourselves at odds with each other. Too often women
on the inside stereotype activists as humorless, man-hating
dykes-on-bikes, and we return the favor, seeing insiders as
self-serving, suit-wearing female impersonators. We need to
recognize how powerful we can be working in tandem and
complementing, rather than fighting, each other. If we could
establish better lines of communication and coordinate our
strategies better, there'd be no stopping us!

Let me give an example from the post-1992 elections period.
NOW and other women's rights groups were determined to
make sure President Clinton kept his promise to appoint more
women to the cabinet. Other women's organizations took the
job of gathering names and résumés for consideration. While I
appreciated their effort, I thought we were far beyond the point
where anyone in the administration could argue with a
straight face that they couldn't find enough qualified women,
so NOW focused on building pressure for the general principle
of having a fair share of power for women, rather than promoting particular women.

After the first few cabinet appointments had been made, Ellie
Smeal received an important phone call from someone she
knew on the Clinton transition team. Her insider friend told
Ellie that too few women were making the cut when the lists of

potential nominees were pared down for final consideration. She called Ellie to deliver this information, but also to ask for help: She wanted those of us on the outside to turn up the heat on the new administration in order to strengthen her argument as she tried to get more women on the short lists.

Ellie contacted me and everyone else she could think of who might help. We started flooding Clinton's Arkansas offices with phone calls and faxes. The president of the YWCA made an appointment for a group of us to meet with the head of the transition team, Vernon Jordan, to make our case for more women in the cabinet. Ultimately, the combination of women pushing from the inside and the outside was successful. Clinton appointed a record number of women and people of color at all levels of his administration, including the cabinet. But I want to describe the process in a little more detail, because in addition to showing how effective a coordinated inside/outside strategy can be, the story also illustrates the conflicts that can arise over the different roles we play, even among outside groups.

Our meeting with Jordan was scheduled for a Monday in the afternoon. That Friday and over the weekend before the meeting, Ellie and I had both been quoted publicly about our concerns over whether Clinton would keep his promise to name a cabinet that looked more like the country. Almost immediately, I began hearing from other political activists. "Give the man a break," they said. "He needs our support, not our criticism." I argued we were trying to support him in making the right decisions, but I could tell they weren't buying it.

The morning of the meeting, Ellie appeared on the *Today Show* to talk about the appointments. The host asked her what percentage of the cabinet she thought women should comprise. Ellie tried to avoid the question at first. But she finally said that a cabinet in which at least a third of the positions were held by women would be "a good start." Since women are more than half the population, she thought that was pretty conservative.

"I thought I was too soft," Ellie told me after the show.

Vernon Jordan didn't think so. Listening to the show that

morning as he shaved, he apparently nearly cut himself when he heard Ellie. Once Jordan arrived at his office, calls started going out to moderate women's groups to say that the upcoming meeting was supposed to be for *supporters* of the president.

Ellie got a call from one of the meeting's organizers.

"We've got a problem, Ellie. Jordan's office says that if you're part of the delegation, he's going to call off the meeting."

Ellie reached me less than an hour before we were supposed to be at the transition team's offices. When she told me what was going on, I couldn't decide who made me madder: Jordan for refusing to meet with Ellie or the other women leaders for being so anxious to be included that they were willing to let him get away with it. Ellie herself had already decided not to press the point.

"Having the administration hear our concerns is more important than my being in the room," she told me.

"Well, if what they mean by 'support' is blind allegiance, then I don't want to be there myself," I told her. "Besides, I don't want them to think they can so easily divide and conquer us."

We got on a three-way call with Antonia Hernandez, executive director of the Mexican-American Legal Defense Fund, who also questioned whether any of us should go if Ellie was excluded. But in the end, we decided that it was important for a few of us who were not so easily intimidated to be at the table. I'd also been pushing to get Michelle Tingling-Clemmons, a board member of the National Welfare Rights Union, invited to the meeting. Either by foresight or oversight, nobody from Jordan's staff had ever gotten back to me about it, and I wanted to be there to make sure she got in. I knew she'd speak up strongly, too.

The meeting went just about as I had thought it would: lots of talk, no commitments from Jordan. The atmosphere was tense. Jordan began by asking, smugly, "Where's Ellie? I thought she'd be joining us this afternoon." Knowing that his office had demanded that she not appear, I found this a strange comment. But it seemed to have the effect of scaring several of the women there—some of whom seemed more interested in ingratiating themselves than in taking an uncompromising position on cabinet nominations. A common form of introduction was, "I'm so-and-so, from such-and-such group, and I think the president-elect is doing a *wonderful* job, and my organization has been getting *all* kinds of calls from his wonderful transition team." Michelle added to the tension when she introduced herself: "I'm Michelle Tingling-Clemmons. I represent poor women, and nobody's been calling us." I was glad she and I had been able to talk our way past the security guards and get her into the meeting. ("Her name's missing from the list? Well, I'm sure it was inadvertent. She was cleared by the guard at the reception desk, and she's supposed to be at this meeting!")

Jordan assured us that we wouldn't be "disappointed" with the final makeup of the cabinet (although, when Antonia asked about possible Latina appointments, she was told that it wasn't in the cards). Jordan also emphasized that everyone who was appointed, man or woman, would have to be a "Clinton supporter." "Ellie Smeal, for instance, will not be appointed to anything," he added. Clearly, she had gotten under his skin, and his comment had gotten under mine. "Believe me, she doesn't want to be," I snapped back. Jordan didn't respond, but some of the women glared down the table at me.

Jordan also told us that the president was going to nominate another woman that very day. On cue, he had his staff bring in a TV so that we could watch Clinton name Hazel O'Leary as secretary of energy. Unfortunately, he couldn't get the set to work. But we later learned that, after his introduction of O'Leary, Clinton had lashed out at those of us who were pushing so hard and so publicly for more women appointees. Although it was widely reported as a spontaneous outburst on the president's part, I wonder to this day whether the remark had been planned and Jordan had wanted to see what our immediate reaction to being called "bean counters" on national television would be.

As the meeting came to a close, Jordan told us that the press was waiting outside, and, he said, he hoped we would all have something positive to say about the meeting. Despite our differences, I had no need or desire to slam the new administration. On the contrary, I felt that the best posture would be to say that we fully expected Clinton would do the right thing. But Jordan's obvious anger at Ellie bewildered me, and if I was going to put a positive spin on our meeting for the media, I honestly needed to know what she had said that had upset him so much. But when I tried to get an answer, some of the other women acted as if I'd insulted our host, and Jordan was able to slip away without answering.

As we left the building, we saw a circle of microphones set up on the sidewalk for our group to address the press. Maybe it was my imagination, but I could have sworn that the others were standing obstructively, in a way that kept me from getting anywhere near a mike. The press, of course, wanted to talk about "bean counters" and quotas, but the other women weren't taking the bait. Instead, they talked euphemistically about Clinton choosing "the best *person* for the job." "They can't even bring themselves to say 'woman,'" I thought as I managed to worm my way over to a live mike. Maybe it was the look on my face that made the reporters, sensing a good quote, immediately turn their attention to me. And the other women, sensing trouble, immediately began to edge their way out of the picture.

I started out innocuously enough, saying our plan was to build the support necessary for the president to keep his campaign promise to appoint more women to cabinet level positions, but then the frustrations of the day spilled over, and I translated my own comment for the reporters. "That's a nicer way of saying we intend to hold the president's feet to the fire." My quote made network news that evening, and the clip showed me standing alone. By the time I'd finished the sentence, the other women were halfway down the block.

If we had staged the whole thing, it would have been fine with me. Whether we play it with women on the inside or with more confrontational women's rights advocates on the outside, I think a game of good cop/bad cop can be very effective on occasion. By taking an uncompromising position and using more militant tactics, those of us who take the outsider's role can make the insiders look more reasonable and strengthen their hand. But this was no role-play; in the meeting and on the sidewalk, these women were genuinely perturbed at me, and, I suspect, at Ellie for violating the first rule of women's socialization and creating social tension. I was frustrated with them, but also a bit with myself. I believe in my own strategies, but I also believe we must always leave a little room for doubt that our views are the only valid ones. Who can know for sure what approach or combination of approaches will lead to progress?

NOW clashed with the administration and U.S. Senate, too, over the ill-fated nominations first of Zoë Baird and then Kimba Wood to be the first-ever woman attorney general of the United States. Baird was forced out of the running for illegally hiring undocumented workers as household help and not paying the proper social security taxes for them. "If she was Joey Baird instead of Zoë Baird, the question of her domestic help would never even have come up," I steamed as I watched the Senate Judiciary Committee members quiz her. And, as it turned out, I was right; subsequent press reports showed that Ron Brown had a similar problem, but when he was nominated as secretary of commerce, no one had thought to ask who cleaned his house, and he had been confirmed. Then when the administration withdrew Kimba Wood's nomination without even a hearing, I went ballistic.

"It wasn't illegal to hire undocumented workers at the time

she did it," I ranted to anyone who'd listen. "What was she supposed to do? Use her woman's intuition to predict they were going to make it illegal and comply in advance with a law that hadn't even been passed yet?"

NOW put out a press release questioning the double standard that holds women—but never their husbands—responsible for household and family care. NOW did not criticize Clinton, but took our whole culture to task for the double burden we put on employed women and for the double talk about how much we all support motherhood. But the media was having too much fun with "Nannygate" to make subtle distinctions. They reinterpreted our message to be "Feminists Say Prez Has Double Standard."

A couple of days later, I found myself on *Nightline* opposite presidential adviser Mandy Grunwald. When I walked into the green room before we went on the air, Grunwald did not return my greeting. During the show, host Chris Wallace asked her about my ongoing efforts to get a woman attorney general.

"I actually am very disappointed, as a woman and as a political strategist," Grunwald replied. "The Clinton administration in three weeks has done more for women than Ronald Reagan and George Bush combined in twelve years, and by trying to push this to the front of the agenda for women, I think she does a terrible disservice to the women of this country."

I countered that I didn't think it was a disservice to women to make sure that her boss kept his campaign promises, and we remained at loggerheads for the rest of the show.

This kind of conflict between insiders and outsiders has existed in the modern women's rights movement from the beginning. Insiders tend to bristle when we criticize them. And we outsiders tend to be very judgmental when they compromise too soon or too far from what we believe women really need. We put them on the defensive, not only about their bosses, but about themselves as women. Career-wise, women in positions of power may identify with successful men, rather than with most other women. Such women may even deny that they've been discriminated against, and along with that comes a denial that they have been helped at all by the women's rights movement.

Other reasons exist for insiders shying away from the influence of outsiders. The corporate culture, which dominates our government as well, rewards conformity and comes down hard on anything or anyone who clashes with that culture. As the old Japanese proverb says: *Any nail that sticks out will be hammered down.*

Women on the inside need our support. On the other hand, influential insiders need to leave doors of communication open to those on the outside who, by speaking the unvarnished truth to power, shift the entire culture and enable insiders to promote our common agenda in more diplomatic ways. Once channels of communication are open, we often find that we *can* work effectively together—in our very different ways—for progress that will benefit us all.

The third time was the charm for Clinton in naming his attorney general, and Janet Reno is among the most powerful women working inside the government today. After President Clinton nominated Reno, I ran into Secretary of Health and Human Services Donna Shalala at a Rainbow Coalition leadership conference in Washington, D.C. After the debacles with Zoë Baird and Kimba Wood, I was excited about Reno's nomination. For me, her nomination had the added spark of having someone I knew from Miami making the historic breakthrough as the first woman to reach this level in my profession.

When Shalala asked what I thought about the new nominee, I was positively effusive. I told her, as an example, about Reno's leadership as state's attorney in pulling together a task force on violence against women on which I had served. She had recognized the connection between family violence and crime, with 40 percent of the homicides in Dade County involving the murder of a woman by her husband or boyfriend. Reno had gone beyond a narrow view of her job as prosecutor to do something about prevention.

Shalala listened, nodding, until I paused to take a breath, then leaned forward and asked, "But isn't the answer to the question 'Are you a feminist,' 'yes'?"

For a moment, I was stopped in my tracks. At a Rose Garden news conference announcing her nomination earlier that week, Reno had not directly responded to a reporter's question about whether she considered herself a feminist. With an answer that began, "My mother always raised me to be the best person I could be . . ." she had ducked the label.

In the same way that many women (and men) in positions of power are ambivalent about calling themselves feminists, I am of two minds about what Janet Reno or anyone else calls herself. Because I know the political and media spin on the word *feminist* can be so negative, I understand why Reno avoided that question. I told Shalala that of course my first choice is to have more "out" feminists in the cabinet and in the world. But no matter what Reno called herself, I said, based on what I had seen her do as state's attorney in Miami, I believed she'd be a great attorney general. And I think I was right.

That doesn't mean that on occasion I have not been frustrated with Janet Reno. It does mean that I appreciate the constraints of her job and the legal system in which she works. But that was the case even before she joined the Clinton cabinet.

In 1989, a large group of Operation Rescue members were arrested for blockading a clinic in the Miami area. Reno was state's attorney for Dade County at the time. I was sure we wouldn't have the same kinds of problems with her we'd encountered with other prosecutors around the country; she wouldn't let these people go with a mere slap on the wrist.

But to my surprise and dismay, the Dade County police just took the crowd of Operation Rescue people to the Orange Bowl, fed them lunch, and let them go. Janet Canterbury, who was by then a national board member of NOW, called Reno to complain.

"What's going on here? It looks to me as if the Dade County taxpayers just treated a bunch of terrorists to a free picnic!"

"Janet," Reno replied calmly, "we didn't have any choice. We treated them the same way we treated any first-time offenders: booked them, then released them on their own recognizance. If you don't like it, try to change the law."

R eno confronted the same kinds of legal and political considerations, and we at NOW experienced the same kind of frustration, after she was confirmed as attorney general. Especially after the nightmare years of both the Reagan and Bush Justice Departments, NOW's hopes were high that Reno would involve the FBI in curtailing attacks on abortion clinics, rather than relying solely on the Bureau of Alcohol, Tobacco, and Firearms. When Michael Griffin shot Dr. David Gunn in March 1993, Ellie Smeal and I both spoke to Reno about the need to bring the resources of the FBI to bear in ending the escalating violence. Although Reno was accessible and returned all our calls—and although she and President Clinton both issued strong statements against the violence—Reno warned Smeal, "I'm going to take action, but I'm not going to be able to act as quickly as you would like."

These are words no activist likes to hear. But they were far better than the previous administration's refusal to act at all. And Reno was true to her word. In December 1993, when NOW's attorney, Fay Clayton, argued our racketeering case against Operation Rescue before the U.S. Supreme Court, an attorney from Janet Reno's Justice Department argued on our side—a far cry from the days of the Bush administration when the Justice Department, under Dick Thornburgh, had gone to court on the side of Operation Rescue to argue against the use of federal marshals to keep the clinics open. As I sat at counsel's table that day, I looked up to see another powerful Clinton appointee, Ruth Bader Ginsburg, on the bench.

Later, when the Freedom of Access to Clinic Entrances Act and the Violence Against Women Act passed with Janet Reno's active support, I felt as if we had turned a corner, not only in combating the violence, but also in the politics of the nation.

The pressures of being on the inside are high, and the risks of doing battle with your superiors on the job can be terrifying. In so many important ways, it all comes down to power—not over others, but over yourself.

I know that I had little power as a flight attendant. And I know that while I had some power as a lawyer, that power was tempered by the desires of my clients and my firm. I chose not to run for election to the Florida House of Representatives because I knew I'd just be another comparatively powerless first-year legislator there, worrying about getting reelected every other year. Instead, I left the inside world for the outside, because I wanted to be able to change things and, at the same time, never to have to keep my mouth shut again. That doesn't mean I don't value women who choose to work for change from the inside, only that it doesn't suit me any longer. From a feminist perspective, I see power as the freedom to set my own agenda—and I want to extend the same to other women.

I can say that I have more real power in my personal and political lives because I have taken control of my life and begun to go after what I want for myself and other women. But I believe we can all do that from whatever position we're in. And I also believe that if insiders and outsiders can learn to work more effectively together, all women will be empowered one day.

After winning big in the 1992 elections, we felt certain that we'd be able to translate some of the gains we had made in public opinion into public policy. We planned on turning more of our resources toward pressuring Congress and the White House to make that policy.

Our confidence seemed well placed: During his first week in office, President Clinton signed several executive orders reversing some of the onerous antiabortion policies of the Reagan and Bush administrations.

But 1993 and 1994 brought us important lessons on how easy it is to get pushed backward and how important it is to maintain our vigilance.

Before Clinton's inauguration in January 1993, the Supreme Court had issued its ruling in *Bray* v. *Alexandria Women's Health Center*, one of the NOW-initiated cases against Operation Rescue under the Klan Act. The Supreme Court's decision overruled a federal appeals court in Virginia, which had upheld an injunction issued against Operation Rescue. In effect, the Court said that all of the antiabortion attacks did not violate women's civil rights.

Legally this ruling was a blow to NOW's litigation strategy: We had used the same civil rights law against Operation Rescue in New York, Maryland, and the District of Columbia, as well as in Virginia. But politically it was just as devastating: Antiabortion terrorists characterized the decision as a signal that their tactics of violence and intimidation were somehow acceptable forms of legitimate social protest.

NOW warned that this ruling would be interpreted as a green light to antiabortionists to increase their destruction and mayhem. In fact, following this decision there was a striking increase in clinic attacks, including bombing and arson, as well as an alarming increase in the incidents of stalking of patients, doctors, clinic staff, and their families. Death threats against abortion providers increased after *Bray*, from eight in 1992 to seventy-eight in 1993. Bomb threats rose from twelve to twenty-two. And, for the first time, the antiabortion violence escalated to murder: that spring, Michael Griffin shot Dr. David Gunn three times in the back outside a Pensacola abortion clinic. We watched in horror as the earlier gains of our litigation strategy seemed to slip away.

A year later, we regained some of the legal ground we had

lost. In December 1993, attorney Fay Clayton argued brilliantly on NOW's behalf in the U.S. Supreme Court and won a ruling that allowed NOW to use the powerful federal racketeering law against the violent antiabortion extremists. Even more surprising than the relatively short period it took for the Court to render their decision in *NOW* v. *Scheidler* (a mere six and a half weeks) was the final vote: 9–0, in our favor.

With a unanimous Supreme Court decision, we finally had some strong legal ground under our feet, not to mention the prospect of forcing antiabortion organizations to pay triple damages. But the case had other, nonlegal results as well. Although not an accurate legal interpretation, the public had seen the *Bray* decision as confirmation that the antiabortion terrorists were really a legitimate social protest movement, like the civil rights marchers of the sixties, not like the Klan; just as inaccurately and just as importantly, the *Scheidler* opinion was viewed popularly as confirmation that the antiabortion extremists were not engaged in civil rights work but in organized criminal activity—just like the Mob.

The Supreme Court victory was especially sweet for me. Back in 1986 when we began the case, I had argued adamantly, but unsuccessfully, that we should include racketeering in our complaint. It was in the brief period when I had taken over as lead counsel, before passing that role on to Fay, that we had amended the case to include the counts of racketeering. By 1994, we had lost in court on our antitrust and our anti-Klan/ civil rights complaints. Only my racketeering theory had survived.

As it turned out, however, our win in *NOW* v. *Scheidler* was a bright spot in an otherwise dismal period. In addition to the escalation of antiabortion violence, domestic violence made headlines in 1993 and 1994. In October 1993, Lorena Bobbitt cut off the penis of her abusive husband, John Wayne Bobbitt, after she said he'd raped her. The case became a media sensation. But the national obsession with John's genitalia obscured Lorena's sad story: a tale of abuse, dependency, and desperation.

At one point in their marriage, Lorena testified at her trial, she had considered leaving John; she hadn't done so, though, because she was from Venezuela and her immigration status depended on her marriage. (Protection for immigrant women whose status depends on abusive husbands was one of the disputed provisions of the Violence Against Women Act—the Senate had threatened to eliminate it.) Lorena Bobbitt's case reminded me of my doomed client Ling Lo, who had taken her own and her husband's life so many years ago, and I wondered once again what the full story behind that tragedy might have been.

During her trial almost everyone involved—the prosecutor, all four psychiatric experts, and a score of defense witnesses—agreed that Bobbitt had repeatedly beaten, raped, and verbally abused his wife throughout their five-year marriage, and that he'd raped her again the night she attacked him. Lorena Bobbitt was eventually acquitted. But six months after her trial, we had still not been successful in passing the Violence Against Women Act and getting the legal protection and the resources it would provide to keep women like her from feeling they had to resort to such desperate measures.

Then on June 13, 1994, Nicole Brown Simpson and Ron Goldman were found brutally murdered outside her home in Brentwood, California. Like the rest of the country, I watched transfixed as her ex-husband, former pro-football player O. J. Simpson, led the police on an eerie slow-motion chase along the Los Angeles Freeway.

NOW used the high visibility of this case to highlight the problem of violence against women, and to point out the continued failure of Congress to pass the Violence Against Women Act. We asked our chapters to write letters to the editors of their local newspapers and to call in to radio and TV talk shows.

Every person who called our offices about the murders was also urged to call Congress.

While we didn't know who had murdered Nicole and Ron, we did know that O. J. had admitted and been convicted of battering Nicole and that the system had failed them both. He had been given a thirty-day suspended sentence, paid a laughable seven-hundred-dollar fine, and been ordered to get counseling, which he was allowed to complete by telephone. What would have happened, I asked at a widely covered demonstration on Capitol Hill, if police, prosecutors, and judges had received the training in recognizing and handling wife-abuse cases provided under the Violence Against Women Act? It was too late to save Nicole, I argued, but not too late for millions of other women.

In July 1994 I was out of the country on leave—writing this book—when NOW's action vice president Rosemary Dempsey and national secretary Karen Johnson called with devastating news. Abortion provider Dr. John Bayard Britton and clinic defender Jim Barrett had been murdered by a shotgun-wielding antiabortion terrorist in Pensacola, Florida. June Barrett, also a clinic defender and NOW member, lay in a hospital bed, wounded. For the first time, NOW members had been cut down for defending abortion rights. Heartsick, I ended my leave early and flew back to the United States.

That August Congress finally passed the Violence Against Women Act. It authorizes money for rape education and battered women's shelters and for law enforcement and judicial training. But the big gain (and one of the sticking points on the Hill) is that the act recognizes that violent crimes against women based on sex are hate crimes—and therefore a violation of the victim's civil rights. Civil rights violations are grounds for lawsuits in civil courts, where the standard of proof is less than the "beyond a reasonable doubt" requirement in criminal cases. It also guarantees protection for immigrant women by disconnecting their legal status as immigrants from that of their husbands.

During the debates on the bill and in the wake of the 1994 elections as Congress has tried to cut $50 million from Violence

Against Women Act funding, some have asked why a federal law was needed at all, why state laws don't suffice. Among the reasons: Now a man can no longer escape across state lines to evade prosecution for these crimes. (The first man prosecuted under the Violence Against Women Act beat his wife and drove to another state with her shoved in the trunk of his car. Under the act, that was now a federal offense, and Janet Reno's Justice Department was willing to prosecute. Even if he hadn't been convicted, under the criminal provisions of the act, his wife could have grounds to sue for civil damages.) Passage of the act was a long-awaited triumph.

But I knew from the murders of Barrett and Britton just two months after passage of the Freedom of Access to Clinic Entrances Act that passage of this bill didn't necessarily mean women would be any safer than we'd been before. As if to confirm my growing apprehension, in October Baltimore Circuit Court Judge Robert Cahill sentenced convicted murderer Ken Peacock to an unbelievable eighteen months. Peacock had come home unexpectedly one evening to find his wife, Sandra, in bed with another man. After chasing him away, Ken spent the next eight hours or so drinking beer and arguing with Sandra. At some point in the night, he fired a shot into the wall behind their bed. Along toward morning, he shot Sandra in cold blood. Judge Cahill lamented having to sentence a "noncriminal" at all and recommended that Ken be allowed to serve his sentence on work release.

On October 31, 1994, I checked into Pensacola's New World Landing. An old, converted warehouse on the waterfront, the hotel reeks of vintage Gulf Coast: Large vases of dried cotton plants line the halls; photos of the cotton trade from past centuries decorate the walls. Founded in the sixteenth century, Pensacola is one of Florida's oldest cities. Hilly, full of stately old homes, situated between bayous and bluffs on Escambia Bay, it is arguably one of the most beautiful. It's also a favorite target city for antiabortion terrorists—one which I've visited all too often during my years as an activist.

That Halloween I was there with Florida NOW lobbyist Ann Gannon. I'd asked Ann to meet me in order to monitor one of the most wrenching murder trials in my experience. On that crisp autumn day, as Ann and I walked down Pensacola's picturesque Main Street, I was afraid. This was the place where, three months before, Jim and June Barrett and Dr. John Bayard Britton, whom they were escorting to work, had been gunned down by antiabortion terrorist Paul Hill. The two men died; June was wounded, but she had survived.

Paul Hill had already been convicted in the first case brought by the Justice Department under the new Freedom of Access to Clinic Entrances Act, and that case had attracted huge crowds of reporters and abortion rights activists. I knew that the state murder trial starting today would draw far fewer supporters, and I wanted to be there so that Ann and I could not only discuss strategy with local activists, but also make sure they did not feel abandoned.

Pensacola's ugly history hovered in the background. The New World Landing had icons of Mighty Cotton, but nothing to memorialize the slaves who had lived and died servicing the crop. This is a town where annually on Martin Luther King Day the memorial to him is defaced. A place where the Klan picketed the abortion clinic, but made sure we all knew that they were only selectively antiabortion: J. D. Adler, a spokesperson for the United Klans of Florida said the Klan did not care if black or Jewish women had abortions. And less than two years earlier, Pensacola abortion provider Dr. David Gunn had become the first doctor to pay for his dedication to women's health care with his life.

As Ann and I walked down the few blocks to the courthouse—a Southern classic surrounded by huge Spanish moss–draped oak trees—my eyes darted around, nervously searching for anything that seemed out of the ordinary. I'm often asked if I get scared working in crime-ridden Washington, D.C., and, when I practiced law in downtown Miami, some women who lived in the suburbs refused to come to my office for NOW meetings because they were afraid. Of course, I have the same general daily misgivings as any woman living in a society where violence against us is a common occurrence. But I have never felt quite the same fear for my own life and safety leaving my office in Miami or D.C. in the dark of night as I did in Pensacola on that bright, sunny day.

My fears weren't eased when we arrived at the courthouse, which was surrounded by police barricades. Security was tight; tension was everywhere. Ann and I made our way across the wide expanse of lawn, past the shady trees, and into the building. We placed our briefcases on X-ray conveyor belts, walked through metal detectors, and gathered our belongings together before heading for the elevators.

As we got off on the fifth floor I immediately spied David Trosch. A Roman Catholic priest who espouses the murder of abortion providers and pro-choice supporters alike, Trosch was a potential witness and had been temporarily excluded from the courtroom by the prosecution. He is a pasty-skinned man, and his face and neck overflow his rigid white collar. He gives the impression of being made of dough at first, but, at closer range, he projects a poisonous fleshiness. His white hair is wispy. He wears small glasses that reflect light and your own image back at you. We didn't acknowledge each other. Yet, as I recognized the look of smug self-righteousness on his face, my fear turned to anger. And I felt glad in a way: Under the circumstances, anger was a much better emotion than fear. After all, I'd be spending the next several days sitting in a courtroom surrounded by people like Trosch who believed that the murders of people like Jim Barrett and Bayard Britton, people like me, were justifiable homicides.

Several weeks earlier I'd appeared on the TV talk show *Rolonda* to discuss antiabortion violence. Trosch had been on that program, too, along with Flip Benham, then national director of Operation Rescue. Benham, a self-ordained minister from

Texas, sports an Elvis-style pompadour. Before and after the show he stood outside in the parking lot waving his Bible around, verbally accosting me and everyone else who happened to walk by. "Pray for Patricia Ireland! Pray for her to see the light! Pray for Jesus to save her!" I couldn't help noticing that his touching concern for my immortal soul disappeared as soon as the television cameras shut down.

David Gunn Jr., son of the murdered Dr. David Gunn, and Dr. George Klopfer, an abortion provider from Illinois, were also on the show that day. When the program began, Trosch and I were seated on opposite sides of a small coffee table—a distance that was fine with me. But during the first commercial break the table was removed and our chairs pushed closer together to make room for the other guests. Sitting so close to a man who advocated my murder made my skin crawl. As I looked over at David Gunn Jr., and at Jim Barrett's son Bruce, sitting in the front row of the audience, I felt a physical revulsion toward Trosch like I'd never experienced before. Both David and Bruce had lost their fathers to this madness. I could hardly bear to be so near Trosch. Remembering that show, I was happy to avoid him now as he paced the courtroom hallway.

The cast of other antiabortion characters at the trial was truly extraordinary. Daniel Ware, an unemployed taxi driver from Houston, Texas, would have been funny with his big stomach, red suspenders, three-inch sideburns, body odor, and hair combed over his bald spot—except that he had already been arrested in Houston's Hobby Airport, heavily armed, after reportedly traveling to Pensacola for an attack on abortion providers meeting there. Prosecutors had failed to get a conviction, and Ware was in and out of the courtroom throughout the trial.

I noted with as much amusement as I could muster under the circumstances that all the antiabortion spokespeople were women. For years, NOW had highlighted the fact that men dominated the leadership of most antiabortion groups. Sensitive to the imagery involved, these groups had finally begun putting forward women to speak on their behalf. Behind the scenes, though, nothing has changed: The antiabortion leadership is overwhelmingly male and white.

One of these newly anointed spokeswomen is Donna Bray, who represents a group called the Defenders for Life. Donna has black-penciled eyebrows, a mouth made to crack gum, and a tough demeanor more suited to a black leather motorcycle jacket than the pink dresses she favored during the trial. When someone chided her outside the courtroom for smoking—and asked whether her church approved—she immediately snapped, "Well, what's *your* vice?" Quality runs in the family. Donna's brother-in-law is Michael Bray, who served eight years in prison for conspiracy to bomb ten clinics in three states and the District of Columbia and for obtaining the destructive devices to do so.

On the second day of the trial, Donna and I appeared—by satellite, from (thankfully) different locations—on a 6:30 A.M. Segment of *CBS This Morning*. When we arrived at the courthouse later that morning, she walked up and introduced herself as if we were supposed to act like mutually respectful colleagues or worthy opponents. I was taken aback. Didn't she understand that the struggle we were engaged in was a very real matter of life and death? She seemed to expect some response from me beyond my decidedly cool "hello." But what can you possibly say to someone who wants you dead?

The local Pensacola antiabortion spokesperson was Vicky Conroy, who has the face and build of a prizefighter with a personality to match. She has been known to picket the clinic wearing a skirt splashed with red paint. Vicky claims to reject the use of violence, but her actions don't match her words. She had stalked Bayard Britton at the Pensacola airport, snapped his picture, identified him via his license plate, and put out Wanted posters listing his name, address, home phone number, and work schedule. During the *Rolanda* show, when Trosch's presence nearly made me physically ill, she was in the audience; she had the temerity to complain that I was unfairly associating her and other peaceful pro-lifers with violence. I could barely control my fury at her phony facade of innocence. But I managed to keep my voice steady as I responded that, while she may not have pulled the shotgun trigger, she might as well have pinned a target on Dr. Britton's back.

Conspicuously absent from the trial was local antiabortionist John Burt. This former Klansman had been a major presence at the trial of Michael Griffin ten months earlier for the murder of Dr. David Gunn; Griffin's defense team tried to portray Burt as a kind of antiabortion Svengali who had manipulated Griffin into shooting Gunn. This particular defense tactic failed to save Griffin from conviction and a life sentence for murder. Also conspicuously absent was Flip Benham. Thank goodness for small favors.

I had expected it would take some time to select a jury for this case because the prosecution was seeking the death penalty. To my surprise, though, a full jury had been seated by midafternoon of the first day. All twelve jurors (and both alternates) were white; every black woman in the jury pool had been excluded because of her stated opposition to the death penalty. I scanned the jury, trying to size it up.

During the three days of testimony from twenty-seven witnesses (including June Barrett) the story of what had happened outside the Ladies Center clinic on the morning of July 29, 1994, was presented to the court and jury. Paul Hill had been a familiar figure at the Ladies Center. He'd picketed there for months (beginning shortly after Griffin killed Gunn on March 10, 1993). But Hill hadn't limited himself to the Ladies Center. He'd also been spotted walking around, wearing an empty pistol holster, at a NOW rally in Pensacola on Mother's Day 1993, which we'd staged to protest Gunn's murder. The turnout had been extraordinary: Three thousand marchers participated, and Paul Hill had lurked among them. Officer Steve Ordonia testified Hill had told him, at the time, that the empty holster represented the need to use violence to protect the unborn. I shivered. I'd been at that rally; NOW had used it as a kickoff for one final push in our successful campaign to pressure Congress into passing the Freedom of Access to Clinic Entrances Act.

Deputy Stephen Wilmer, a veteran of seven and a half years as a county and city police officer, testified that he'd talked to Hill while working as a security guard at the Ladies Center. Hill had carried picket signs that read EXECUTE MURDERERS, ABORTIONISTS, ACCESSORIES. When asked who he meant by "accessories," Hill replied that Wilmer himself was an accessory. Wilmer then asked Hill if that meant he ought to be executed. Hill had shrugged and said, "Read the sign." Other signs found in Hill's garage after the murders included one that read MURDERERS DESERVE DEATH, ABORTIONISTS ARE MURDERERS.

Although it did not come out at the trial, I'd also seen a videotape (taken by NOW escorts at the Ladies Center) in which Hill said on camera: "I should have the 'right to choose' to shoot every one of you in there."

All in all, this is hardly the portrait of a man who deserved the right to bear arms. But on July 27, 1994, without a hitch, Hill bought a Mosberg pump shotgun at Mike's Gun Shop in the small nearby town of Milton, where John Burt runs a group home for pregnant women. Hill also purchased five boxes of Winchester and one box of Remington double-ought twelve-gauge 2/3-inch shotgun shells. Then he headed off to hone his aim at the International Shooting Range in Santa Rosa County, just east of Pensacola.

Meanwhile, the decent people whose lives he was about to ruin prepared for other work. June Barrett, a retired nurse, had worked for more than twenty years in the Public Health Service. Jim Barrett had served thirty years in the air force, attaining the rank of lieutenant colonel, then taught high school math and science for fifteen years before retiring. Both were in their early seventies. They were active in their church, the Pensacola Unitarian Universalists' Fellowship. June's son from a previous marriage had died of AIDS; both June and Jim were active in an AIDS group and in P-FLAG (the Parents and Friends of Lesbians and Gays). When June mentioned during her testimony that she and Jim were Unitarians, several men sitting in court near David Trosch smirked and nudged each other. When she mentioned her involvement with P-FLAG, these same men poked each other again; one of them turned toward me and rolled his eyes, sneering.

June and Jim became active with Escambia NOW's clinic defense project shortly before the murder of Dr. David Gunn in 1993. I'd actually seen them once before, when I'd come to Pensacola after that first shooting. I remembered June as a small woman who exuded energy beyond her years. She was tiny-waisted and glowed with maternal warmth. Jim had a round, kind face. Although he'd spent three decades in the military and owned a gun, his involvement with June and with their church had made him more committed to a philosophy of nonviolence. By the time he was cut down by Paul Hill, Jim no longer carried a gun.

June and Jim had known Bayard Britton for about fifteen months. Dr. Britton lived in Fernandina Beach, Florida, a small community near Jacksonville. His elderly, impoverished rural patients remembered him as someone who'd make housecalls, someone who didn't try to collect if you couldn't pay. He flew into Pensacola regularly to provide abortion services at the clinic there. As volunteer escorts, June and Jim would pick him up at the airport on the last Friday of each month. They also volunteered at the clinic, helping patients and staff push through crowds of antiabortion picketers, confirming patient appointments before letting people in.

On the morning of July 29, June and Jim had picked up Bayard at the Pensacola airport just after 7:00 A.M. When she greeted him with a hug, June could feel the bulletproof vest he wore. When they arrived at the clinic in their pickup truck, Paul Hill was standing in the driveway waving something that looked like a pamphlet.

"Now Paul Hill, get out of the way, you know us. Get out of the way," Jim said under his breath. They'd spoken before; Hill had seen them transporting Britton on many occasions. He stepped away and let the truck drive by. After they moved past, June noticed Paul holding something up to his face. She thought, "He's pretending to shoot us." Then she saw the shotgun's recoil, and heard three loud shots. Jim had already stepped out of the truck; he was hit by the first blasts. June fell to the floor in the backseat. The next thing she heard was Bayard asking if Jim had brought his gun. No, she answered. Three or four more shots rang out.

Looking up, June saw what she described to the court as "the drip drip drip of blood." "Doc, are you OK?" she whispered. But there was no response. She asked again. The only answer was the sirens speeding toward the clinic. And she said to herself, "No, he's not OK." As the sirens got closer and she heard voices, June sat up and called out, "Help me."

Several other witnesses heard the shotgun blasts that morning. Elizabeth Pinch, who worked in the deli at the Del Champs supermarket across from the Ladies Center, was one of several people who called 911. She and several others also followed Hill or kept him in sight, afterward, to make sure he did not escape.

Officer Bruce Martin, who had been on the Pensacola police force just eleven months, was about a quarter of a mile away from the Ladies Center when he heard the alert on his radio. Driving toward the clinic, he saw Hill approaching. The killer was staggering southbound. Several people were following him, waving their hands frantically to get the officer's attention. Martin stepped out of his car, drew his own weapon, and ordered Hill to lie on the ground.

When veteran Officer Mark Holmes arrived, he found them like that: Officer Martin with his firearm drawn, trained on Hill, who was facedown on the ground. Holmes proceeded to cuff and search the suspect. Later, when they lifted him to his feet, Hill smiled. "I know one thing. No innocent babies are going to be killed in that clinic today."

"What did you say?"

"At least there'll be no more babies killed there today," Hill said.

On the stand, June was remarkably composed. She broke down only once, describing the deaths of her husband and the doctor. Listening to her, I raged inside. I was impressed that she allowed herself to show only a small hint of anger: when she identified Paul Hill to the jury as "the blond man over there, with the smirk on his face," Hill's supporters groaned. But it was an accurate description: The murderer did have a mysterious half-smile, and others noticed it.

After three days of testimony, the jury took less than two hours to convict Hill of first-degree murder in the deaths of Bayard Britton and Jim Barrett. Hill was also convicted of the attempted murder of June Barrett and of shooting into an occupied vehicle.

That evening, I met with local NOW activists, as well as organizers from the Feminist Majority at the Ladies Center clinic to plan future strategies. As daylight faded, word spread among our clinic escorts outside that the new doctor was on his way.

As we awaited his arrival, I could feel our tension mount. Still, I was unprepared for the tangle of emotions that swelled inside me when he finally did appear. First, an extremely muscular man in a tight T-shirt and SWAT team jacket burst into the room with his gun drawn, surveyed the scene, then waved in his colleague accompanied by the clinic's new doctor. Compared to his bodyguards the man looked terribly small and vulnerable. My God, I thought, he's so young.

Despite the elaborate precautions and preparations, the door to the clinic area was locked, and no one seemed to have the key. The doctor had glanced at me as he was hurried through our small group. Waiting for the door to be unlocked, he openly stared at me.

"Do I know you?"

"I'm Patricia Ireland," I said, trying to sound calm, "the president of the National Organization for Women."

"I thought so! I want to thank you and your folks for what you're doing."

The door was finally unlocked. Police escorts whisked him through.

That door would not be unlocked often. Nor would the doors at his home.

Outside, Vicky Conroy and her antiabortion crew were already carrying Wanted posters for Pensacola's new abortion doctor—the same posters that had turned out to be death warrants for his predecessors.

Throughout the trial, one witness who did not take the stand was Paul Hill himself.

In fact, the only words anyone heard from Hill during the entire proceeding were the three sentences he read to the court after his conviction.

"You have a responsibility to protect your neighbors and use force if necessary to do so," Hill read. "You may mix my blood with the blood of the unborn. May God help you to protect the lives of the unborn as you would want to be protected."

This came at the close of the penalty phase of the trial in which the jury had to decide whether or not to recommend death for Paul Hill. (NOW was opposed to a death sentence. Our news statement in Pensacola said that state-sanctioned violence wouldn't put an end to antiabortion violence but would only reinforce the belief that violence is an appropriate solution to problems if you think you're right.) Prosecutor Jim Murray argued that Hill's crime was especially heinous, atrocious, cruel. He described Hill standing over the body of Jim Barrett surveying his deadly handiwork, before reloading his shotgun and striding around to the front of the truck. Perhaps Bayard was unwilling to abandon June in the back of the truck. Perhaps he was frozen in fear. For whatever reason, he sat and watched as his executioner came across the clinic parking lot. Hill crouched for better aim and pulled the trigger.

* * *

I stayed in Pensacola to hear the testimony in the penalty phase of the trial. Then I flew back to Washington. My plane was still in the air when the jury returned and recommended to the judge that he sentence Hill to death in the electric chair.

In the taxi from National Airport to my apartment, I felt numb. When I got home I flipped on the TV, hoping to hear what the jury had decided. The first images on the screen were of debris and body parts strewn over the Pennsylvania countryside: A USAir flight had ended in a fiery, deadly crash. A few tears rolled down my face as I watched. Then the floodgates opened inside, and I found myself sobbing in utter despair. In that moment, I felt as if everything I'd done had come to nothing. All of my organizing, all of my rhetoric, all of my best efforts had simply not been enough to stop the murders and the violence. I felt like a total fraud: Here I was holding myself out to the world as a leader, but none of my strategizing or hard work seemed to have made any difference.

I realized I'd thrown myself into work all that summer and fall to keep my emotions at bay. I'd done that all my life; now, though, my feelings were closing in on me. I'd gotten to know some of the family Jim Barrett had left behind. They were wonderful people—and I felt I'd been partly responsible for their grief and loss. The clinic escorting project the Barretts had participated in was initiated by Escambia NOW as part of the national Project Stand Up for Women I had developed. I felt as if I'd put them in harm's way. I also had to confront my own fear. It could easily have been me dying in a pool of blood. How many times had I defended a clinic? I had passed through anti-abortion picket lines at the Ladies Center itself.

For me, this was another taste of the bitter costs women pay when we try to gain political control—or even control over our own bodies. It took me a long time to recover from the terrible anguish of this experience. But the pain I felt was not for myself alone, nor was it just for the families of those murdered activists; it was for brave people everywhere who dare to take a stand against right-wing terrorism and brutality. After all, I was one of the people urging them to fight.

A week after the Hill trial ended, feminist candidates suffered extensive defeats in the 1994 elections. And six weeks later "pro-lifer" John Salvi opened fire at two clinics in Brookline, Massachusetts, murdering Shannon Lowney and Lee Ann Nichols, and wounding five others.

I t wasn't easy to pull myself out of that emotional nosedive after the Hill trial, the elections, and the shootings in Brookline. In fact, it took months. I'd wake up sometimes feeling depressed and empty. But I finally regained some equilibrium. I did so by looking back over the past few years and reviewing some of the concrete gains from the work we had done at NOW. I made a mental tally sheet of good things and bad.

After Anita Hill's confrontation with the Senate Judiciary Committee, we had organized people's outrage to convince Congress to pass once again the new Civil Rights Act previously vetoed by President Bush—and to force him to sign it this time. Women who faced sexual harassment and other job discrimination now had the right to have their claims heard by a jury and the right to damages.

We had focused the horror at David Gunn's death into pressure on Congress to pass the Freedom of Access to Clinic Entrances Act. With clearer jurisdiction, the Justice Department was now taking stronger action to counter antiabortion extremists.

And with the helpful support of the first woman attorney general, we had been able to translate Nicole Brown Simpson's terrible tragedy into passage of the Violence Against Women Act, which had languished in Congress for years.

Each of these major progressive laws had been instituted, after many fruitless attempts, only after terrible suffering and in some cases blood sacrifice. Knowing that the humiliation of Anita Hill and the deaths of David Gunn and Nicole Brown Simpson had not been in vain helped me pull myself together.

We had made real, measurable progress. And if we had not been able to prevent the deaths of Nicole Brown Simpson, Ron Goldman, David Gunn, John Bayard Britton, Jim Barrett, Shannon Lowney, and Lee Ann Nichols, that was a measure of how much remains to be done and how important it is that we continue our work.

I'd always known there was no magic wand we could wave, no final victory we might win, that would mean women's lives and our rights would finally and forever be safe. None of the laws passed meant that harassment at work or domestic violence or antiabortion terrorism would automatically end. If the carnage of 1994 taught us anything, it is that we can't stop with changing laws—that's just a first step. We have to change the entire culture that supports and legitimates discrimination and violence against women. And change doesn't happen just because laws are passed or because time passes; it happens because we make it happen.

I also knew that if I let myself become dispirited or discouraged, I could never be an effective leader. Even if it's sometimes hard to see the progress, we must understand that the work itself is important. I had to remind myself that years before, during the ERA campaign, I decided that I wanted to do this work for its own sake. Now, I had to reaffirm my faith that it would make a difference in the long run—even if I did not live to see it. In the meantime, I had to rededicate myself to the sheer joy of fighting back.

I focused on the memory of leaders who had inspired me. I thought of Susan B. Anthony, who never lived to see women win the right to vote, and of Martin Luther King Jr., who somehow knew that he would not live to see the fulfillment of his dream. But both had built bridges between a troubled time and a better future. That was what I had to try to be, too: a bridge. We may not reach the other side, but if we don't build those bridges, sometimes at great cost, no one will ever get across.

The deaths of so many reminded me of how fragile life is—and how ephemeral. And short. All the more crucial, then, to live a life full of meaning, a life both fulfilling and significant.

AFTERWORD

I n 1995, as we celebrated the seventy-fifth anniversary of women's right to vote in this country, I thought often of my grandmothers. They were young women, already mothers, before that hard-earned right was won. I have had so much more opportunity in my life than they did. And for some of us the differences between our world and the world in which our grandmothers grew up is even more profound and shows even more clearly how far we have come.

I first met Congresswoman Carrie Meek during the campaign for the Equal Rights Amendment, when she was a pro-ERA legislator from Miami. I was proud to campaign with her when she first ran for Congress in 1992. Congresswoman Meek's grandparents were slaves. Her parents were sharecroppers. Carrie and her sister both worked as "domestics," household help in someone else's home. Now Carrie Meek brings her important perspective to the U.S. Congress.

But we don't have to look back to the days of our grandmothers for encouragement. So much progress has been made just in my adult lifetime. The 1963 Equal Pay Act and Title VII of the 1964 Civil Rights Act prohibit discrimination on the job. Title IX, the federal equal education law passed in 1972, opened up professional and other schools and athletic scholarships for women and girls. The Supreme Court finally recognized the right to abortion in 1973, following decisions confirming the right to birth control for married couples in 1963, then for all people in 1972.

The Equal Credit Opportunity Act in 1974 gave women a basis for challenging discriminatory consumer lending practices, and in 1988 Congress extended equal opportunity laws to cover commercial credit as well. The Pregnancy Discrimination Act of 1978 and the Family and Medical Leave Act of 1993 were additional steps in the still unfinished business of creating workplace equity and a better balance between our families, our health, and our work.

The Supreme Court confirmed that sexual harassment is illegal job discrimination in 1986, and between the Court and the 1992 Civil Rights Act, women now can sue for damages in cases of harassment in school and on the job. The Violence Against Women Act, passed in 1994, brought additional funding and attention to the pervasive problem of violence in our lives and a historic breakthrough in acknowledging the role violence plays in limiting women's civil rights.

Legal gains at the federal level have been matched by progress at the state and local levels. Programs for so-called displaced homemakers, rape crisis centers, and battered women's shelters were created and funded. State legislatures and city councils have passed lesbian and gay civil rights laws.

Women have entered previously all-male bastions—everything from the soapbox derby and Little League to MacSorley's Ale House, West Point, and Annapolis. Women in increasing numbers have moved from city councils, state legislatures, and county courts to the Congress, the Cabinet, and the Supreme Court.

In addition to changing the laws, feminist activists have changed our language and our culture. Like the civil rights movement, the women's rights movement recognized that language is not trivial (and, of course, the entire legal system is built on the same principle). By insisting that adult females be called "women," we helped shape a view of us as adults, fully capable of making our own decisions and participating as equals in our society. We popularized slogans like "Every mother is a working mother" and descriptive phrases like "women who work outside the home" to underscore the real value of women's traditional roles in the family. As we shifted from talking about policemen, firemen, and mailmen, to police officers, firefighters, and letter carriers, more little girls and grown-up women could picture ourselves in these untraditional roles as well.

In my early years as an activist, when women would win some breakthrough vote in Congress or a landmark decision from the Supreme Court, I didn't always have a ready response when reporters would call for a quote. Sometimes it was difficult to get accurate information in time; sometimes I was reluctant to reduce a complex situation to a one-line opinion. Eventually Janet and I came up with an all-occasion sound bite: "We've come a long way, but we still have a long way to go."

It's as true now as it was then.

When I look at how far we've come, I am thrilled and inspired. And I am optimistic about meeting the challenge of our future. But we must be realistic about how serious the threats to women's progress are. The progress we have made was not inevitable, and it is not irreversible.

We have indeed come a long way from the early days of our country, but some things haven't changed. From the birth of our country to the present day, women's efforts to empower ourselves, and resistance to those efforts, have continued. Many of us are familiar with Abigail Adams's admonition to her husband, John, that he and the other founding fathers should "Remember the Ladies" in drafting our country's founding documents and laws. "Do not put such unlimited power into the hands of husbands," she wrote. "Remember all men would be tyrants if they could." Fewer of us are familiar with John's reply, which is noteworthy both for its astuteness in assessing the possibility that "the ladies" would be remembered and for its honesty. "Depend on it," he wrote back. "We know better than to repeal our masculine system."

For centuries, power has been held in a very narrow range of hands; they are the hands of men like John Adams—rich, white, able-bodied, and apparently straight. Some of them have been good men, men who believe in abstract concepts of equality, liberty, and justice, but whose experience nevertheless represents a very limited part of the total life of our country and its people.

Questions of power and control are at the heart of the current attacks on women's rights and women's progress in dismantling John Adams's "masculine system." As those of us who don't look like John Adams have made some inroads and gained some tiny toeholds in the arenas of real power, the strength and vehemence of the response is one measure of our progress. If we are not only to avoid losing ground but indeed to continue moving forward, we must learn from our history.

A hundred years ago, in 1896, the Supreme Court's decision in *Plessy* v. *Ferguson* heralded the end of the post-Civil War Reconstruction era and cleared the way for the firm establishment of racial segregation. Jim Crow laws, passed throughout the old Confederacy, established legally separate facilities for whites and blacks, while throughout the North the same segregation was enforced in fact, if not in law. Voting rights of African Americans were curtailed, and African Americans who had been serving in Congress and state legislatures lost their seats. Legal segregation was not ended for more than sixty years, and seventy-six years passed before Barbara Jordan from Texas and Andrew Young from Georgia broke through as the first blacks elected to Congress from the South since Reconstruction.

In speaking of the struggle for freedom and progress, abolitionist and suffragist Frederick Douglass warned, "Power concedes nothing without a demand; it never has and it never will." History bears him out. We didn't abolish slavery, we didn't win the right to vote, first for African American men and

then for all women, because we had a few good men in the
Congress or in the White House or on the Court, but because we
had strong individuals and strong movements that demanded
change. Now it is our turn to continue making that demand.
We have the ability and the responsibility not only to take control over our lives, but literally to change the course of history.

After more than seventy-five years of women's suffrage, I
think our slogan heading into the next century must be
"Women's Vote: Use It or Lose It!" because all of our rights
hang in the balance. Since the 1994 elections, the conservative
onslaught in Congress and in the states threatens all of the
progress we have made. The specifics of the attacks are important, but the atmosphere and attitudes of those in power in
Congress can be as revealing.

After the 1992 elections resulted in a doubling of women in
Congress, Dick Armey, a Texas Republican who now serves as
majority leader of the House, complained that the Congress,
which was still 90 percent men, had become too "femcentric."
It was also Armey who called Barney Frank, then one of three
openly gay men in the House, "Barney Fag." Armey said he
just mispronounced the last name, and Congressman Frank accepted his apology, although Frank did note that there are
many ways to mispronounce his name, none of which is Fag.

And what are we to make of Newt Gingrich's opinion, re-
vealed by his mother on national television, that Hillary Clin-
ton is a bitch? Based on what we have seen him act out in
Congress, I think it means that Newt Gingrich cannot stand
Hillary Clinton or any other woman *Being In Total Control of
Herself.* And as we said to Newt on a T-shirt we put out,
"That's Ms. Bitch to you!"

Despite Newt Gingrich's attempted revolution, we have
fought successfully to save many of the Violence Against
Women Act programs. But Congress slashed millions of dollars
in funding for urgently needed training for state and federal

judges in how to deal effectively with family violence, and funding for battered women's shelters has been cut even though shelters are already having to turn away beaten and frightened women every day.

Family planning funding was threatened in the House as well. Congress has voted to restore antiabortion policies from the Reagan–Bush era and passed a bill outlawing an abortion procedure that for some women who face a risk to their health or lives late in pregnancy may be the safest, most effective medical procedure. Among the more punishing changes was a Republican-led reversal of the requirement that states provide Medicaid–funded abortions for poor women who are pregnant as a result of rape or incest.

If not for the Constitution, I have little doubt access to abortion would be even more severely restricted, if not eliminated totally, and the extent of continued constitutional protection depends on the outcome of future elections and presidential politics. The landmark *Roe* v. *Wade* decision has already been eroded by the Supreme Court. How narrowly the Court will interpret our constitutional rights in the future will depend on appointments made by the president and confirmed by the Senate.

We are also facing challenges to our ability realistically to choose to have and raise our families. Nutrition programs for pregnant and nursing women, infants, and children; Head Start; school breakfast and lunch programs; public education; school loans; health care for the elderly and people with disabilities—all have been on the chopping block. President Clinton signed the Republicans' welfare repeal bill, but the issue of how to end poverty remains. Democrats and Republicans alike seem in need of basic sex education; they seem to think that babies come from welfare checks. They act as if it does not count as real work for a poor woman to raise emotionally and physically healthy children, keep them in school, out of gangs and off drugs (although middle-class and wealthy women are supposed to stay home with their children). We haven't seen the last of the punitive proposals from politicians of both parties who argue that poor women must be forced into the paid workforce, without adequate child care, health care, transportation, education, or job training, much less jobs that pay a living wage. The federal safety net that had been in place for sixty years has been ripped out from under all of us.

At the same time, opponents are trying to slam closed in our faces some of the doors that affirmative action has opened, however narrowly, for women and people of color. A bill to repeal affirmative action has been filed in Congress, the California Board of Regents has eliminated affirmative action in the state university system, and a deceptively worded anti-affirmative action ballot measure, disguised as a civil rights initiative, passed in 1996. Speaking of the affirmative action ballot measure, Newt Gingrich has been quoted as saying that the winds of political change often start in California and blow east. We must give him an updated weather report.

Many of us, men and women, are feeling economically insecure as the income and wealth gap widens between the middle class and poor, on the one hand, and the rich and super-rich, on the other. Fewer and fewer of us envision that we will do better than our parents or that our children will do better than we have. Current efforts to roll back affirmative action, like the attacks on poverty programs, seem to me to be cynical attempts by politicians to scapegoat women and people of color and divert attention away from the impact of their proposed tax and spending cuts that may further widen the gap between rich and poor.

"You're having trouble keeping your family together and your heads above water?" their argument goes. "Don't look up at those of us who are setting policy! Look over there at that undeserving poor woman who's taking your tax dollars, that undocumented worker or someone who seems 'foreign' to you, that unqualified woman or person of color who got your job through affirmative action—it must be their fault!"

Aid to Families with Dependent Children, or AFDC, commonly known as welfare, accounted for only about 1.1 percent of federal expenditures, and studies by the bipartisan federal Glass Ceiling Commission provide objective evidence that at the highest levels of the biggest companies in our country, 95 to 97 percent of the senior managers are still men, virtually all of them white. Still, we have to work hard to ensure even the barest level of continued sustenance for poor women and their families as well as to provide legal support for those trying to break into skilled craft jobs or through the glass ceiling.

The Supreme Court has made it harder, although not impossible, to maintain affirmative action. It has also narrowed application of voting rights laws in redrawing district lines to maximize election of African Americans and other people of color.

We must act to reverse these trends, and we must act quickly. Some of us may feel there is little we can do, that we are too weak to take on the entire Congress and the Supreme Court, too. Some of us are probably too overwhelmed with our own lives to imagine meeting one more challenge. But we don't have to resign ourselves to shrugging our shoulders and saying, "Well, Newt happens!" All of us have the power of our voices and our votes. Newt happens when 63 percent of the eligible voters stay home, as they did in 1994. Women, who were 54 percent of the voters in 1992, dropped to 51 percent in 1994. Women were 52 percent of the electorate in 1996, but nonvoters outnumbered voters within the voting-age population.

Participation in electoral politics is critical to the kind of world we will live in. Of course, if the choices on our ballot are Tweedle Dee and Tweedle Dumber, we've lost before we ever cast the first vote. So, some of us must run for office, too. I've long joked that our efforts to recruit women to run have been hindered by women's belief that to run a candidate has to be qualified. Looking at some of the current incumbents, I can only say women should set aside all humility and run. We are qualified. We don't need graduate degrees in law or political science. Believe me, there are plenty of lawyers running around in Congress and state legislatures and on local school boards. We need the experience of more teachers, child-care workers, nurses, social workers, and mothers, more of women's traditional work and experience in life represented at the table when public policy is set.

While I frequently see and hear in the media the question, "Can women *have* it all?" what I hear from women from all over the globe is, "Why do women have to *do* it all?" We have underpaid jobs in the workforce and unpaid jobs at home. Then I come along with the suggestion that we should all be political activists, too, and I know that some people will feel like running away, screaming.

But I want to assure all of us that the payoffs for taking control over our own lives, and making a difference in the future for all women, are enormous. Figuring out how to incorporate into our already busy lives the things we feel passionately about is well worth the effort. Fortunately, there are many ways to start, and we can all find ways to take part.

Whether we decide to correct a boss at work who calls women "honey" or to raise a fuss when the local laundry charges more to clean women's blouses than they charge a man for his shirts, life provides us with many opportunities to help make our society fairer and more equitable. We just have to decide which battles we want to take on.

Like many women, I took my first successful stand not out of any idealistic plan to save the world, but because of a concrete need. I had a strong and clear interest in the situation. After talking to the local NOW chapter, I knew I wasn't alone and I had the law on my side. I figured this all gave me a pretty good shot at winning, so I decided it was a fight worth waging.

Deciding when to draw a line in the sand depends on subjective as well as objective factors. When the time just doesn't feel right, I've learned to trust that impulse. As a flight attendant, sometimes I was just too tired to argue with the crew bus driver who asked if we "girls" had had a good trip (as he reached to take the heavy bags from my weary hands). As a lawyer, I sometimes decided that my interest in making partner—and my firm's interest in keeping our clients happy—outweighed the short-term satisfaction of telling someone off.

The first step for all of us is to figure out what we want and to pick the battles that will move us toward getting it. But the most important decision is to get started, to do something, to begin to develop our skills and confidence, and then to take the next step, whatever that is for us, however small it may seem. They all add up.

Some of us have moved into positions where we have some power and influence in a wide array of fields: law, medicine, science, media, religion, education, business, labor, the arts and humanities. We have an opportunity to serve as role models and mentors and to help change these institutions from the inside. Some of us, on the other hand, will never be in positions traditionally regarded as powerful, but we can still have an impact.

All of us can improve our own lives and the lives of other women by influencing the people around us every day. We can keep a straight face when someone tells a racist, sexist, or homophobic "joke" and suggest that the person explain it, because we just don't see the humor. We can tell the truth about our lives and be proud of overcoming violence, incest, or rape. We can refuse to be intimidated by harassment or lesbian-baiting and refuse to be forced into denying our sexuality. All of these things can help move public opinion and ultimately public policy.

As individuals, we can enjoy the satisfaction of expanding our personal power. And that power is multiplied when we take collective action. Not everyone wants to join in demonstrations or picketing or direct confrontations outside an abortion clinic. Some people may participate by joining in a consumer boycott of a business that gives money to antiabortion groups. Some of us may be more focused on issues like getting our daughter's soccer team the same quality coaching and equipment as our son's. All of it is valuable, and all of it moves us forward.

There will inevitably be times when conflict and confrontation cannot be avoided. Making progress for women means challenging some of our most deeply held beliefs about women and men, about how we relate to each other, about our relationship to the society as a whole. When we step outside the traditional bounds of our sex, we create conflict. When we push for change, even positive change, we make ourselves and others uncomfortable. It's been painfully difficult for me to learn to be willing to create social tension and to deal constructively with the conflict that results. Self-examination is the key. I still experience the same initial fear and anguish when I find myself in conflict. But recognizing these emotions in advance, knowing where they come from, has made them less frightening. And lots of practice has allowed me to experience these emotional responses without being controlled by them.

I have spent a lot of time in this book describing my battles with the right wing, and especially the violent antiabortion movement, to make another point: There are times when we simply have to speak up and to fight back, because it will be catastrophic if we don't. These situations can be scary, but we must confront them—even when others tell us we are being paranoid, or want to ignore what's going on or are too afraid to speak up themselves. Harassment and violence, whether personal or political, have much greater and more far-reaching consequences if they're allowed to go unchallenged.

As anticommunist violence built up in Miami, too many of us, myself included, failed to speak up or take a stand. I tried to tell myself it wasn't my problem. Similarly, as antiabortion violence burgeoned around the country, too many of us looked the other way. Abortion rights supporters and providers too often tried to convince themselves that if they kept their heads buried in the sand, the storm would blow over without touching them. How many family members and friends pretend not to see the obvious signs of family violence until it's too late? If more of us had the insight and courage to fight back sooner and harder, lives might be saved.

This lesson was driven home to me during a trip to Europe with Ellie Smeal, Molly Yard, and Peg Yorkin. Our group met in Paris with high-ranking officials of Rousell-Uclaf, the large pharmaceutical company that manufactures RU-486, the abortion pill. We also met in Bonn with representatives of Rousell's parent company, Hoechst. Abortions with RU-486 are non-surgical and can be performed earlier in pregnancy, which adds up to greater safety for women patients, so we were trying to convince the companies to export RU-486 to the United States or to license another company to make it available here. But at the time company officials were worried about the Bush administration's antiabortion stance, and they were equally afraid of threats by the antiabortion movement. Antiabortion thugs had accosted some of Rousell's workers in the parking lots, in broad daylight, at the Paris plant.

With these unsuccessful discussions fresh in mind, I went to an exhibit at the Women's Museum in Bonn entitled "2,000 Years of Bonn Women." There I found myself intrigued by three stone figures of female deities worshiped by the Frankish tribes in Bonn before the Romans conquered the region. Modern-day problems faded from my mind as I wandered past relics, works of art, and documents tracing women's history in the two-thousand-year-old city.

But near the end of the exhibit, I was brought back to the present abruptly. I'd reached the section focusing on the build-up of Nazi strength and Hitler's ascension to power. Posters from that era trumpeted the appropriate sphere of activity for women: *Kinder, Küche und Kirche*—children, kitchen and church. Medals honoring Aryan "super-mothers" who had borne a half dozen or more children for Hitler's youth corps, were on display. By the time I reached the display of women's shoes, family photographs, and other poignant mementos of those murdered in the Holocaust, my eyes were filled with tears.

How clear the need to take on such evil. How utterly illusory the perception that we can be safe by not drawing attention to ourselves, by refusing to get involved. I left the Women's Museum more committed than ever to feminist activism, more determined than ever to rally opposition to antiabortion violence and to hate crimes and political violence everywhere.

As we near the close of the twentieth century and the beginning of the twenty-first, we find ourselves at a critical point in history. Women are called upon to defend every bit of progress we have made against particularly virulent attack. But we must also hold out a vision, put forth a positive agenda of what women need and want, and then move forward toward that dream.

I would like us to construct a practical bill of rights for women, and I think we should include at least the following rights: to be fairly compensated for our work and to have safe, affordable day care and other societal support for the roles we play in our families;

to be respected as fully competent, moral decision-makers; this means the right to reproductive freedom, as well as the right to make informed decisions regarding our own health;

to have a fair share of political power and policy making in the public and the private sectors;

to be free from discrimination based on race, religion, national origin, ethnicity, disability, sexual orientation, childbearing capacity or choices;

to be free from harassment and violence;

to have a constitutional guarantee of equality so clear that even this Supreme Court cannot mistake its meaning.

I want us to demand equality measured not by a male standard that provides no protection when women and men are not similarly situated, for example in pregnancy, child bearing, and rearing, but by a standard that asks whether a law or policy disadvantages women or whether it dismantles barriers that keep us from equal participation in our society.

Some will ask whether this is the time to be looking at a constitutional amendment strategy. I would urge that the need was never more apparent. With all the fights on our hands, when was it ever easier to explain why we need to have women in the Constitution? Why should we have to keep refighting these same battles over and over again? As important as it is not to let ourselves be pushed backward, I think we all get tired of playing defense. And I think a good offense is in order here.

I want us to move forward and to continue fighting for justice in those areas where triumph has so far eluded us. I want us to feel the urgency of taking action now to prevent the loss of everything we've gained over the past thirty years of progress and struggle.

I want us to feel not only our power, but the absolute necessity of using it to the fullest.

I want each of us to connect what is happening politically in the world and in our country to what is happening and will happen in our own lives, to understand the real, practical meaning of the aphorism "the personal is political." Our actual everyday lives, our ability to live in a satisfying way, to fulfill our hopes and dreams—our ability to pursue happiness—are dramatically affected by the policies of the government and of the other institutions that shape our society as well. Likewise, the choices we make daily for freedom in our individual lives shape our whole society.

What we do individually and collectively does make a difference. Each of us can, and must, play a role; we face challenges on so many fronts, and we have so much to do.

Just as we began this century by winning the right to vote, I want us to end this century by taking real political and personal power.

INDEX